EVAN MARSHALL is from Northern Ireland and has worked in television and archiving for many years. He was film archivist on a range of social history documentaries and series for DoubleBand Films and curated various expansions of Northern Ireland's Digital Film Archive. In 2013 he established his own production company, Clackity Films, which makes sport-based documentaries. He produced and directed the acclaimed *Spirit of '58: The Story of Northern Ireland's Greatest Football Team* and followed it with a book of the same name. Evan is currently working on a documentary about the Northern Ireland football team in the 1980s, due out in 2022. His journalism has included work for *Record Collector, FourFourTwo* and the *Belfast Telegraph*. He works for Northern Ireland Screen and he and his son are ardent followers of Dundela FC in Belfast.

GW00502621

FIELDS of WONDER

EVAN MARSHALL
WITH A FOREWORD BY MARTIN O'NEILL

·THE·
BLACK
·STAFF·
PRESS

In memory of Ben and Edna Marshall
who watched these games with me during a glorious
summer when I was young and dreaming.

First published in 2022 by Blackstaff Press
an imprint of Colourpoint Creative Ltd
Colourpoint House
Jubilee Business Park
21 Jubilee Road
Newtownards BT23 4YH

Printed and bound by CPI Group UK Ltd, Croydon CRO 4YY

A CIP catalogue for this book is available from the British Library

ISBN 978-1-78073-240-4

www.blackstaffpress.com

CONTENTS

FOREWORD

March 1980. It's a struggle. A desperate struggle. We have been driven back into our own penalty area like sheep being corralled into a pen. We knew it was going to be a tough match, but no one had anticipated how little possession of the ball we would have just now. It's scoreless in eastern Tel Aviv but Israel are in command of this game, the opening qualifying match of the 1982 World Cup. There are twenty long minutes left and only our resilience is keeping Israel at bay.

Suddenly the stadium is plunged into darkness. A floodlight failure has come to our temporary rescue. Gathered together on the touchline we draw breath, form a circle and convince ourselves that not only will they not score, but that a point away in Tel Aviv will be as important as any we might gain going forward. Fifteen minutes later, the game restarts. We find that inner strength to withstand the Israeli attacks and see it through to the end.

On the face of it, a scoreless draw doesn't seem to be a

watershed moment in anyone's footballing life, but as we sit here in the foyer of the Sidi Saler hotel in Valencia, awaiting tomorrow's possible history-making match against Spain, it's Tel Aviv, 1980, not victories against Sweden and Portugal at Windsor Park, that is the topic of conversation.

It's been a long two years, during which time we've forged relationships with each other that will last forever. Billy Bingham, in his second spell in charge of the Northern Ireland team, has instilled a strong willpower in the group. Although, with players like Jennings, Jim and Chris Nicholl, McIlroy and Armstrong, I think there was plenty of character in the squad in the first place. But, in truth, he is exactly what we needed back in 1980. Play to our strengths and cover up our weaknesses is his maxim. And even in the short time he has been with us in preparation for international games, this remains his focus and it has carried us here.

It's been a glorious period for Northern Ireland's football history. The brilliant 1958 team has been the reference point for so many years but by qualifying for the 1982 World Cup we have at least identified ourselves with Peter Doherty's squad. Can we emulate them by reaching the quarter-finals? Well, tomorrow the answer will be provided.

Armstrong, Billy Hamilton and Sammy Nelson are in deep discussion. If Nelson is around, fun will follow and, right on cue, the table, waiting for Sammy's punchline, bursts into paroxysms of laughter. Any passer-by would not believe that all these men around the table will, within twenty-four hours, take the field in one of the biggest games of their lives. But, despite the joviality, we are prepared for what is coming. Only a win can get us into the quarter-finals and that win will have to come tomorrow evening, just a few miles down the road in the storied Mestalla Stadium, against Spain, the host nation.

If we think about it too much it might overwhelm us. But, honestly, we believe we can do it. The mentality is strong. Our physical condition, honed with a tough pre-tournament training schedule in Brighton, matches anyone at this competition. And in Norman Whiteside, the youngest player ever to play at the World Cup, beating Pelé by 208 days, we have an ace in the pack. He is a man in boy's clothing but his impact at this World Cup so far has been immense. He cannot wait for the game. Neither can David McCreery who continues to be outstanding for us.

We are about to leave the table. I say quietly to Armstrong, that warrior of all warriors, that we need him to continue his brilliant form in the tournament. 'You can depend on me, Martin,' he replies with a big smile. 'I think I might even score the winning goal.' 'Now *that* would be brilliant,' I say.

Martin O'Neill
April 2022

TROUBLE AHEAD

In the world of international football, small nations can often only dream about having a moment in the sun. This might come in the form of a victory against a mightier opponent; securing a team of players so talented that they exceed the country's expectations; or, that rarest of achievements, a chance to hold their own on the world stage for a short time. Should such a moment ever be experienced, it would be savoured and remembered for generations, with little expectation that it would ever be repeated. Such are the fortunes of the minnows.

For Northern Ireland, with a population of just one and a half million people and no professional football league, fans could have been forgiven for thinking that their moment in the spotlight had been that outstanding period in the 1950s when the side, then on par with England as the top team in the British Isles, reached a level of success few had ever thought possible. With an inspirational manager and a highly skilled and motivated first team that included superstars of English football such as Danny Blanchflower, Jimmy McIlroy, Harry Gregg, Wilbur Cush, Peter McParland and Billy Bingham, they had enjoyed a thrilling run to the quarter-finals of the 1958 World Cup. Along the way there had been a famous triumph over a seemingly invincible England team at Wembley in 1957 and victory over double World Champions Italy in the pulsating final qualifying game. The drama continued, at first along farcical lines. A faction within the IFA launched legal action to try to stop their own team from competing at the World Cup as they would be playing matches on the Sabbath Day. Then tragedy struck when two of the star players of the national team were involved in the Munich Air Disaster, which took the lives of so many of Manchester United's famous Busby's Babes team and ended the career of Jackie Blanchflower.

There had also been something irresistible about the manner in which this great team achieved its success. In a crucial game to qualify for the quarter-final, stand-in goalkeeper Norman Uprichard had damaged his ankle ligaments in the first few minutes. He then broke his hand at the start of the second half. With no substitutes allowed, he hobbled around on one good leg and only able to use one arm for the rest of the game, right on through to the end of extra time. The Northern Irish physio, a famously mercurial character by the name of Gerry Morgan, had been treating the ankle damage on the pitch by pouring whiskey onto it. When Gregg was forced to return for the quarter-final he literally set aside a walking stick to do so and went out onto the pitch to secure his place as Goalkeeper of the Tournament, just four months after he had pulled survivors from the wreck at Munich. And through all the adversity there was always the humour, with Blanchflower quipping after a game against Czechoslovakia, 'Our tactics have always been to equalise before the other team scores.'

It had been the stuff of dreams – an epic saga that would be told and retold by those lucky enough to have borne witness, sporting ecstasy that soon passed into memory and half-believed legend. But sometimes, just sometimes, the minnow is granted a second and even more dazzling path to immortality, and while Northern Ireland might have to wait a few decades, their chance would come again.

In the years that followed 1958, however, the team began to run out of steam. There were always campaigns to be fought, but ultimately these ended in disappointment. The squad as a whole just could not compare with the team that had brought such glory in the 1950s. There was, nevertheless, a constant sprinkling of stardust that was just enough to keep the fans believing, and there were plenty of talented players, with more coming up through the ranks.

In this period, the landscape of British football was very different. If footballers from Northern Ireland, Scotland, Wales or the Republic of Ireland made the grade, their talent was often nurtured and developed by the biggest clubs in England (compared with modern times when aspiring young players must compete against players from Europe, South America, Africa and Asia for Premier League signings). So, while Northern Ireland often had to fill some roles in the team with players from what was then called the Second Division, the nucleus of the squad was always taken from the cream of England's top teams and, as the stars of 1958 began to disperse, Northern Ireland could still dream big thanks to a core of players who were regular first team picks for competitive clubs. On their day they could achieve fine results and, although actual glory and success were receding further into history, they were far from being on the lowest rungs of the international ladder.

In particular, Northern Ireland seemed to have a habit of producing their best football when playing against the best teams; yet they struggled against familiar or lesser opposition. Their results in the British Home Championship – or Home

Internationals as they were often known – throughout the 1960s make for particularly grim reading. Only occasionally could they rouse themselves to a memorable result against either England or Scotland, more often achieving a 'moral victory' in a narrow defeat. It was undoubtedly a period of struggle when some heavy and embarrassing losses were inflicted upon them by their neighbours.

The 1962 World Cup was always going to be a big ask for Northern Ireland. Some of the 1958 team were now veterans and others had retired from the international stage altogether. Being drawn against West Germany – winners and semi-finalists in the last two tournaments – conjured even less optimism. Yet Northern Ireland lost both games by only a narrow margin: 4–3 in a thrilling game in Belfast (where Billy McAdams was unfortunate enough to score a hat trick and still end up on the losing team), and 2–1 in West Germany. Typically, it was a defeat against Greece, after the first of the German games, that effectively killed their campaign and demonstrated what was to become an all-too-familiar weakness – an inability to close out games against teams they were expected to beat.

When the legendary Peter Doherty stood down as Northern Ireland manager in 1962, there was a sense of continuity with the great team he had moulded in the appointment to the role of one of its most accomplished players, Bertie Peacock. The ex-Celtic legend had returned to local football as player-manager of his hometown side, Coleraine FC, before also taking on the international job and, as another who had achieved greatness on the pitch, he was well respected by the squad.

Peacock managed the team through the 1964 European Championship, which was still in its infancy (in those days it was a straight knock-out tournament, played across two years). Northern Ireland eased past Poland with a comfortable 2–0 victory and secured a wonderful 1–1 draw with Spain in the away leg of the next round, but were undone by a single goal in the return fixture in Belfast. Nevertheless, it bade well for the future, as the new players settled in beside the last few remnants of the 1958 team. Harry Gregg and Billy Bingham were both now in the twilight of their careers, but the charismatic Derek Dougan had been to the World Cup as a youth and was a front man capable of leading the new team for many years to come.

Unfortunately, Northern Ireland's familiar pattern of achieving reasonable results against continental opposition, and heavy defeats in the British Championship, continued. Following the impressive performances against Spain, the next result was an 8–3 demolition at Wembley against England. It hadn't helped that injury was beginning to take its toll on Northern Ireland's superstar goalkeeper, Gregg, and for the next game against Wales, no one from the '58 team was in the starting line-up.

Peacock had rung the changes successfully with new kid on the block Pat Jennings (then at Watford but about to begin a long tenure at Tottenham Hotspur), and Manchester United's George Best, both of whom made their debuts for Northern Ireland on 15 April 1964. Jennings was a talented up-and-comer, who would go on to become one of the most outstanding goalkeepers in Britain, if not the world; Best would light up British football for a decade with his unique skill. Stability at the back and flair going forward. Suddenly, the future looked bright.

When qualifying came round for the 1966 World Cup, Northern Ireland had at its disposal, a circle of new talent to call upon, and with England set to host, this was the closest they could ever possibly come to having a 'home' tournament. They were confident that they would qualify, especially following a series of improving results in the British Championships.

At this time, the legendary Jimmy McIlroy was experiencing something of an Indian summer in his club career and was brought back out of international retirement. In the 1950s and early 1960s, as he guided his beloved Burnley to an unlikely First Division triumph, McIlroy had been considered one of the true artists and thinkers of the game. Now playing for Stoke City, it suddenly seemed possible that a further World Cup campaign could provide a fitting sunset to his sublime talent.

The story of how Northern Ireland failed to reach the 1966 World Cup – one for which McIlroy provided the experience, and Best the emerging genius – in a country that was the established home of their entire team, with easy access for their fans to follow them, is almost too heartbreaking to tell. Going into the final qualifying game, Northern Ireland simply needed to beat Albania away from home to finish level with Switzerland and set up a play-off game. Albania had lost every single one of their previous games, so the Irish would certainly have been favourites. Instead, after leading 1–0 in atrocious and stormy conditions, Northern Ireland conceded a late equaliser and their hopes tipped into oblivion.

We may never know what would have happened in that play-off game, and there is no guarantee Northern Ireland would have triumphed, but the young Best was becoming a more accomplished player week by week. Just a few months later he played for Manchester United in a European Cup quarter-final against the mighty Portuguese champions, SL Benfica. This was a team who counted the legendary Eusebio among their ranks and they had never lost a single European game in their home fortress that was known as the Stadium of Light. The nineteen-year-old Best tore them apart and scored the opening two goals as United thrashed them 5-1. The Portuguese press latched on to his pop-singer hairstyle and declared, 'A Beatle called Best smashed Benfica.' It's likely that such a fearless young talent would have tipped the scales in Northern Ireland's favour against the Swiss.

The sad reality is that while Northern Ireland had some great players, a few good ones, and commendable team spirit, they just didn't have enough to get them over the line. There were limits to what a small nation like Northern Ireland could produce. As

Peacock acknowledges, 'The pool's just not big enough. It's all right being a manager, but if you've not got the personnel, you're in trouble. Ron Pickering was once asked what made a good coach, and he said, "A damn good pupil." And he was right!' Following a winless run in the 1967 British Championship, Peacock felt he had done all he could and stepped down to concentrate on his role at Coleraine, eventually winning the Irish League title with them in 1974.

By the end of 1969, things were looking up for Northern Ireland as they were on target to qualify for the 1970 World Cup in Mexico. If they could just win their final game away against the Soviet Union in Moscow, they were guaranteed a place in the tournament. Even a draw would have been enough in the end. But they stumbled in the final game – due, in no small part, to the loss of George Best, who missed the trip to Moscow through injury – and lost the match 2–0. They had been within touching distance of another World Cup appearance and this was a depressing end to the campaign. For the players and the fans, it wasn't so much the despair of failing again that caused frustration but the endless hope of always being on the brink of better things.

The manager at the time was another star from the 1958 team, Billy Bingham. A member of the famous 'Bank of England' team of stars at Sunderland in the 1950s and a league winner at the end of his career with Everton in 1963, Bingham had always been well suited to management. He had been a keen student of the game and he managed the international side in addition to his full-time duties as a club manager, first at Plymouth Argyle and then in local football, winning the league with Linfield in 1971. Under his management, Northern Ireland recorded a fairly decent win ratio (greater than that of Peter Doherty), but despite the talent of his players, he was unable to shape them into a cohesive unit that could win important games, and in 1971 he left for the fresh pastures offered by the Greek national team.

There were moments along the way, though, that continued to entrance those on the terraces, such as a famous game against Scotland at Windsor Park in October 1967. It was Bingham's first in charge and the team were up against a strong Scottish squad, which included Denis Law and four of the Celtic team who had just become the first British club to win the European Cup. Northern Ireland won 1–0 thanks to a goal from Dave Clements, but Clements' contribution has been almost obliterated from history as the match became known as 'The George Best Match'. Best took the visitors apart almost singlehandedly in a mesmerising display of his talents. Tommy Gemmell, the legendary Scottish defender attempting to shackle Best that day, described it as, 'like trying to catch the wind'.

In one of Bingham's final games, a British Championship match against England at Windsor Park in May 1971, Best would again make history. England keeper Gordon Banks had carelessly tossed the ball in the air to kick it, but Best was at his side, saw his chance and knocked the ball over Banks. He then raced the keeper to head into the empty net. However, the referee saved the great goalkeeper's blushes and disallowed the goal – clearly the wrong decision – and a relieved England eventually squeaked home 1–0.

Having been agonisingly close to qualifying for two successive World Cups with managers who had played in 1958, the Irish Football Association (IFA) now looked to the current squad to fill the role and in 1971 promoted captain Terry Neill, who was just twenty-nine years old. Following a long career in the Arsenal defence, Neill had already dipped his toe into management as player-manager of Hull City and he now fulfilled the same role for his country. However, it was at this stage that everything changed for Northern Ireland, and this time there was nothing that any player or manager could do about it.

It is simply impossible to continue a narrative about sport in Northern Ireland without also mentioning that period of political, military and societal destabilisation known as 'The Troubles'. Northern Ireland had been pitched headfirst into civil disorder and sectarian tension, followed by open violence, killings and bombings. It was a dark time for everyone: businesses, families, neighbourhoods and, of course, the legions of the bereaved. But it would be wrong to say that it had no impact upon the national team, and football in general within Northern Ireland. Those players training and playing in England would have been shielded from the day-to-day misery of this period, but each home fixture in the broken and scarred city of Belfast, combined with visits to family and conversations with their international team-mates, would have focused their attention on the anguish, despair and suffering of their birthplace.

The team did their best, striving to lift the gloom of the populace and always searching for the spark to reignite the glory of times not so long past, but the off-field circumstances helped push any dreams of success – already limited for a small nation – well beyond the expectations of even the most optimistic player or fan. It can be no coincidence that Northern Ireland's footballing fortunes began to fall in the early 1970s, despite having a useful team. George Best, Derek Dougan, Pat Jennings, Pat Rice and Allan Hunter were the bedrock for the side, and they were supplemented by players of decent quality but, from 1971 onwards, the political and security situation in Belfast necessitated Northern Ireland playing all their home games at various grounds in England. Robbed of home advantage, and with their own impassioned fans unable to travel to the games in any significant numbers, these were the nomad years of Northern Irish football. That they should intersect with a period when their two greatest players, Best and Jennings, were at their peak is a sporting tragedy.

For the fans, already enduring the grim and unrelenting headlines of shootings, bombs, instability and disorder, even the limited solace of sport had been taken away from them. The chance to delight in Best's enchanting skills for an hour and a half was given to ex-pats and curious locals in half-empty provincial grounds in the north of England, rather than to a surge of impassioned fans spilling forth from the streets around Windsor Park.

The political and security situation continued to deteriorate throughout 1971, and in Michael Walker's excellent collection of Irish footballing stories, *Green Shoots*, Terry Neill recalls the atmosphere that October, when the Soviet Union visited for a Union of European Football Associations (UEFA) European Championship match. 'A lot of countries were starting to get worried … and we could understand it. The IFA worked closely with the security forces, but what could they guarantee? The Troubles loomed over us. We'd a couple of security men from the RUC with us who travelled on the bus from the hotel to the games.'

One of the officers on that security detail was later killed in an explosion outside his home, and with the death of someone the players had known personally, the reality of the Troubles began to make itself felt. 'Belfast, then? You wanted eyes in the back of your head going into the ground and coming away,' recalls Neill. 'You were uncomfortable, and you were unsure because you never knew where or when anything was going to come from.'

The Troubles had an even more direct impact on Northern Ireland's most famous son, George Best, when in late October 1971, the IRA issued him with a death threat, explaining that if he took to the pitch for Manchester United against Newcastle United on 23 October, he would be killed. A rumour had circulated that Best had donated money to the Democratic Unionist Party (DUP), the just-formed venture of Reverend Ian Paisley. This, apparently, was enough to mark him for death, and it didn't matter that the stories were a complete fabrication. The resulting threat seemed in deadly earnest and Best was given police protection. The Manchester United team bus was broken into, and had to be thoroughly searched, so Best was offered the chance to sit the game out. He declined, determined not to give in to the terrorists' demands, but later noted, 'Typically of me, having let the team down so many times, when the manager offered me a Saturday off, I insisted that I wanted to play.' But he was nervous taking to the pitch and later admitted that the high-rise flats overlooking the ground made him fear a sniper attack, 'I never stopped moving on the field. Somehow, I felt that I should not stand still. Even when there was someone on the floor injured, I kept running around.' He scored the only goal that day and, according to Best, after the match Newcastle United manager Joe Harvey 'broke the ice at the press conference when he said, "I wish they'd shot the little bugger."'

The threats against Best didn't stop. There were reports that figures armed with a gun had been spotted in Manchester asking where Best lived, and the *Manchester Evening News* received a letter saying that he would be knifed in the back if he played in Northern Ireland's forthcoming European Championships qualifying game against Spain in Belfast that November. As it turned out, the plug was finally pulled on home games at Windsor Park and the game was instead played in England the following February.

Best wasn't the only Northern Ireland player who received death threats. Pat Jennings recalls how he became aware of a tit-for-tat warning from loyalist terrorists, 'At that time, I had the same threats. If anything was going to happen to George, it was going to happen to me in retaliation. I got a call from the club secretary [at Spurs] one morning. The police had been in touch with the club to say this threat had come through to Scotland Yard. They wanted to give me police protection.'

Loyalist paramilitary elements also turned on Northern Ireland's Protestant manager. 'I'd been quoted in the paper,' Neill remembers, 'referring to ourselves as "Ireland" and some nutcase – subsequently traced and arrested – started sending me little parcels with wire showing. It was amateur, but I'd to call the police in. There were notes too. So, for a month or so I had to have a reflector under the car, and every now and again the coppers at the ground and at my home. You can dismiss it as "just some nutter", but we'd just had our first two kids. It wasn't funny for my wife Sandra, with two young kids.'

The idiocy of this situation was that 'Ireland' was actually the IFA's preferred name for the national team – it had always been billed as such for Home International games and only began to use the name 'Northern Ireland' in the 1950s for World Cup qualifying, as FIFA insisted that two nations couldn't compete under the same name in case they ended up meeting each other later in the competition. However, the squad who ended up going to the 1958 World Cup would forever refer to the team as Ireland and the name was used throughout the 1960s for games against British opposition, only petering out in the early 70s.

Terrorists from both sides of the conflict threatening to kill star players and manager alike didn't help the team focus on the football, and no longer having a home stadium was another impediment to success. Neill reflects, 'Once we made the decision that we couldn't play home games at home we just had to go on the road.' The rescheduled match against Spain in February 1972 was held at Boothferry Park, Hull, thanks to Neill's connections to Hull City, and for each new game against continental opposition a different ground was required. The next year, the team would play at Coventry's Highfield Road, Everton's Goodison Park and Sheffield Wednesday's Hillsborough, with the match at Hillsborough against Bulgaria that September offering a particularly demoralising experience for the 'home' team, when only six thousand spectators came to the high-capacity ground.

Despite the dispiriting experiences of playing in these grounds, Neill is full of praise for the generosity of the clubs in helping them out and the support from opposing nations: 'Those people couldn't have done more. That needs to be said. In all those games, the ovations we got were tremendous. The Coventry game [against Portugal], Eusebio said, "I'm sorry we're not in Belfast." The Spanish game the same, and the Bulgaria players and the Cypriot players, they were all sympathetic. The football fans in those cities and grounds were brilliantly supportive. We were very welcome everywhere except home.'

In the end, between November 1971 and April 1975, Northern Ireland played eighteen games in a row away from home, yet even in those sombre times, the team spirit remained strong, especially for the younger players coming into the squad. Martin O'Neill (who made his debut in 1971, in the final game played in Belfast) recalls the get-togethers that the team would have before the Home International games in England, 'Whether we were successful or not, all the gatherings that we had were terrific. In my early days, George Best participated, and of course that's a great experience for young people like myself, to be in the company of George Best. It was fantastic ... There was a camaraderie between all the players. Being young I was glad to be a part of it. We just accepted that, because of The Troubles, we had to play these games away from home and that at some stage we could return.'

The closeness of the squad is something that Neill also acknowledges. 'When we were the nomads, the togetherness got us through. It certainly felt an added bit of burden to perform well. We'd always say, "Give the people back at home something to cheer about." We'd all been through the euphoria of victory and the despair of defeat but that was not just a question of being happy with a win. What's going to happen to our country? Are things going to get better or go down the tubes?'

With the horrific levels of violence within Northern Ireland, it wasn't just the national team who suffered. The domestic league was also thrown into chaos. In October 1972, Derry City resigned from the Irish League. Since September 1971, following other teams' refusal to travel to Derry's Brandywell Stadium owing to the volatile security situation in the city, the Irish League had forced the team to play their home games in Coleraine. The fans did not follow, and attendance dwindled to almost nothing. The security forces greenlit games for the Brandywell once more, but the motion to allow the team to return was rejected by the other teams, and Derry City would spend thirteen years in the soccer wilderness.

Meanwhile, in Belfast, Distillery FC had been firebombed from their ground at Grosvenor Park (the place where Derek Dougan and Martin O'Neill had ignited their young careers, and where the latter had still been playing, before his move to Nottingham Forest). The team would spend most of the next decade in enforced groundsharing with nearby local sides.

Violence on and from the stands was an ugly problem at the time as well. In the 1970/71 European Cup Winners' Cup, Billy Bingham's Linfield competed against mighty Manchester City. After a now famous 2–1 home victory, Linfield would go out narrowly on away goals, but at the Windsor Park match, City keeper, Joe Corrigan, was forced to endure an onslaught of bottles being fired at him by the home fans. With the game on the brink of being abandoned, Bingham left his dugout and shouted himself hoarse in front of the stands, pleading with the fans to show some sense.

Direct rule was introduced to Northern Ireland in 1972. As a result, the IFA decided to voluntarily withdraw its teams from European competition in the 1972/73 season, in what must surely have been a pre-emptive strike against the inevitable barring of games in the country.

Other incidents in local football reflected a sickness within society. Future Northern Ireland international Terry Cochrane was a rising goal-scorer for Belfast giants Linfield, and in August 1973 he married his sweetheart, Etta. She was Catholic and in marrying her Cochrane had immediately made himself an unwelcome figure at the club. Management asked him to leave. As he recalled in his autobiography, *See You at the Far Post*, 'It actually wasn't their policy to ask a player to leave for this reason, but they felt I would get too much stick if I stayed. I was pretty upset as it didn't seem any business of theirs whom I married, although I did appreciate that they were a staunchly Protestant club and had been pretty honest and open with me. I would very much have liked to stay with Linfield as I was really happy there, but it was not be.'

Incredibly, against this background, Northern Ireland international star and former captain Derek Dougan tried to organise a friendly match between an all-Ireland team and World Champions, Brazil. The idea was to bring together footballers from both communities, from Northern Ireland and the Republic, under one banner in a one-off game to help promote healing and reconciliation. Given that his international manager had been subject to a death threat just for using the word 'Ireland', this certainly represented almost foolhardy bravery. However, Dougan – a star from the streets of Protestant east Belfast – was a maverick who would often be attracted to a cause just because he was told he shouldn't be.

No one could doubt his sincerity or backbone, and he found no problem interesting both Catholic and Protestant team-mates from Northern Ireland in combining their talents with the best of the Republic of Ireland. However, the IFA showed little enthusiasm for the venture when the proposal was put to it. As Dougan recalled, '[There was] the possibility of contributing to the healing of division. People would come together and, in a society in which neighbours were rent apart by the bigotry and hate of the Irish situation, a temporary sporting unity would be a major achievement. The response of Harry Cavan [IFA President] was precise and well-focused. He informed me, tersely, that he would put the discussion to the members of the IFA. Mr Drennan [IFA Secretary] warmly told me that he would be in touch ... but the issues raised that night have never been discussed again. Neither man came back to me.'

Dougan persevered, forming a team that featured Pat Jennings, the young Martin O'Neill, Johnny Giles and Don Givens. They played Brazil at Lansdowne Road, Dublin, on 3 July 1973, narrowly losing 4–3 to the Brazilians (who fielded nearly all of the side that had so famously taken Italy apart to win the 1970 World Cup). However, all mention of Ireland had been removed from their billing and they were forced to take to the pitch as Shamrock Rovers XI due to opposition behind the scenes from Harry Cavan. In the build-up to the match, the longstanding FIFA President, Sir Stanley Rous, had been on a television programme with Dougan and told him afterwards, 'What are you doing upsetting Cavan? He is on the phone to me constantly trying to get the Irish match called off.'

Dougan reflected, 'I knew immediately that the man at the top of Northern Ireland soccer had tried to obstruct the possible progress of trust and togetherness. Cavan tried to get the match cancelled purely and simply because he felt that it was going to be a precedent, that the north and south was going to come together after that. It was very selfish. He may have changed the name of the team, but what he couldn't do was take away that memorable day.'

As Martin O'Neill (who was named man of the match in the *Belfast Telegraph*'s report of the game) recalls, 'Derek Dougan didn't have a sectarian bone in his body. It was very forward-thinking of him at the time. Obviously, it couldn't be called Ireland, but it was a mixed religious team ... and we played in this magnificent game. A wonderful thrill for me.'

Dougan, however, felt that organising the game led to him being overlooked for international duty and sent him into exile. As he recalls, 'After it, I probably had a couple of my best years at Wolves, but I never played for Northern Ireland again.' While it's true that he never pulled on the green shirt after this, he had already been overlooked for recent games, and none of the other players involved suffered deselection. However, given the tensions surrounding Northern Ireland games and the threats being made, it was perhaps a blessing in disguise for Dougan that he did not become a target for the extremists by playing again for his country.

Such was the state of the nation and its football in the early- to mid-1970s. For a new young generation of footballers emerging from the streets of Northern Ireland, the siren call of the big clubs from across the Irish Sea represented not just the chance to parade your skills before vastly larger stadiums, or the chance to earn a huge salary, but also, sadly, escape. And not just for themselves but for the families they were worried about back home.

Sammy McIlroy came from the Newtownards Road area in east Belfast and arrived at Manchester United in 1969, just as the unrest was kicking off in earnest. He recalls, 'When I went back home during 1969 and 1970, the Troubles were well under way with people marching the streets at night, and my dad, who was no spring chicken, was having his door knocked on at night by men who were calling on him to go on vigilante duty. I was worried sick and thought, this was not for me. So, I asked them [my parents] if they would come over and they said yes.'

A few years later, in 1974, Jimmy Nicholl, from the Rathcoole housing estate in north Belfast, joined the same club. He, too, worried about his family, but manager, Tommy 'the Doc' Docherty, worked to allay his fears. 'I was only sixteen when he helped get them out. I got the message from home about how things were beginning to cut up rough. I used to go home every month and got the message, don't come back for a wee while. After a game at Preston, I went back to the Doc and said, "If I don't go back now, I will be going back for funerals." Things were starting to creep into Rathcoole. I told them I was away and went back home. The club told me to bring my ma and da back with me because they had a house for them in Sale.'

Against such a backdrop, Northern Ireland's chances of becoming a competitive team once more were being undermined by events outside their control. Hope was just been around the corner, but the remainder of the 1970s would turn out to be a rollercoaster of contrasting fortunes.

DEEPER AND DOWN

With their continued exile from Belfast, it is not surprising that results for Northern Ireland were mixed. The first qualifying campaign affected had been that of the 1972 European Championships. It was a challenging group, and Northern Ireland lost away games against the Soviet Union and Spain. Perhaps they would have been able to turn this around with victories back in Windsor Park, but there was to be no Belfast fixture for the second tie, and the Soviet Union match was overshadowed by escalating violence. Instead, the team could only manage spirited draws, which kept their pride alive but did nothing for their chances of attending the summer tournament.

The 1974 World Cup qualifying campaign was the stage for another demoralising blow, when fans were denied the small consolation of seeing George Best pull on a green shirt. Best had his own well-documented problems, his inner demons, and had lived his life in the spotlight for the best part of a decade. He was still unquestionably the most photographed and written about footballer of the age, and he was struggling to cope with the demands upon him. His Manchester United career had gone into a tailspin, especially once Sir Matt Busby stood down as manager, and his international career had petered out without him ever having played in a World Cup. For a few seasons he played only occasional games for lowly sides hoping to boost their gate receipts, despite only being in his late twenties. Starved of the weekly regime of training, and lacking any kind of match fitness, the tragedy is that he fell out of contention for international duty at the very age when a footballer is considered to be entering his peak.

One glimmer of light during this period was Northern Ireland's performances in the British Championship. Following on from the 1958/59 tournament, Northern Ireland had finished bottom eight times out of eleven seasons; but in the three seasons under Neill – from 1971/72 to 1973/74 – they secured four wins, one draw and four defeats across the nine games. On paper it was only a modest recovery, but to achieve these results while playing every game away from home was actually a notable achievement.

Overall, though, Neill's time as player-manager for Northern Ireland was neither good nor bad. He scored the winner in a memorable victory over England at Wembley in the 1972 British Championship, but this was followed soon after by several embarrassing defeats. Northern Ireland started the qualifying campaign for the 1974 World Cup with losses to Bulgaria and lowly Cyprus – teams they should have been able to beat. They then recorded two draws against Portugal which, had they won both games against Bulgaria (the eventual qualifiers), would have been enough for them to qualify. Once more, their Achilles heel was their inability to perform against lesser opposition.

It was time for Neill to move on. He played his last game for Northern Ireland against Wales in 1973 and stepped down from the manager's role in September 1974. He had attracted the attention of Tottenham Hotspur, surprisingly appointed ahead of Danny Blanchflower, and would manage them for two seasons. He then laid down a distinguished record as manager of Arsenal from 1976 to 1983, where he led a memorable team centred around Liam Brady, featuring many Irish players from north and south of the border.

Doherty, Peacock, and Bingham had all taken the reins of the national team after their playing careers but, in 1975, Northern Ireland appointed their second successive player-manager, Dave Clements. Aged just twenty-nine when he took on the role (his predecessor Neill had been the same age), he was still playing midfield in the First Division for Everton.

In Neill's final game as manager of Northern Ireland – the opening game in the 1976 European Championship qualifiers – the team had lost to Norway, but Clements instigated a quick turnaround with an away win against Sweden, followed by victory over Yugoslavia. The latter was of huge significance as it not only put the team firmly back into the frame for qualification but was also the first international game to be played at Windsor Park for three and a half years. It was April 1975.

The violence in Northern Ireland was still at a horrific level. The Troubles' bloodiest year had been 1972, when almost five hundred people lost their lives in some of the most infamous acts of the conflict. And even though the death rate had come down to under three hundred a year in 1973, and again in 1974, the figures were still significantly higher than the almost two hundred deaths in 1971 that had prompted Northern Ireland's footballing exile. The change of attitude to staging games in Belfast might perhaps be explained by a normalising of the background violence. People were, sadly, used to it. The security forces were also more confident, knowing what public events they could and couldn't police. Or perhaps it was reckoned that the people, after more than half a decade of suffering, needed some glimmer of normality.

Whatever the reason, international teams were now willing to travel to Belfast again, and the Yugoslavs won many admirers for bravely testing the lay of the land. Clements even organised his team into a guard of honour for the visitors as they took to the pitch, in appreciation of the risk they had taken.

Neill also attended the game in Belfast, no longer as manager, but in solidarity with his countrymen at their return home. As he recalls, 'I think there was a feeling all around … that as a society we were beginning to see some daylight. That was more important than winning football games. But football definitely helps, it unites people.'

The home crowd certainly made a difference, and Northern Ireland won 1–0. The only real blot on Clements' promising first year record was a narrow 2–1 home defeat to Sweden in a game they had been winning. Unfortunately, it was to be of great significance. Thanks to an impressive 3–0 home victory over Norway, Northern Ireland still had a chance of qualifying as they went into the final game of the campaign away to Yugoslavia, although they needed a two-goal margin of victory to overturn the goal difference. However, it was perhaps too much of a long shot and the Irish lost 1–0, failing to qualify for a tournament in the final game for the third time in a decade.

Despite this disappointing end, there was a sense that Northern Ireland were slowly turning the corner, with some good results recorded both within the British Isles and abroad. During the 1974/75 British Championship – which saw both England and Wales playing in Belfast (Scotland would continue to refuse to play there when their turn came round in the 1975/76 tournament) – Northern Ireland had a fairly encouraging campaign: one victory, one draw and one defeat.

Northern Ireland's momentum was entirely lost during the first half of 1976, however, when Clements accepted an offer to cross the Atlantic and play with the famous New York Cosmos. It was a new and exciting platform in the North American

Soccer League (NASL), and Clements would be playing in a team alongside the legendary Pelé, so it was, understandably, an offer impossible to turn down, though Clements did try to perform his duties as Irish boss long distance. This arrangement, however, was quickly ended following a disastrous 1975/76 British Championship tournament in which Northern Ireland lost all three games without scoring a goal in reply, including heavy 3–0 and 4–0 defeats to Scotland and England respectively. Clements realised that the commute across the Atlantic wasn't going to work and that it was time to stand down.

For the first time, Northern Ireland hired a manager who wasn't either a current international or a recently retired star, and they recruited possibly the biggest name they could turn to in Irish football: Danny Blanchflower. Blanchflower had coached at his beloved Spurs upon retiring from the game as his mentor, Bill Nicholson, had suggested to the board that the Irishman be his successor. When management of Tottenham – the only job in football he had been interested in – was surprisingly given to his fellow countryman Terry Neill, Blanchflower had walked away from the game, although he remained a constant presence in the public eye through his insightful and intelligent journalism.

Now, though, Northern Ireland needed him and a poll conducted by the *Belfast Telegraph* indicated that he was the public's clear favourite to take over. The part-time role wasn't going to be financially rewarding, but he was keen to accept the challenge; to give something back to the local game that had given him everything. As Pat Jennings recalls, 'Danny was such a nice bloke, a real charmer and he was so committed to Northern Irish football, wanting us to do well … he did the job to help out the national side, and we wanted to respond to that.'

Blanchflower had spent most of his career in football as a thorn in the side of authority. As a young player at Barnsley he had been labelled as a troublemaker for insisting on training with the ball (in the early 1950s such a practice wasn't common); he had been a vocal critic of the cap on player wages; and he had been an implacable opponent of what he saw as unqualified officials and administrators hampering the beauty and playing of the game. This included taking aim at his new employers. In his 1961 autobiography, *The Double and Beyond*, he had ruthlessly exposed the amateurish organisation of the national team in Belfast, so the IFA would have been all too aware that it was hiring an individual with strong views on how the game should be organised. However, such were the dire straits of Irish football in the mid-70s that the IFA now had no choice. When the committee met to discuss contracts and bonuses, Blanchflower wasted no time in cutting to the chase, telling it that since Northern Ireland never won anything anyway there was little point in discussing such terms. He told the press, 'Since they know I'm not in the job for the material rewards, I have their respect and with it a healthy new spirit.'

Blanchflower's playing credentials were impeccable: he was captain of the famous 1961 double-winning Spurs team; the side won the FA Cup again the following year, and the European Cup Winners' Cup the year after that. His was a glittering career, which had seen him lauded as one of the best midfielders of his generation – when he had joined Spurs from Aston Villa, his transfer fee had been a British record price for a midfielder.

As captain of the Northern Ireland team of the 1950s he and his great idol and friend, Peter Doherty, had instigated a transformational era both on and off the pitch. They instilled a sense of professional pride into everything they did, taking a broom to the decades of slipshod amateurism and careless attitudes that had been endemic within the international framework under the old system of IFA selectors picking the team instead of the manager.

Under the twin guiding lights of Blanchflower and Doherty, Northern Ireland had evolved. Throughout the 1950s, the team went from being an embarrassment to taking their place among the eight best teams in the world in the quarter-finals of the 1958 World Cup. At the tournament's end, Blanchflower proudly took his place alongside Harry Gregg as the only two British players selected for the official Team of the Tournament. And, always, Blanchflower's graceful skill on the pitch was accompanied by his sharp intelligence and wit. Appearing in 1960 as a guest on BBC Radio 4's *Desert Island Discs*, he had remarked upon the famous victory over England in 1957. 'When we get defeated it's a moral victory for us. We try to change it into one. This was one of the blackspots when we sort of defeated ourselves by winning.' His views on all aspects of the game made him the first thinking man's footballer and it was no surprise when the highbrow BBC interview programme *Face to Face*, normally reserved for the movers and shakers of the political and arts worlds, selected him to hold forth on subjects such as the wage cap.

The appointment of a legend such as Blanchflower was a huge lift to the beleaguered international squad and there was a new-found optimism at what might be achieved. On top of this, the squad was beginning to mature into a useful band of players, many of whom were playing for top English sides of the day. For instance, both Manchester United and Arsenal had three Ulstermen in their first teams, and more besides in the reserves. Blanchflower was even able to revive the international career of the prodigal son, George Best, who was back playing regular football and having an entertaining spell at Fulham in between stints in US soccer. Blanchflower clearly had pulling power if he could make even the likes of George Best obediently come running.

Blanchflower's first objective was simply to stop the rot and instil some self-belief in the squad again, just as Doherty had done over twenty years earlier. Blanchflower knew it was an uphill task, but he was refreshingly honest with the press about what he wanted, 'I know I am putting my head on the chopping block.

I won't gain anything financially or in reputation by doing this job. I don't know if I can cope, but I must try. I want to explain my attitudes to playing for your country and towards football. I want to explain about the reasons behind those attitudes. I will tell them, too, that we cannot expect to win everything. That is not logical with our limited resources, but I will hammer home the point – and this is vital – that I would expect them to do their best within their own terms.'

Blanchflower's contract would see him through to the World Cup of 1978, but the chances of attending that tournament were low. To qualify, Northern Ireland were up against the Netherlands (the 1974 World Cup runners-up) and a decent Belgian side. However, to some extent, with victory and qualification not expected, Blanchflower had the freedom to try something different. His very first game in charge, against the Netherlands in October 1976, was the most daunting of all: away, against a squad full of rare talent, including Johan Cruyff, the player many considered the best in the world at that time. Nevertheless, the baptism of fire, played at the Feyenoord Stadium – where Blanchflower had lifted the European Cup Winners' Cup for Spurs in May 1963 – was a memorable night for both Blanchflower and Irish football.

Going into the game, Blanchflower told the press, 'In the past we have been swamped in our own half. I promised to do something about this. I want my players to respect team discipline and, within that general framework, since no one expects us to win, I tell the boys to go out with heads high and attack the opposition. That way we may achieve the unexpected instead of cowering defensively in our own half, hoping to scrape a draw. To me that is undignified. It is better to lose by doing this than by negative, boring defence. If we lose then we do so in a determined manner.'

That night, the players were true to this new philosophy, buoyed up by a new manager they all respected as a footballing great, stirred by his stories of past successes against the odds and energised by his warm and larger-than-life personality. Although a much inferior team to the Dutch opposition, the Irishmen went toe to toe with them in a pulsating, attacking game, first taking the lead, then falling 2–1 behind, before levelling matters for a well-deserved 2–2 draw. However, it was Best in particular who caught the eye as he gave one of the finest displays of the autumn years of his career, perhaps with an eye to showing Cruyff who was the better of the two.

Unfortunately, only a couple of minutes of game footage is still circulating online, and this concentrates only on the goals and near misses. It doesn't record one of the main talking points of the game, namely Best's torturing of the two greatest Dutch players: Cruyff and Johan Neeskins. The nutmegging of either one of these would seem fantastical enough, but Best managed to put the ball through the legs of both during the match in an outrageous show of cheek; one that he had predicted before the game. Best had been telling journalist Bill Elliot how good Cruyff was but when Elliot asked if he was better than Best himself, the Irishman replied, 'You're kidding, aren't you? I'll tell you what I'll do tonight. I'll nutmeg Cruyff the first chance I get.'

Elliot reported, 'Five minutes into the game, Best received the ball wide on the left. Instead of heading towards goal, he turned directly infield, weaved his way past at least three Dutchmen, and found his way to Cruyff who was wide right. He took the ball to his opponent, dipped a shoulder twice and slipped it between Cruyff's feet. As he ran round to collect it and run on, he raised his right fist in the air. Only a few of us in the press box knew what this bravado act really meant.'

Neeskins, too, was embarrassed by Best's audacity. As Pat Jennings fondly recalls, 'Neeskins was doing a man for man marking job on him and he must have nutmegged Neeskins five or six times during the match. Neeskins tried to kick him and came in under him and George jumped and came down on top of him. Neeskins was lying on the grass complaining about being stamped on and George took his sock tie off and threw it to Neeskins and said, "Here, tie them together" – his legs, you know. George absolutely ran the match that night.'

The *Belfast Telegraph* the following day reported a very pleased Best saying of Neeskins, 'I hear he is receiving treatment for bad knees. They kept knocking every time I nutmegged him.' As Martin O'Neill, who watched with other non-playing members of the squad from the stand that night, remembers, 'George was maybe only at seventy per cent of his fitness by then and yet he ruled that night.'

Blanchflower's preparation and tactics, along with his simple footballing philosophy of attacking at all times, had paid instant dividends. He told the press, 'We have none of those long team talks no one understands. I tell them they are all wearing the same-coloured shirts so they might as well pass to each other.' It was, however, unlikely that this famous talker and conversationalist would keep the message so brief, and George Best confirmed this with the press. 'It's fun to play for Ireland again under Danny. He says the same things as Sir Matt Busby used to at Old Trafford: "Go out and be yourself on the field." The only difference is he takes twice as long to say it!'

The night in Rotterdam showed just what Northern Ireland were capable of. However, to record such a result with their limited squad they needed everything to go right for them, for every player to be at the top of their game. As Jennings recalls, 'We had the nucleus of a decent side, so it was always possible for us to have a good game, but the problem was doing that consistently.'

The following week was less successful. They played away to Belgium in Liege and, although they gave a good account of themselves, they ultimately lost 2–0. Their next match, in the spring of 1977, was a friendly in West Germany against vastly superior opposition. Although they commendably held on at 0–0 for a full fifty-five minutes, unlike the Dutch game, where they met opponents who joined in with the free-moving attacking football, the German approach was clinical, and they took Northern Ireland apart in a brutal 5–0 win.

Going into the German game, Blanchflower had once more said, 'It's better to lose having a go than be defeated concentrating on defence as Ireland has done so often.' However, the players were beginning to question the wisdom of this approach. As much as they all adored Blanchflower as a person and as a footballing idol, they needed to start notching up some results. As Jennings recalls, 'He'd rather lose 5–4 than 1–0, the only trouble being that we weren't capable of scoring four, but were always capable of letting five in. A lot of the players weren't too keen on that, especially as things went on, because you don't want to keep getting hammered. We weren't good enough to take the game to the likes of West Germany and I don't think his tactics were right for us. It didn't suit our players.'

Jennings had particular reason to worry about the tactics. As the man repeatedly picking the ball out of the net, it was more demoralising for him than most, particularly when, following the 5–0 defeat, Malcolm Brodie of the *Belfast Telegraph* wrote a scathing article with the headline 'Auf Wiedersehen, Pat' suggesting that it was time to call an end to Jennings' twelve-year reign as Northern Ireland's first-choice keeper. Brodie was a whole-hearted supporter of Blanchflower's attacking philosophy, so the argument that this tactic didn't suit the Northern Ireland personnel was brushed aside and the blame laid instead at Jennings' feet.

The criticism stung Jennings. 'A friend of mine brought me back the *Belfast Telegraph*, coming back from Belfast, and said, "Pat, can you believe this?" I'd played maybe sixty games at that stage for Northern Ireland and I wasn't just written off the international team but was written off as a footballer ... I have nothing but admiration for Malcolm. He was a brilliant writer and I used to read him in the *Belfast Telegraph* and *Ireland's Saturday Night* before I was any sort of age. We never fell out over it and he sort of apologised for it.'

Blanchflower tried to protect his squad from criticism and told Jennings, 'You forget the press, I'll talk to them, you just do your best,' but there was little doubt that Blanchflower's deserved and hard-won respect for past glories was shielding his tactical choices from criticism in the Irish newspapers, and it was the players who were picking up the blame instead.

Bad results kept coming with the 1976/77 British Championship series in which Northern Ireland recorded only a solitary point against Wales. They had been on course for a credible draw in the match against England but conceded the winner with just four minutes to go. However, it was now six games under Blanchflower without a win and things became markedly worse when the World Cup qualifying resumed against lowly Iceland. Without Best, who had now returned to the US from his spell at Fulham to resume playing for the Los Angeles Aztecs, they suffered a soul-destroying 1–0 defeat, with all the early optimism of the previous year now evaporated.

According to Jennings, 'The problem with attacking all the while was that we had some beatings like the West German game and that knocks your confidence. It takes a while to get that back again and if you keep getting beaten badly, you can't get over it. But Danny wouldn't change the style. I wanted a good defensive unit around me ... but he wouldn't change his principles. We had players like Allan Hunter, who was as good as anyone in Britain, and he didn't want to be carrying the ball up to the halfway line while everyone dropped back. He wanted to look for lads up front to take the pressure off.'

Martin O'Neill also recalls being left bewildered by Blanchflower's approach: 'Danny had a very attacking philosophy. Maybe in hindsight he should have taken a little bit more notice of Northern Ireland's limitations. We once played a game against England at Wembley where we played like a 4-2-4 formation and he basically told the four of us forwards to stay up the field and not to worry about getting back. So, essentially, we watched the game with binoculars as most of the match was played in and around our penalty area.'

Tactics on the training ground were often even more bizarre: on one occasion the players were instructed to try and dribble with two balls at once. Gerry Armstrong, like the rest of the squad, deeply admired the man but found his training eccentric. 'He made you feel special. He was a breath of fresh air, but he was a bit of a dreamer. Danny was always trying to think outside the box. Pat was in goal and we were setting up a wall for some free kicks. Danny said, "Hold on. I've got an idea. Move the wall back further." Pat says, "What do you mean?" So Danny said, "Instead of making it ten yards, let's make it fifteen yards. Move it back further. We've got Pat Jennings in goal, the best goalkeeper in the world." So he says, "Who's left footed?" and Sammy Nelson steps up. "Okay, Sammy, go and hit one, bend it over the wall if you can." So, Sammy smashed it with his left foot, right over the top of the wall into the top corner, Pat couldn't get anywhere near it. Pat says, "Hold on a wee minute, Danny. Get that wall ten yards again. Forget fifteen yards." Danny said, "Okay, we tried it, just an experiment." He loved to try things.' Another experiment was to leave half the team upfield when defending a corner. Thankfully, such ploys never made it into an actual match.

The first win under Blanchflower eventually came during September 1977, in the reverse fixture against Iceland at Windsor Park with Northern Ireland winning 2–0. After the game, Blanchflower blasted Iceland's tactics and what he perceived as a cowardly show of defence. 'That's not the way I would have played under the circumstances. They came to save their face, not to entertain, but I suppose that's the name of the game today.' He couldn't comprehend the changed footballing world in which he now found himself. Entertainment always trumped results to his thinking.

Three weeks later, on 17 October 1977, a landmark game was played, although its significance wasn't known at the time. Against Holland and its shining star Johan Cruyff, George Best pulled on a Northern Ireland shirt for the very last time. The men in green rose to the occasion with another spirited performance, but this time the superior guile and skill of the Dutch won out in a narrow 1–0 victory and Best left the international stage. In thirteen years, he had notched up a mere thirty-seven appearances and his talent had never been given the platform it deserved. Despite the narrowness of the defeat to the second-best team in the world, the report in the *Belfast Telegraph* criticised most of the team, although this time Jennings was spared. The word 'embarrassment' was bandied around, as if the players were at fault for not being as good as one of the greatest footballing nations in the world. The disconnect between the demands of local journalism and reality couldn't have been greater and the dispiriting criticism of the team after a narrow loss to such illustrious visitors cannot possibly have helped the morale of the squad.

An impressive victory did come soon after when, in November 1977, Belgium were beaten 3–0 at Windsor Park with young striker Gerry Armstrong grabbing two of the goals. However, expectations were brought down to earth as Northern Ireland again recorded only a single point in the 1977/78 British Championship. Although the defeats were both narrow 1–0 losses, the inescapable truth was that Blanchflower's record as boss stood at two wins, three draws and eight defeats from his thirteen games in charge.

Blanchflower stayed on as manager for the European Championship qualifying campaign, held throughout 1978/79, as there wasn't any other viable candidate with the credentials or the desire for the job. He did make known, however, that this would be his final tournament in charge, and it looked set to be a tough one. Drawn in a five-team group alongside England, with only one team qualifying, their chances already looked slim. On top of that, they were to face Denmark, Bulgaria and the first-ever fixtures against the Republic of Ireland. This pairing in particular once more raised the question of whether there should be a single team to represent the island. Blanchflower showed that he had lost none of his famous wit when he responded: 'Terrific! I'm all for it. If they let us play twenty-two players in a united team, I think we will have a chance to beat the world!'

The opening fixture was in September 1978 when Northern Ireland played against the Republic at Lansdowne Road, Dublin. It was a very tight affair, with neither of the Irish sides wanting to lose this historic game, which was played under heavy security for the visiting squad. While the 0–0 result was the product of a largely forgettable match, it provided a springboard for Northern Ireland to improve. A morale-boosting 2–1 home victory against Denmark followed in October 1978, and when the first away win of the Blanchflower era was obtained in November 1978 with a 2–0 triumph in Bulgaria, Northern Ireland suddenly found themselves sitting top of the group.

With Northern Ireland now seen as an improving unit under Blanchflower's guidance, an unexpected offer came in from First Division strugglers, Chelsea, who decided to take a gamble on the manager. The Northern Ireland job was, to the IFA, only part-time and so didn't stand in the way of Blanchflower doing both jobs at once (in the same way as Bingham had double-jobbed a decade earlier, and as Peter Doherty had in the 1950s). However, the end of the year would turn out to be the high-water mark of Blanchflower's managerial career before a renewed run of poor results kicked off with a 4–0 thrashing by England at Wembley in February 1979, which helped to put into perspective the chances of Northern Ireland qualifying. Although they bounced back with a 2–0 win over Bulgaria in May 1979, they were at the end of another morale-sapping 4–0 defeat to Denmark in Copenhagen that June, which effectively killed off their chances of making it to the 1980 European Championships in Italy and finished the 1978/79 season on a low. Before that, there had been another fruitless campaign in the British Championships which saw them pick up a single point and remain winless for the third straight year under Blanchflower.

Part of this lack of success may, as Pat Jennings recalls, have been owing to the inferiority complex he and his team-mates would often suffer from when playing against other home nations. 'It was always on the cards that England might wallop us – you looked at what they had on the bench and what we had on the field and that set it up for us. We knew them and what to expect. Perhaps ignorance was bliss at times – when we played Belgium or Bulgaria, we didn't know what was coming, what their strengths might be, and so you weren't overawed and just played your game.'

Meanwhile, things had started badly for Blanchflower at Chelsea and just kept getting worse as the season progressed. His opening game had been a humiliating 7–2 defeat at Middlesbrough and he finished the season with just three victories from the twenty-four league games he managed. Chelsea finished bottom of the First Division and were relegated, forced into selling their prize asset, Ray Wilkins, to Manchester United.

Blanchflower had a reasonable start to the 1979/80 season, then experienced a run of poor results and in September fell on his sword and left Chelsea, perhaps finally coming to realise that the way of playing football that he held so dear was no longer effective. He was now free to concentrate on the remaining few fixtures of his time with Northern Ireland but, a month after stepping down at Chelsea, he experienced the trauma of a 5–1 trouncing at home by England.

All that remained was the final fixture of the campaign, a match against the Republic in November 1979. The two Irish teams went into the game level on points so there was a definite purpose in both teams trying to win and finish ahead of the other in the group. In the end, Blanchflower was allowed to bow out with a sense of dignity and relief following a 1–0 victory, courtesy of Armstrong, and Northern Ireland finished second in the group. The results against the top team aside, it had actually been a reasonable campaign, but they'd had no answer when asked to match England, and Blanchflower's attacking philosophy left them badly exposed to heavy defeats when playing against opponents of that stature. As Pat Rice, the Arsenal defender and Northern Ireland stalwart, explains, 'European football was very defensively minded at that stage and the goal-scoring opportunities weren't there for us. When George Best finally went, we didn't have the players up front.'

Blanchflower resigned as manager immediately after this game, with the pride of a win behind him. He had taken the job out of a sense of national service and given his all, but his approach was so out of tune with contemporary footballing reality that it could never be enough. While everyone wanted to believe in the dream that he could steer Northern Ireland towards success, it was always doomed to failure and it was a sad sight to see this played out in the full glare of journalists who delivered damning verdicts. As he departed the international stage for the last time in the final days of 1979, it became clear that Blanchflower's philosophy was a product of earlier decades. Football in the 1980s would only feel his influence through the inspiration of those memories.

Yet Blanchflower was philosophical about his tenure, 'It was time to go. I had done my best. I had paid off my [footballing] debts. I had made some friends among the players. We could shake hands and behave like sportsmen. It does not matter about winning and losing so long as the Irish spirit of fair play sparks some admiration and affection in others.'

It should come as no surprise that this honourable man left the role still beloved by everyone who had worked under him. He would be missed by the players, even if they had disagreed with his tactics. As Jennings said, 'If I'd wanted to win for any of the managers I'd played under, it would have been Danny. There wasn't an ounce of badness in him, he just wanted what was good for Irish football ... It was an enjoyable experience, a privilege and an honour to play for his teams.'

Rice echoes this view, 'What he really did was brighten up Northern Irish football ... there was a lot of happiness, joviality about the camp, a great spirit and a sense of comradeship among the players, and I think that stood the team in good stead after he'd left.'

Northern Ireland now had to find a worthy successor to kick off the new decade, and the unenviable task for any incoming manager was how to retain the spirit of the squad and marshal the abilities of a small group of players. The inescapable truth was that the country didn't have quite enough good players to compete and win consistently at the highest levels. But could they somehow find a way to make better use of what they did have? The team had tried the tactics of the timorous and the adventurous throughout the 1970s and both had failed. Was there a third way to advance the nation's cause in the 1980s?

PUTTING THE BAND TOGETHER

As the IFA began its centenary year in 1980, the matter of replacing Blanchflower as manager was far from clear cut. The job represented something of a poisoned chalice and the five managers since Doherty had each resigned when they realised that they couldn't take the team any further. Although the political situation in Northern Ireland wasn't as dangerous and volatile as it had been a decade earlier, it was still a grim time of violence and division – not an ideal background for building the nation's sporting aspirations.

Although it was reported the day after Blanchflower resigned that Billy Bingham would be interested in the job, he was considered an outsider, with a younger man much more likely to take it. By far the most obvious choice was Terry Neill, another former manager who had been capped and tutored under Peter Doherty. Neill was easily the most successful club manager of Northern Irish heritage. He also had a number of Northern Ireland internationals on the books at Arsenal and had guided them to two successive FA Cup finals, winning the 1979 competition in one of the most memorable finals of all time with a 3–2 win over Manchester United. However, Neill moved quickly to distance himself from the speculation, telling the press, 'My total devotion is now taken up at Highbury, it's a massive job, although the Northern Ireland team has always been close to my heart. I can't see any way where I could take over, but certainly if I could help out in any other way, I will be only too glad.'

Six weeks later, with a new decade ushered in, the IFA had only half-heartedly looked into appointing a new manager and, despite Neill having already ruled himself out, the International Committee seemed intent on offering him the job. Two former goalkeepers were also in the frame, however. Iam McFaul, a coach at Newcastle United and former understudy to Pat Jennings in the national team, had been given permission by his club to travel to Belfast for talks. The other was the hero of the 1958 squad, Harry Gregg, a former manager at Swansea, Shrewsbury and Crewe, now a goalkeeper coach at Manchester United. Gregg was certainly the choice of the *Belfast Telegraph*, which asserted that he was 'the disciplinarian and inspiration required to sort out the international squad'. He was a familiar sight to the three regular Northern Ireland internationals playing at Manchester United and to the other fellow countrymen playing in their reserves, including a young up-and-coming teenager called Norman Whiteside, just fourteen, who was already being spoken about as the future of Northern Ireland's attacking line. Martin Harvey, a former international during the 1960s, who had picked up thirty-four caps and was now on the coaching staff at Carlisle United, was the other candidate being mentioned as a possibility.

Meanwhile, the IFA had other matters on its mind. Despite

Harry Cavan's hostility towards Derek Dougan's 1973 all-Ireland project, talks had been ongoing for at least two years between the IFA and its counterpart in Dublin, the Football Association of Ireland (FAI), on the viability of unifying and creating a single team to compete in international competition. Formal talks had been held on the subject during the recent fixtures between the two nations and were followed up early in 1980 when the IFA presented the FAI with a detailed document outlining what it saw as potential hurdles.

High-profile players from both religious backgrounds, such as Best and Jennings, had been public supporters of a single team, and the Republic of Ireland team at this stage in its history had suffered from the same problem as its neighbours in the north – a squad that contained some excellent players, but was lacking strength in depth and always falling agonisingly short of qualifying for the major tournaments. Should the best players from both teams compete together, they could form a side that was on the same level as Scotland, who regularly qualified for such tournaments. Northern Ireland had a good defensive line playing in front of Pat Jennings but struggled going forward, whereas the Republic of Ireland team was strong in this area, with players such as Arsenal's Frank Stapleton and Liam Brady, and Liverpool's Steve Heighway.

Perhaps predictably, finances seemed to be the main stumbling block for the IFA. Should a unified Irish team play in the British Championship, the money available to local football in the north would be diluted. The IFA argued that the money it earned from the TV rights of this tournament was the lifeblood of the local football framework, with proceeds trickling down to club and amateur level. This seemed an insurmountable problem, despite a willingness from both sides to explore the possibilities of unification.

Of course, the romantic notion would almost certainly have been unworkable from a security point of view. Whereas a single national rugby team based in Dublin had always been accepted, the idea that the merging of the two football sides would have occurred without trouble was perhaps naïve. Policing any games in Belfast would unquestionably have presented a problem. The mood in the press once the IFA documents were presented in January 1980 was of extreme pessimism and the proposal was soon dashed on the rocks.

The IFA now finally addressed the vacant manager's position and offered the job to Neill, who considered it, but ultimately felt that he needed to remain focused on the excellent squad he had assembled in north London. He was quoted in *Ireland's Saturday Night* as saying, 'There is no point in trying to do it if I cannot do it properly. I'd thought of perhaps taking it on for the period of the World Cup, but then this would not be right either. You [need] to devote a lot of time to this job.'

Another former manager, Dave Clements, then entered the frame. The ex-New York Cosmos star was still living in the US, playing and coaching in Denver, but was reportedly deciding whether to abandon his sports shop business and return home. It was expected that he would be a serious contender if he did.

So, with a supposed shortlist of four – Clements, Gregg, McFaul and Harvey, with McFaul being promoted as the frontrunner – the international committee was to meet at the end of January to discuss the issue. There was under two months to go before Northern Ireland's World Cup campaign was due to start and the dragging of heels began to agitate the press. Malcolm Brodie made his feelings clear in his weekly column in *Ireland's Saturday Night* when he complained, 'For almost a year now there has been stagnation. Quite bluntly, the international build-up has ground to a halt. The message is crystal-clear to the Irish FA – appoint the manager and let him get on with the job, a mammoth one of rehabilitation.'

With the press focusing attention on the four contenders, it came as something of a surprise when the announcement was made that the job had been offered to Bingham, who was quickly confirmed in the position on 7 February. After leaving his twin interests in Northern Ireland in 1971, when he had resigned from his positions at Linfield and the national team, he had spent a few turbulent years as manager of Greece before, in May 1973, returning to the north west of England, close to his Southport home, to take on a high-profile job as manager of Everton. Everton had finished seventeenth in the 1972/73 season, perilously close to the foot of the First Division, but Bingham marched them up the table to finish a respectable seventh in his first season in charge. Building upon this he had looked almost certain to win the title the following year, only to see his team falter with the finishing line in sight, picking up only two wins in their final ten matches as Derby County were crowned champions.

After this near-miss, results weren't as impressive the following season as Everton slipped back into mid-table in eleventh position. A run of eight league games without a victory the year after saw the board lose patience and Bingham was sacked towards the end of January 1977. He wasted little time, though, in securing a new position and returned to Greece where he took on a club challenge at PAOK Thessaloniki. He lasted just six months in the job before being replaced, but shortly afterwards took control at struggling Mansfield Town in February 1978. Mansfield were a team with relegation written all over them and Bingham was initially unable to stem the flow of defeats.

Although he did oversee some better results towards the end of the season, it wasn't enough to stop Mansfield finishing second bottom of the Second Division and slipping down a rung of the footballing ladder. Bingham stayed with them but was unable to turn things around the following year, and when Mansfield could only manage eighteenth place under his guidance in the Third Division he quit and bided his time doing consultancy work on foreign players for a team in the north of England. He would be out of management for a year before answering the call of his country once more.

Although the position was, as always, offered only on money-saving part-time terms, Bingham relished the prospect of devoting all his energies to the task ahead and told *Ireland's Saturday Night* in the days before he signed his contract, 'This time I shall be doing the job virtually full-time instead of fitting it in with club duties and that has to be good. It's the only thing on your mind.' Having done the job before his eyes were certainly wide open to the problems he faced, but he was fiercely optimistic nevertheless. 'We are realistic in Northern Ireland. We know our position in world football – we are one of the little people. But sometimes small nations come to the fore – like Holland have done – because a certain group of players come together at the right time. Maybe that cycle will happen to us again.'

For World Cup qualifying, Northern Ireland had been drawn in a five-team group that also contained Scotland, Portugal, Sweden and Israel. Northern Ireland would probably have been considered fourth favourites in this pool. However, this was to be the first World Cup expanded from sixteen to twenty-four teams, which meant more places available for European nations. Previously a team would have had to win the group to qualify, but second place would be enough this time. Bingham was alert to this change in circumstances and told the press, 'Certainly it is not an outstanding group, and with traditional Irish spirit, hard work and organisation, we must be in with a great chance. If you have two qualifying, as is the case in our group, then you have a great chance. Let's get the right side, a settled side, and one which is properly organised, then there is a positive chance of qualifying. These players can put themselves into history like those of us in 1958.'

The IFA had originally agreed to appoint an assistant alongside Bingham, a younger man with the potential to take over in the future. Bingham's choice was Martin Harvey, who accepted the position when it was offered to him. However, he was now caretaker manager at Carlisle, who agreed that Harvey's arrangement of release would only come into effect with the British Championship in May rather than for the forthcoming fixture against Israel in March. It is possible that Carlisle assumed Harvey would be replaced as manager by that stage anyway, but when a series of improved results saw Harvey being kept on in his position, they began to develop cold feet regarding the agreement. By the time the match in Tel Aviv came around it was clear that Harvey would be unable take up the role later in the year and the idea of having an assistant was dropped.

The team Bingham inherited in 1980 contained a few familiar faces from the end of his previous spell in charge almost a decade before. Mainly, however, this was a new squad, which had settled themselves in under Neill, Clements and Blanchflower. Any sensible manager wants to build his team from the back with a solid defence, and Bingham was lucky in that the personnel were already in place to provide that bedrock for the team. As an added bonus, many of them were already team-mates at Arsenal or Manchester United and therefore possessed an understanding of each other's game. The solid core of what, over the next six years, would become the Bingham team, were players mainly of the same age – mid-twenties – and about to hit their peak season as footballers. In many ways it was similar to the team of the 1950s who grew up together at international level.

Few would suggest that, as individuals, the 1980s team were on the same level as the team Bingham had been a part of in the 1950s, but collectively they were a solid squad of seasoned professionals playing mainly for top English clubs and with experience in plentiful supply. The players may not have been, in most cases, the stars of their English clubs, but there was little doubt that they had genuine quality of their own. They were useful members of the team who worked hard and held down their places.

Of the players potentially available to Bingham, the two longest-standing members of the international squad were Best and Jennings. Best's career had been erratic to say the least since his ten-year spell at Manchester United ended in acrimony in 1974 when the club was under the management of Tommy Docherty. Aged only twenty-eight when he left United, Best was still within his peak playing years, but for the next two years played only a handful of games for clubs of little standing, including the Jewish Guild in South Africa, Stockport County and Cork Celtic. In 1976, US soccer offered him a lifeline and he signed for Los Angeles Aztecs, playing later for Fort Lauderdale Strikers and then San Jose Earthquakes. From 1976 to 1977, he had an entertaining spell back in English football, playing for Fulham in the Second Division while Bobby Moore was manager. He left Fort Lauderdale Strikers in 1979 and signed for Hibernian in the Scottish Premier Division that November.

He was certainly, inevitably, one of the first names Bingham was asked about upon taking up the reins of the national team, and the new manager responded by saying, 'I'm aware of what he is doing with Hibs. They seem to be satisfied but I've got to look at the international involvement where the standard could be higher than in Scotland. Best will be looked at like the others.'

Unfortunately, Best picked a very poor time to go off the rails again. That weekend, the first after Bingham had been appointed, Best went missing and didn't turn up for a game. However, Bingham must have found the lure of a potentially rejuvenated Best hard to resist, and in February 1980 he travelled from his Southport home to Edinburgh to watch the midfielder play for Hibs against Ayr United in the Scottish Cup. But the night before the match, Best had embarked upon a drinking binge of epic proportions, accompanied by Jean-Pierre Rives (the captain of the French rugby union team, who were in Edinburgh at the time) and, reputedly, Debbie Harry of Blondie. The revelries finished at eleven in the morning with Best due to play a few hours later. He was immediately sacked, although this was later reduced to a suspension and eventually he continued to play for the club. Bingham's response was not quoted in the press – it is unlikely to have been favourable – but it was doubtful that he, a hard taskmaster and disciplinarian, would be inclined to include Best in his first squad.

A year older than Best but much more dependable, and still in top physical shape, was the country's number one goalkeeper, Pat Jennings. Jennings had played Gaelic football at school but would find his true calling in soccer. As a teen, he had a successful season with Newry United before moving into the Newry Town team, attracting the attention of bigger clubs and making a debut for the Northern Ireland Youth team. A transfer to England's Third Division followed when he joined Watford Town, where he so impressed in his first season that he signed for London giants Tottenham Hotspur in the summer of 1964.

That same year, just a few months earlier, he had made his debut for Northern Ireland and by the end of 1979, at the age of thirty-four, he held an incredible eighty-two international caps. It was a remarkable total, especially considering that he played in a time with fewer international fixtures. He was recognised as being one of the most outstanding goalkeepers in English football and had collected a fair few medals along the way: the FA Cup in 1967, the League Cup in 1971 and 1973, and the UEFA Cup in 1974, all with Spurs. His time with the club even included a rare goal when he kicked the ball the full length of the field at Wembley to score against Manchester United in the 1967 Charity Shield. He was personally honoured with the coveted Football Writers' Association (FWA) Footballer of the Year Award in 1973 and the Professional Footballers' Association (PFA) Player of the Year in 1976.

In 1977, however, Jennings was suddenly bundled out of Spurs, who told him he was to be sold to Ipswich Town. Manchester United and Aston Villa were also reportedly interested but

Jennings had other ideas. After being snubbed by the club's directors in the car park when he went to say farewell to his team-mates, he made the short trip across north London to the club's rivals, Arsenal. 'There was only one place I was going after that,' he recalls, 'and that was over the road to suit me and hopefully create a bit of embarrassment for Tottenham.' Arsenal won 5–0 on his first return to White Hart Lane and Jennings extended his honours at his new club with an FA Cup winner's medal in 1979.

The first name on the team sheet was therefore a formality. Bingham had relied upon Jennings during his first spell as Northern Ireland manager, and would have no worries doing so again. Bingham also had no concerns about who might replace Jennings in the long term or stand in for him if he was injured. Northern Ireland's second-choice goalkeeper was a First Division player of some stature in his own right, Jim Platt of Middlesbrough. He had won the Second Division title with them in 1974 and the Anglo-Scottish Cup in 1976 and was now at his peak as a shot stopper. But, just as Iam McFaul of Newcastle had been limited to only six caps by being unlucky enough to be on the scene at the same time as the brilliant Jennings, so Platt now also found his chances severely limited. Having made his debut four years earlier in 1976 against Israel, Platt had only been able to add caps from the three games of the 1978 British Championship series and no more. However, despite his lack of appearances, Bingham knew enough about Platt's ability to realise that he had a replacement of good standing should Jennings ever be unavailable.

Among the veterans in the squad were several outfield players who had played regularly since the tail end of the 1960s. Bryan Hamilton and Allan Hunter were both now thirty-three but had still been regulars under Blanchflower. Both had played at Ipswich together until Hamilton moved on to Everton then slipped down into the less rigorous Third Division with Swindon Town.

Hunter was still at Bobby Robson's incredible Ipswich team, but with a highly competitive squad at the high-flying club, he was no longer a regular first teamer, despite holding the captain's armband for his country. Hunter was a well-known figure in the English game and had even, alongside Jennings, been one of two Northern Irishmen to represent The Three in a prestige friendly against The Six – a now forgotten game from 1973 at Wembley which celebrated the United Kingdom, the Republic of Ireland and Denmark joining the six original members of what was then called the European Economic Community.

It may not have been immediately obvious from some of the heavy defeats in the Blanchflower era, but it was in defence that Northern Ireland was particularly strong. Pat Rice and Sammy Nelson were two long-serving members of the international squad. Rice had made his debut in 1968 and was now aged thirty while Nelson was the same age but first played for his country in 1970. Both fullbacks were first team picks in an excellent Arsenal side, and they had been with the club their entire careers. They had enjoyed honours there, with Rice a part of the legendary First Division and FA Cup double-winning side of 1971. He was an FA Cup winner again in 1979 and also picked up two runners-up medals in 1972 and 1978. Nelson had been an understudy during the double year but by 1975 had established himself in the first team and had stayed there ever since, playing in both FA Cup finals at the end of the decade, including the 1979 victory. With Rice, Nelson and Jennings on board, Northern Ireland had three fifths of the Arsenal back line and couldn't have been more fortunate. Better organisation at international level should stem the flow of goals.

The other chief centre back for Northern Ireland at this stage, besides Hunter, was thirty-three-year-old Chris Nicholl of Southampton. Despite the small pool of players to choose from, the IFA at this time tended to almost exclusively pick players who had been born in Northern Ireland. Nicholl was an exception. Born in Macclesfield, he qualified for Northern Ireland through parentage and was a solid hard-working pro who finally climbed the footballing ladder with a no-nonsense work ethic. Initially signing for Burnley in the 1960s, he worked his way to Halifax Town and then to Luton Town before finding himself captain of Aston Villa during a highly successful period. They were promoted out of the Third Division, where the once great club had been languishing, and in 1975 won promotion back to the First, as well as triumphing at Wembley in the League Cup Final.

Two years later they returned to the final and, in an epic game against Everton, which ended up going to two replays, Nicholl scored one of the great Wembley final goals of all time, cutting in from the wing and smashing a shot from forty yards into the far top corner. During this season he also became an answer to a great pub quiz question when he scored all four goals in a 2–2 draw against Leicester City, his two own goals balancing out the two conventional goals he scored in the match. He dropped back down to the Second Division when he signed for Lawrie McMenemy's Southampton in 1977 but was back in the First Division by the end of the season when they were promoted, and back for yet another League Cup Final at Wembley when Southampton lost 3–2 against the top side of the period, Nottingham Forest. Nicholl had made his debut for Northern Ireland in 1974 and, although now in the autumn of his career, he represented a model of consistency and effort.

The Northern Irish defence was packed with quality, but it was beginning to get somewhat long in the tooth. The average age of the back five named above was thirty-two. In the short term they could do the job, but they would all be two years older by the end of the forthcoming World Cup campaign. Fortunately for Bingham, there was already a first-class defender of younger years playing in the First Division, Jimmy Nicholl – cousin to Chris Nicholl – of Manchester United. The younger

Nicholl had been born in Canada to Northern Irish parents, but had been living back in Belfast from the age of three. He signed for Manchester United in 1974 and made his debut the following year when the club unexpectedly found itself in the Second Division. By the 1976/77 season he had established himself as first-choice right back and picked up an FA Cup winners' medal in a famous 2–1 victory over treble-chasing Liverpool. He had remained a regular ever since and had just tasted defeat in the 1979 final. Although a natural right back, Nicholl's great strength was his versatility and he often slotted in as a centre back for Northern Ireland if Chris Nicholl or Hunter were injured or unavailable. To have a young player with such top-level experience was a boon to Bingham who knew that his back line would need tweaking going forward.

He would also have been encouraged by reports of a new generation of Northern Irish defenders coming through the ranks of English teams, with Mal Donaghy at Luton Town and John O'Neill at Leicester City both showing promise in the Second Division.

If Bingham could be reasonably pleased with Northern Ireland's defence, he would also have been greatly encouraged when he looked to the centre. He had inherited as its anchor a pair of central midfielders who would have been the envy of almost any First Division club of the time. The first of these was Martin O'Neill, who had enjoyed a stratospheric rise in a career that, like that of Jennings, had started in Gaelic football. O'Neill had played for several GAA sides, then for amateur soccer league outfit Rosario in south Belfast. In 1971, he joined Irish League side Distillery. As he explains, 'I think I always wanted to play soccer, it was a professional game. I enjoyed my Gaelic days greatly … But it was a life choice to follow professional football in England.'

He enjoyed a successful period at Distillery and scored twice when they won the 1971 Irish Cup with a 3–0 victory over

Derry City. In the following season's European Cup Winners' Cup, Distillery were handed a daunting but lucrative fixture against the glamorous Barcelona. The Irish side lost the first leg 3–1 (and would go on to lose 4–0 in Barcelona a fortnight later) but the scorer of the single Distillery goal was O'Neill, aged just nineteen. This brought him to the attention of English clubs, and he was sold to Nottingham Forest.

O'Neill scored on his debut for Forest in November 1971, but they were a team in decline, and they were relegated that season, remaining in the Second Division for the next five years. However, in 1975 came the appointment of Brian Clough, the outspoken manager who succeeded in turning things around for the club, which was promoted back to the First Division in 1977 (albeit via the unconvincing route of third place in the Second, winning the Anglo-Scottish Cup along the way). The next year, however, with a remarkable group of players now gelling together, they won the First Division and the League Cup for good measure. The following season Forest began a then-record of forty-two unbeaten league games, a sequence that spanned two seasons, lasted thirteen months and that only came to an end in December 1978. They were runners-up to Liverpool in the league that season, but by May 1979 had added a second successive League Cup to their honours, as well as the European Cup. Unfortunately, O'Neill had been recovering from injury and was only able to make the subs bench for the final against Malmö, but he was present in the first of two legs when Forest added the 1979 UEFA Super Cup to the bulging trophy cabinet by defeating Barcelona.

His record for Northern Ireland was also impressive. He had been studying law at Queen's when he was drafted into the squad to face the Soviet Union in October 1971 – he was a late replacement and appeared in the game as a substitute. This was, of course, the final game in Belfast for several years, so when he scored on his full debut in March 1973, in a 'home' game against Portugal, it was, unfortunately, in front of a less than full stadium in Coventry, rather than before the Belfast faithful. Nevertheless, he was now a regular under the stewardships of Neill, Clements and Blanchflower, and Bingham would have wanted him to bring his experience of winning at the highest level as inspiration to his international team-mates.

Alongside O'Neill, Bingham had inherited another experienced and much-admired midfielder from the top rungs of English football, Sammy McIlroy of Manchester United, who had notched up forty caps and could act as a central midfield lynchpin around which the team could be built. McIlroy, originally from east Belfast, was the final Busby Babe – the last of Sir Matt Busby's signings for Manchester United. He graduated to the first team in 1971, playing alongside his hero George Best, and scored on his debut in a thrilling 3–3 derby against Manchester City. After the club's relegation to the Second Division in 1974, he established himself as a regular in the team as they bounced back into the top-flight.

He played in all of United's trips to Wembley when they notched up three finals in four years in the FA Cup, picking up two loser's medals and one winner's. In the 1979 final against Arsenal – where he played against several of his international colleagues – he personally gained a moment of glory when his stunning individual goal equalised for United in the dying seconds of the game. Twisting past two defenders and leaving them both lying on the ground, McIlroy had slid the ball past Jennings, who was diving at his feet, only to agonisingly see Arsenal regain the lead in the final minute, resulting in a 3–2 defeat.

McIlroy's international call-up came during Terry Neill's spell as manager and after he had made just eight full senior games for his club. His debut came against Spain in February 1972 in the first of the exile games where he played alongside his famous United team-mate, George Best. As he states in his book, *Manchester United: My Team*, 'At 17 years and 198 days old, I became the second-youngest British footballer to claim an international cap. I made sure I was on the 8.40 a.m. train from Manchester's Victoria station, even though George Best missed it, and I arrived to find that I would be rooming with Martin O'Neill, so two new boys were given the chance to get to know each other, as well as their team-mates.'

McIlroy's former Manchester United team-mate, David McCreery, would add a third established star to the centre of the field. The diminutive but tough and energetic midfielder made his debut for the Manchester club during their one-season sojourn in the Second Division in 1974 and was an important squad member over the next few campaigns back in the First, often employed as a substitute. He came off the bench in both the 1976 and 1977 FA Cup finals but, as these were the days when only a single substitute could be named, he didn't make the named team of twelve for the 1979 final and was sold to Queens Park Rangers that summer. Now playing in the Second Division with the London club, McCreery, still only twenty-two years old, had half a decade of experience at one of football's glamour clubs and was now playing every week as an integral part of the team.

His Northern Ireland appearances dated back to the British Championship of 1976 and incoming manager, Danny Blanchflower, retained his services for his first game in charge against Holland. The teenage McCreery had been tasked with marking Johan Cruyff. Not only did he have an admirable game in this highly unenviable role, but he memorably jinked his way into the Dutch penalty area and took the ball towards the byline to cross for the equalising goal in the closing moments. With twenty-five caps to his name already, McCreery was another dependable figure for Bingham to rely on.

Providing some outlet on the right flank of midfield was Terry Cochrane. Having moved from Derry City to Linfield to Coleraine in 1976, Cochrane had come to the attention of Second Division Burnley, a club that was second only to Manchester United in providing a home for talented young Northern Ireland players. Cochrane's displays impressed Middlesbrough who, in 1978, brought him up a level into the First Division.

He had made his debut for Northern Ireland back in 1975, then spent three years waiting for his second cap, but his performances with Burnley and Middlesbrough encouraged Blanchflower to make him a regular from 1978 onwards. Now aged twenty-seven, he was at his peak and gaining experience in the top division.

Completing the midfield line-up in recent seasons, alongside veteran Hamilton, were a number of ex-Irish League stars who had moved into English football and beyond. Tommy Cassidy had played for Glentoran as a teenager before, in 1970, getting a chance with Newcastle United, where he had remained for a whole decade. A First Division side, they had enjoyed a strong run as a cup team in the mid-70s: they reached the 1974 FA Cup final, where they lost to Bill Shankly's Liverpool, and the 1976 League Cup final, which they also lost. These two Wembley appearances for Cassidy were accompanied by back-to-back triumphs in 1974 and 1975, in the long-forgotten Texaco Cup. By 1978, however, the team had entered a period of decline and Cassidy was relegated with the club to the Second Division. His international career had been something of a stop–start affair and it had taken him nine years to accumulate his thirteen caps. He had fallen out of favour with the international management for a couple of seasons, but he had recently come back in from the cold to play in Blanchflower's final games. At twenty-nine, and with many years of experience in the top division in England, he was a useful addition to the squad.

Another player who had featured in midfield in many of the later Blanchflower games was young Vic Moreland. He had spent his early years as a successful attacking midfielder at Glentoran before enjoying a loan spell in 1978 at Tulsa Roughnecks in the NASL. That same year, shortly after returning to Glentoran, he was snapped up by Tommy Docherty at Derby County who declared him to be 'one of the most accomplished midfielders in Britain'. Derby, who had been crowned champions of England twice in the mid-70s, had fallen into a very steep decline but they were still a First Division club. Moreland may not quite have lived up to Docherty's accolades, but Blanchflower was impressed enough to find room for him in many of his later first elevens.

Any study of the team options for Bingham up to this point would have been most satisfactory. He had one of the most experienced and able goalkeepers in the world, with strong back-up. The defence had five First Division players to choose from and some promising young players currently playing in the Second Division. Two stars of the game filled the centre of midfield, with several First and Second Division players available to play alongside them. Up front was where the problems began for Bingham and, despite there being some skilful individuals, it had always been the one area where Northern Ireland struggled to find strength in depth, even as far back as the great team from the 1950s.

As Bingham took over there was only really one striker from a first-rank team available to Northern Ireland – Gerry Armstrong. Northern Ireland were fortunate to have Armstrong's services as he had only seriously taken up soccer while serving a four-week ban from Gaelic football (he was involved in a fracas while playing in an Antrim Minor final and had broken his opponent's jaw). Already an eager sportsman who trained hard, Armstrong was taken on by a local side, moved on to play in the amateur leagues for Cromac Albion, then came to the attention of Irish League side Bangor FC. As he surmises, 'Everything happens for a reason.' However, this wasn't the end of Armstrong's involvement with GAA. He spent several seasons with Bangor, but he continued to play GAA once more when his ban ended, and he was a player of some note. According to Armstrong himself, 'I was a much better Gaelic player than I was a soccer player, let's put it like that.' He spent his weekends playing football on Saturday and Gaelic football on Sundays and represented Antrim Under-21 as they won back-to-back Ulster titles, losing the All-Ireland final in 1974 and narrowly losing the semi-final in 1975 in a game in which Armstrong was singled out for rave reviews. He only gave up GAA when he made the move to England.

In 1975, when Terry Neill was managing Tottenham Hotspur, word reached him of Armstrong's efforts for Bangor and he bought him for the north London club in November of that year, although Armstrong would have to wait until the following August before making his debut. By that stage, Neill had taken on the Arsenal job and Spurs went into a tailspin, finishing bottom of the First Division. Armstrong was part of the team that won promotion back on the first attempt, but he found his chances for first team football limited. He was often employed as a substitute, and his strength, combined with his pace and his usefulness in the air, meant that the new Spurs manager, Keith Burkinshaw, played him almost anywhere on the pitch. He sometimes appeared for Spurs as a centre half in one game but as a centre forward for Northern Ireland in the next.

He had made his debut for the international team under Danny Blanchflower, playing alongside George Best in the 5–0 drubbing against West Germany in 1977, but scoring twice against Belgium later that year while winning his fifth cap. It still wasn't enough for Burkinshaw. 'He fancied me as a centre half,' says Armstrong, 'but it wasn't challenging enough for me, I wanted to be up front, I liked playing as a centre forward and enjoyed it there. But I ended up playing lots of positions like right back and midfield. In those days there was only one person on the bench, so I was an easy Number Twelve. I even played in goal for Spurs on occasions.'

Armstrong had added a further three goals to his tally before Bingham took over as Northern Ireland manager, but it had taken him another fourteen caps to achieve that. As he was often being played out of position at Spurs, his goal return by the start of 1980 was just nine league goals in his fourth season since making his debut. Of course, he was not playing every week, was often brought on late in a game and usually was not even playing up front, but it was obvious that for all the strengths in his all-round game, he was not a prolific out-and-out goal-scorer. He had fared better during the 1979/80 season, already having scored five times in five appearances in the FA and League Cups, but Bingham knew that his team was going to have problems converting chances. Armstrong was the best they had, but he wasn't being played enough at his club, or in position enough, to develop himself into a more regular goal-scorer.

It seemed that Northern Ireland would have little choice but to stick with a striker who was getting the occasional run-out as a centre half. Other strikers had been selected in recent years, but they were all playing at a lower level. Of these, Tommy Finney had been capped earliest, three managers earlier, in 1974. He had managed to score on his debut in the final game under Terry Neill but had added only one further goal since and, during Blanchflower's three-year reign, had been picked only once, adding his eighth cap. Now twenty-seven, he was unfortunate not to have played in the First Division, having gained promotion with both Luton Town and Sunderland. However, he wasn't a regular starter at either team and had been sold from each before the next season started. He had ended up down in the Fourth Division with Cambridge United, which quickly took him out of consideration for international duty. But under Ron Atkinson, manager at Cambridge, Finney established himself in the first team and two successive promotions saw him back in the Second Division by 1978. He was now once more in contention for his national team and played in Blanchflower's penultimate game as manager – a match against England.

Forward Derek Spence offers a good representation of the problems Northern Ireland had in the attacking line. Capped in 1975 for the first time, while playing for Bury FC, Spence was a very fine player at his level of the game, and he scored a respectable tally of goals for the club. However, Bury had been in the bottom rung of English professional football since 1971, spending three years in the Fourth Division before being promoted to the Third in 1974. The step up to international football from such a level is a steep one and Spence went nine games under Dave Clements without a goal for Northern Ireland. His first goal for the side came during Blanchflower's first game in charge, a moment never to be forgotten as he scored the equalising goal against Holland in Rotterdam with just two minutes remaining. Following this game, Spence was transferred to Blackpool in the Second Division but soon found himself surplus to requirements and was sold to Olympiacos FC in Greece, where he performed well.

But while Spence enjoyed a good spell in Greek football, he was absent from the Northern Ireland team for some time, due in part to some slapdash administration from the IFA. Blanchflower had selected Spence for the squad to play against Iceland in Belfast in September 1977, but the IFA mistakenly sent the telegram to Panathinaikos FC – Olympiacos' deadly rivals – instead. It took several weeks for the telegram to eventually reach Spence, by which time the game had been played, and he then spent a year on the international sidelines before picking up his next cap. Spence returned to Blackpool in 1978, but the club was now playing in the Third Division. Despite this, he became a regular for Northern Ireland from September 1978 to November 1979, playing in nine of the next eleven games and scoring twice. Just before Bingham took over in 1980, the twenty-eight-year-old Spence was transferred to Southend United, also of the Third Division.

The other regular striking option of the late Blanchflower period had been Billy Caskey. His career had seemed entwined with that of Vic Moreland and the pair had played together at Glentoran where Caskey was prolific in front of goal. The two had then been loaned to Tulsa Roughnecks and returned together to Glentoran before being sold together to Derby County and making their debuts in the same game in September 1978. It was while playing for Derby in the First Division, and scoring three times that autumn, that Caskey was first called up to the national team, inevitably making his debut in the same game as Moreland against Bulgaria and scoring to celebrate the occasion. He played six times under Blanchflower, but never scored again. He failed to find the net for Derby throughout 1979 and took the opportunity to return to Tulsa Roughnecks in December, further reducing the pool of striking talent for Bingham to pick from.

Of the four main strikers open to Blanchflower, one was now living in the US, another was playing in the Third Division, one was in the Second Division and the only First Division player among them was often playing in the reserves and being utilised as a defender. Between them they had amassed just eleven goals in a combined fifty-seven appearances. Bingham had unquestionably inherited a squad with many strengths and a lot of top-level experience, but the dearth of striking options was worrying. With World Cup qualifying due to begin the following month in Israel, it was a problem to which Bingham was going to have to find a quick solution.

BRITISH CHAMPIONS

Bingham started his second reign in charge of the national team with a series of team-building get-togethers, the first of which took place in Coventry on 4 March, although not all the players were able to attend due to club commitments. Several more made it to Leicester a week later, but players from Arsenal, Nottingham Forest, Tottenham Hotspur and Ipswich were all conspicuous by their absence as they prepared to push on in European competition.

However, since the delay in his appointment had already cut into his preparation time, these sessions were mostly just a way for Bingham to evaluate those players he was less familiar with. In came several new players: defenders Mal Donaghy and John O'Neill; young winger Noel Brotherston, who was doing well with Second Division Blackburn Rovers and could offer the team speed and width; and twenty-two-year-old striker Billy Hamilton, who had impressed in local football with Linfield, before moving to QPR and then Burnley. Hamilton had been capped once by Blanchflower in 1978 when he came on as a substitute against Scotland and had progressed significantly since then. Tall and strong, he was something of an old-fashioned centre forward, and Bingham needed all the options up front he could muster.

For the players, it was clear that things would change under Bingham's regime. As David McCreery remembers, 'We all got a jolt ... everything, every little detail was covered – even in our team talk going out to the games. Billy was a person who knew how to lift you up and also knock you down. He was hard and he was soft at times. In a training session you had to give your all. You couldn't go there and give fifty per cent ... you had to do your day's graft.'

Sammy McIlroy, who had played under several Northern Ireland managers previously, was also appreciative of the new methods, 'He had a more up-to-date style ... He got us training a little bit differently and organised the sessions and the team how to play and gradually [the team] was beginning to take shape. We had a tremendous spirit, great camaraderie.'

As Billy Hamilton recalls, 'The first thing Billy Bingham did for Northern Ireland was to stop the leaking of goals. He made us very hard to play against and we worked against other teams to close them down. As a forward that may not have been what you wanted. You wanted to see plenty of attacks, lots of crosses, but that was all sacrificed to getting behind the ball and making it difficult for the opposition. As soon as a midfielder went past you in a training session it was the forwards who had to drop back into the midfield and cover the space. It was drummed into you. Now, it lessened your chances of getting international goals because you had less time in the opposition box, but it did make you stronger as a unit, not conceding goals ... He played to our strengths. He was also very meticulous in identifying the strengths and weaknesses of the opposition.'

Martin O'Neill also praises Bingham's pragmatic approach, 'It didn't mean he didn't want to attack, he always wanted to have wide players in the team so we could force the issue. He wanted a centre forward who could hold the ball up … although we had a great goalkeeper, we were trying to make him less busy in games. If we were in tight games for any length of time, then we could wear teams down and beat them.'

The chief problem for Bingham to solve was clearly that of defence. Northern Ireland were blessed with quality defenders and two excellent goalkeepers, so the problems at the back were not down to personnel but to attitude and style of play. As Jimmy Nicholl recalls, this was all about to change. 'I remember Billy saying to me one night when we were away, "You know, Jim, you won't be overlapping tomorrow night. I'll be telling the left back the same thing. We'll have the four defenders on the halfway line when we're attacking and two sitting midfielders. If the ball goes to outside right, the reason he's outside right is because he's a better player than you, because he's more skilful and it's his job to beat the fullback and cross the ball." … That was the first form of discipline I think I had … but when you start winning games and seeing yourself at the top of the group instead of the bottom, you don't mind.'

When Bingham announced the squad in mid-March, out went veteran defender Allan Hunter – captain of the side under Blanchflower – to be replaced by Leicester City's uncapped John O'Neill. Also gone was Derby County's Vic Moreland, who had left the Midlands club and returned to Tulsa Roughnecks to join up with Billy Caskey again. Donaghy and Brotherston both earned call-ups to the squad in search of a first cap but Pat Rice, just one game short of his landmark fiftieth was absent through injury.

The question of who was to replace Hunter as the new captain of the team was answered just a few days before the game in Tel Aviv – a decision that made headlines, when Martin O'Neill became the team's first Catholic captain. These, sadly, were times in which someone's background and religious beliefs were, regrettably, sometimes seen as more important than their ability, and the decision attracted a lot of bigoted outcry. Bingham, however, remained firm. As he recalls, 'Martin was my captain because he was the best man for the job. In my years as manager of Northern Ireland, every decision taken was on the merit of the individual, his suitability as a player, his suitability as captain. The mail we received was abusive, dreadful stuff ... but it didn't stop us, and the majority agreed the decision was the correct one. Martin asked me why I had chosen him. I told him it was simple: he was the best man for the job ... his religion had no bearing on my choice ... and Martin was a superb captain.'

In many ways, O'Neill and Bingham were a perfect fit, their relationship similar to that enjoyed by Doherty and Blanchflower three decades earlier. Bingham, like Doherty, was the inspirational star of a time gone by who could rouse the players with stirring talks. O'Neill, like Blanchflower, was a midfielder of craft and one of the most intelligent thinkers in the game, with a clever wit to boot. Speaking at the time, Bingham told the *Belfast Telegraph*, 'I like the occupant of this position to be intelligent, have an understanding of the game, show initiative, and be flexible enough to change the tactics during a match. Martin is a top player with a top club. This responsibility will make him an even better player. It should be a spur.' Promoting O'Neill to captain was a shrewd choice, and the wisdom would pay dividends in the years that followed.

Today, O'Neill is able to reflect upon the confidence that he and the rest of the team felt at this time, despite the negativity in some quarters, 'No matter how successful I had been with Nottingham Forest, the captaincy would still cause a problem with certain sections. It probably had less effect on me because I was successful at club level ... that gave me incredible confidence. And with Billy coming in we had a collection of players where we felt that, not only could we compete, but we could win. It was always our ambition to qualify for a World Cup and emulate the team of '58.'

Northern Ireland's opponents, Israel, were making their debut in the European qualifying groups for the World Cup. Due to the volatile political scene in the Middle East, and following their exclusion from the Asian qualifying sections, they had spent a number of years in exile. They were managed by Englishman Jack Mansell and featured Liverpool's defender Avi Cohen in their squad. However, they went into the tie with very low confidence, with Mansell even telling the press, 'The average club side here is up to about English Fourth Division standard, no more. I would say with complete honesty that we have only about eight reasonable performers.'

Nevertheless, Bingham played down expectations ahead of the tie, saying, 'This will be a hard match for us – very hard. The Israelis are fit and, backed by 50,000 fans, can rise to the occasion. It won't be easy for us – far from it.' It was a sensible precaution and he was clearly keen to avoid an instant judgement upon his new-look team if things didn't go to plan.

In the end, Bingham did not hand out too many first caps, with only John O'Neill making a debut in a back line that featured Jimmy Nicholl, Chris Nicholl, Sammy Nelson, and Pat Jennings in goal. Midfield had Terry Cochrane and Tommy Cassidy alongside the solid central unit of Martin O'Neill and Sammy McIlroy, while Gerry Armstrong featured in attack alongside Tommy Finney.

Bingham was clear about his expectations going into the game, 'It is important for us to get off to a good start. Psychologically, that would give us a great boost and cause problems for the other teams in the group. Once you get two points in the locker you are in the driving seat. You set the pace for the others. I'm confident we can qualify, especially as two go through from this group. We are capable of beating Scotland, Sweden and Portugal in Belfast. It is what we do away from home that is vital. Morale is high. I've spoken to every one of the players and their desire is to go home not only with a win but a convincing one.'

The feeling that a new dawn was possible was shared by Manchester United's Sammy McIlroy. 'We have taken stick for over a year now. We have been lambasted, particularly in Belfast. Our pride has been hurt. We have to restore it. Israel is not the strongest of soccer countries. Surely, we can turn the tide, end the frustration here in Tel Aviv.'

He was to be sorely disappointed.

Bingham's team, in a game broadcast live on BBC Northern Ireland, had a frustrating afternoon in the Ramat Gan Stadium. Other than a stinging McIlroy shot in the thirty-eighth minute, the Israeli goalkeeper, Arie Haviv, was completely untroubled. Jennings, however, was forced into a number of superb saves to keep the game level, with one thirty-yard free kick, taken by Rifaat Turk, hitting the crossbar. Northern Ireland were further aided when the stadium's floodlights failed, dimming at first before pitching into total darkness. The game was held up for twenty minutes and the Irish benefitted from the break in the rhythm of the game, escaping Israel with a point. There was predictable backlash back home, however, with the *Belfast Telegraph* declaring, 'this is not a point gained but one lost.'

Bingham focused on the positives after the game, pointing out the impressive debut of John O'Neill (whom he predicted would be a bedrock of the team for the next ten years), and reminding fans that 'The potential of the side has still to be realised. We are building on teamwork. It is the only solution when you have a limited choice of players. If we can get a win you will see the confidence rise. These players can do much, much better, of that I've no doubt.' The 0–0 draw had been an uninspiring start to the campaign, with the only consolation being that it could have been worse. Only time would tell if they would rue their inability to win the game or be eternally grateful for escaping with a single point.

★

The three matches of the British Championship held in May 1980 gave Bingham another chance to put his team through their paces. Northern Ireland had long been regarded as the weakest nation competing, which was unsurprising given that they were the smallest, and had only won the tournament once, back in 1914 (though they had been declared joint winners on a handful of other occasions, mainly during the Doherty/ Blanchflower golden age of the 1950s). However, three games in rapid succession, against players with whom the Irish team would have been familiar from playing against them in the English league, would give Bingham the chance to experiment and test his new ideas.

The first match was against Scotland. It held particular significance as it was the first time Scotland had visited Belfast since 1970, and a certain amount of animosity had built up regarding the continued reluctance of the Scots to fulfil their away fixtures at Windsor Park. England and Wales had resumed their journeys to Belfast for the 1975 competition. Not so with Scotland. The Scottish FA (SFA) refused to play in Northern Ireland and missed four successive tournaments in the alternating years between 1972 and 1978. Worse still, Scotland would not play their away match in a neutral stadium – as England and Wales had done when games could not be played at Windsor Park – and instead added an extra home game at Hampden Park to the calendar. This meant that, between 1971 and 1979, Northern Ireland played all their games against Scotland as fully-fledged away games. It put them at a huge disadvantage in the competition, while Scotland benefited from playing all three games at home every two years.

This thoroughly one-sided arrangement might have continued for longer were it not for the fact that Northern Ireland and Scotland had been drawn together in the same World Cup qualifying group. FIFA had already declared several years earlier that Belfast was considered safe for qualifying matches so there was no possibility that Scotland could refuse to play without forfeiting the points, and if they could come to Belfast for one game then it became patently ridiculous not to travel for another. However, even with their hand forced into doing what England and Wales, not to mention many other nations, had already been doing for several years, the SFA urged their supporters not to travel to the match and refused to supply any tickets.

The home players were not daunted by this, however, and McIlroy echoed the team's optimism, 'Time and again we've threatened to do well. Things have looked promising and our hopes have been raised. Yet when it comes to the crunch we've been flattened. This time we are starting at home against Scotland and if we get a result it will be a tremendous boost to us.'

Going into the opening match, several Northern Ireland players were riding high from their fortunes at club level: Martin O'Neill was fresh from the European Cup semi-final where Nottingham Forest had defeated Ajax to set up a date with Kevin Keegan's Hamburg at the end of May; Jimmy Nicholl and Sammy McIlroy had enjoyed a successful campaign at Manchester United in which they had taken Liverpool to the final game of the season, before ultimately finishing as runners-up; and Pat Jennings, Pat Rice and Sammy Nelson had just reached the European Cup Winners' Cup and FA Cup finals with Arsenal, under the stewardship of ex-Northern Ireland captain and manager, Terry Neill.

This success came at a cost for Northern Ireland, however, and Bingham was rocked by the withdrawal of the Arsenal trio in the days before the Scotland game. Arsenal had lost both finals, and their only hope of playing in Europe the following season now rested on finishing third in the First Division to qualify for the UEFA Cup. This was long before the time when all final matches in the league programme had to be played simultaneously, and Arsenal now had a fixture backlog extending beyond the normal end of the season. They needed to win their two remaining fixtures and couldn't spare the talents of three fifths of their defensive line.

While the withdrawal of the Arsenal players was entirely understandable under the circumstances, Bingham faced another complication when Brian Clough refused to release Martin O'Neill from Forest. The manager clearly had one rule for English players and another for the rest of the home nations. The European Cup Final was still two weeks away and Clough had allowed his striker, Gary Birtles, to play in a friendly for England against Argentina just a few days before the Northern Ireland game, and he had granted permission for Larry Lloyd to play for England against Wales the day *after* a game he wouldn't release O'Neill for. Losing these four players was undoubtedly frustrating for Bingham but he used the opportunity to blood new players and to reintroduce some familiar faces.

Taking Jennings' place in goal was Middlesbrough keeper, Jim Platt. He was now given an opportunity to enjoy a sustained run of matches and add to his tally of caps. Mal Donaghy and Noel Brotherston would also debut – they had both been called up for the squad against Israel but failed to make it on to the pitch. Billy Hamilton was given the other forward role alongside Armstrong. His second cap would represent his first home game as an international in front of the Windsor Park crowd. David McCreery failed a late fitness test and so Tommy Finney managed to retain his place in the side, although he had to drop back into midfield. Meanwhile, there was also a unexpected call-up to the squad for twenty-four-year-old centre half, John McClelland, a pleasant surprise for him at the end of a season in which his club, Mansfield Town, had just been relegated to the Fourth Division. Bingham knew McClelland well from his time at Mansfield – he had been responsible for bringing the young player to England the season before.

McClelland had started his career with Portadown in the Irish League, moved to Wales with Cardiff City, and was quickly offloaded to non-league Bangor City. This was in the time before Bangor had joined the newly created fifth tier of English football, the Alliance Premier League (later to be better known as the Football Conference), and McClelland spent three whole seasons playing with them in the Northern Premier League before Bingham brought him to Mansfield. Despite having played under Bingham for a season, McClelland had not entertained the possibility of stepping up to international level. 'I thought there was no chance because I was playing in the Fourth Division ... I never thought our paths would ever cross again. So it was by surprise I got a late call-up for the Home International Championships ... "There's been injuries, you've been called into the Northern Ireland squad."'

Of course the squad, some of whom were also new recruits, sought McClelland's insight into Bingham, as the one who had known him best from club level. 'It was strange meeting up with all these top players. They were very nice and nobody made me feel inadequate. They said, "You know him better than we do, what's he like?" And I said, "You don't want to know! You'll find out!" He was very ruthless. Technical genius, but he was ruthless. Martin O'Neill said that he could be mean, "But if he gets us to World Cups I don't care." Which is right.'

On the day of the game, Bingham held a conference to announce his team and he could tell that the local press already had the knives out. He remarked to Malcolm Brodie, 'I see you are going to be pessimistic.' Brodie replied in his column in that day's paper, 'I cannot be otherwise when assessing Northern Ireland's chances. Look at the facts. A depleted side, new caps introduced, experiments in midfield and a Scotland eleven which is an excellent amalgam of experience and youth ... a team on which manager Jock Stein is preparing for the 1982 World Cup finals,' as if Bingham wasn't doing the same for his

Northern Ireland squad. Nevertheless, it was a fine Scottish side that returned to Windsor Park after a decade away. Scottish league football in this period was played to a high standard, and under legendary manager Jock Stein were players like Alex McLeish of Aberdeen, Danny McGrain of Celtic and, making his Scottish debut, the newly-crowned Scottish Footballer of the Year, Gordon Strachan, also of Aberdeen.

They were supplemented by genuine superstars from the English First Division, such as Graeme Souness and Kenny Dalglish of Liverpool, Joe Jordan of Manchester United, Archie Gemmill of Birmingham City and Steve Archibald of Tottenham Hotspur. They might have been even more formidable if Andy Gray of Wolverhampton Wanderers (the most expensive footballer in Britain after Aston Villa had sold him for almost £1.5 million) had been available. But Gray had been forced to stay in England and play a game against Arsenal at the insistence of Bobby Robson, manager of Ipswich Town, who feared Arsenal would pick up easy points against a depleted Wolves and pip Ipswich for a UEFA Cup place. To demonstrate the quality in Scottish football in this era, there were four other Manchester United first team players – Gordon McQueen, Martin Buchan, Lou Macari and Arthur Albiston – who weren't included in the Scottish starting line-up.

Bingham, though, remained undaunted. 'The Scots are a good side, but it is to our advantage they are playing in Belfast. A team with new caps can often create surprises. We're going out there determined and prepared.'

In front of eighteen thousand spectators, Bingham's words came true. Donaghy had a fine game slotting into the defence, inspiring optimism for the future of the back line alongside other recent debutant, John O'Neill. Noel Brotherston provided menace down the flank on his first cap while Finney played out on the left to successfully neutralise the threat of the speedy Strachan. However, it was chiefly Billy Hamilton's day to remember as, in the thirty-sixth minute, the ball was played down the middle to Armstrong who flicked it on with his head when about thirty yards from goal. 'It was a dream come true,' Hamilton remembers. 'I had my back to the goal and, as the ball came to me, I turned a defender and the ball just sat up lovely for me. So I let fly and in she sailed. It wasn't the best goal I've ever scored, even at Windsor Park. But grabbing the winning goal on your home international debut can't be bad.'

When Hamilton was forced on to the bench after a knock on the head left him concussed, John McClelland was called into action, giving him his first cap. As he recalls, 'I was sitting sunning myself on a seat at the end of a row of players on the Windsor Park track. I thought I was just there for the ride. Suddenly … Billy Hamilton came off and I was told to play centre forward, which really took the pressure off me. If I made a mistake it wasn't going to cost us a goal! The next day my mum, who was listening to the game on the radio, said the commentator thought Billy Bingham had made a mistake. Apparently, the commentator didn't know my name.'

Regarding his head injury, Hamilton says, 'I can't remember a thing after that. All I know is that I was substituted just after the interval suffering from concussion. The only time I ever got concussion in a match in my whole career was that one after I scored and you just want to stay on the pitch and do more, try and get another goal. But I was seeing double and it was time to come off. I was trying to hit the wrong ball!'

It had been a good start for Bingham's new strike force and Hamilton reflects on the role he and Armstrong had to play, 'I think Billy's idea of playing the two of us up front was [for] the aerial threat and the physicality. I think we were supposed to go in there and ruffle feathers. If we could occupy as many defenders as we could it would help out elsewhere … some games I never even got an attempt on goal, but we were playing against teams that maybe on paper were better than us and

Bingham's organisation went a long way towards us getting results.'

Almost more important than the win over a local rival was having McClelland, Donaghy and John O'Neill – three players who would be key to Northern Ireland's defence in the 1980s – play at Windsor Park for the first time. As John O'Neill commented, 'It was a fabulous day for me. All the family came down from Derry for the match, even some of the ones with Scottish connections. As for me, I'd only been to Windsor Park once before in my life – to watch England about ten years ago – but I wasn't overawed by the occasion. I think the fact that I had already made my debut in Israel helped me to settle down and enjoy the Scottish game.' Donaghy was typically modest after his fine debut, saying, 'My colleagues made it easy for me. There were so many good players around me, I could hardly fail. I was a Manchester United fanatic and used to go over by boat to see them. So, playing alongside Jimmy Nicholl and Sammy McIlroy was fantastic.'

The following evening, things got even better for Northern Ireland when Ron Greenwood's England team made the trip to Wrexham to play Wales with their confidence sky-high. They had just convincingly defeated World Champions Argentina, now augmented by the presence of the young Diego Maradona, 3–1 and wouldn't have been too concerned by the threat posed by the Welsh. The game in Wrexham, however, would live long in the memories of all the Welsh fans who packed into the Racecourse Ground. Despite taking a 1–0 lead through Paul Mariner, England found themselves trailing 2–1 by half-time, and matters soon got even worse for England's finest when Phil Thompson of Liverpool turned in an own goal to finish the scoring in a dismal 4–1 defeat.

The magnitude of this wholly unexpected result gave the Irish a surge of belief ahead of their own match against England three days later, at Wembley Stadium.

Bingham sought again to keep expectations rooted in realism when he spoke to the press ahead of the game, 'The lion has been wounded and when he is in such a state, he can be vicious – attempting to seek revenge. He won't, however, devour us. Of that I am certain.' Ron Greenwood, meanwhile, thought the defeat might actually be beneficial to his team. 'We have to be extremely cautious and careful here in our selection. That defeat in Wrexham ended the euphoria of the win over Argentina and, anyway, I thought it was all just a little too fatuous. Maybe it will do us good, make us hungry. Certainly, I'm glad it came in this series to get it all out of the system before the European Championships.'

In the end, the English line-up was almost totally transformed from the one that had faced Wales. Playing against Northern Ireland was Alan Devonshire, who had made a big impact in the recent FA Cup Final for West Ham, earning his first cap; the recalled Ray Wilkins; third choice keeper, Joe Corrigan of Manchester City; and veteran Emlyn Hughes of Wolves as captain. Bingham, on the other hand, named a completely unchanged first eleven as Billy Hamilton had recovered from his concussion and Tommy Cassidy's gashed shin had been patched up.

Playing in front of thirty-five thousand supporters at Wembley, the Irish knew they would be in for a hard night's work and instantly applied themselves to it. Liverpool's Terry McDermott had just become the first ever player to win both the Footballer of the Year and the PFA Player of the Year awards in the same season, and yet Tommy Finney of the Second Division extinguished any threat from him. Sammy McIlroy did a similar job on Trevor Brooking, and provided thrust from midfield to most of Northern Ireland's attacks. Still, the Irish were fortunate that Jimmy Nicholl was well placed to clear from the line just before half-time when a Trevor Cherry effort would have otherwise given England the lead.

As the second half progressed, Northern Ireland grew

increasingly comfortable, and kept up an impressive work rate as they harried and harassed their English opponents. In the seventy-third minute, Bingham made a double substitution as David McCreery and Terry Cochrane replaced Tommy Cassidy and Billy Hamilton. If anything, England became even more frustrated at this point as the terrier-like McCreery rigorously applied himself to breaking up their flow in midfield. In the eighty-first minute, however, disaster struck for Northern Ireland. Hughes had pumped a hopeful ball across the box, which was met by Liverpool's David Johnson, fresh from scoring twice against the Argentinians. Brotherston challenged for the ball alongside Johnson but, as the Englishman shot, it clipped off the Irishman's knee and past Platt to give England the lead. It was a most unfortunate own goal for Brotherston who had been enjoying a good game and who had worked so hard throughout the match.

For the second time in a few days, though, England gave away the lead. Within a minute of going behind, Jimmy Nicholl pushed forward down the right flank and crossed into the box. Armstrong met it and flicked it through into an even more dangerous area where Cochrane was steaming in towards the far post. The Middlesbrough player slid in as the last English defender also challenged for the ball, but he was able to get there first and squeeze it past Corrigan for the equaliser. Northern Ireland then saw out the remaining nine minutes with confidence to register an important draw and leave England winless so far in that year's tournament.

In his autobiography, Cochrane recalled that his goal was, 'the pinnacle of my entire footballing career – to that point at least. In a later interview I even declared, "If you'd have killed me then I'd have died happy!" We do say some silly things, but I think, at least for a moment or two, that I really meant what I had said.' He also recounted how his wife Etta had found out about the goal in Middlesbrough. 'When she was at her bingo session in the town, the MC interrupted to announce that I had scored. The crowd erupted in bursts of applause and cheering despite the goal having been scored against England. They were clearly proud of their local boy made good even if he had scored for his own little Northern Ireland against their mighty England.'

Ron Greenwood was scathing of his own players afterwards. 'After having battled Ireland for so long we got a goal that may have been fortuitous. But it was one that counted. Instead of consolidating we allowed Ireland back into the game, and for that we need our backsides kicking.' Bingham, meanwhile, was obviously full of pride when he said, 'Some of the best teams in the world would be happy to come to Wembley and get a draw against England.' Indeed, the very World Champions had found it beyond themselves to emulate what Northern Ireland had just achieved.

Malcolm Brodie led the charge of tributes in the *Belfast Telegraph* and was gushing in his praise, picking out the performances of Finney, McIlroy and Brotherston in particular. Some of the English press were less than complimentary – one described the Irish as being 'as appetising as a plate of cold Irish potatoes', while another painted them as 'international non-entities' – but under a headline of, 'Irish eyes are smiling – Bingham's boyos leave champs facing the wooden spoon,' David Miller of the *Daily Express* clearly wished the Irish well and pointed out what an appropriate celebration it would be if they could win the British Championship in their centenary year.

Things got better for Northern Ireland the following evening when Scotland defeated Wales 1–0 at Hampden Park, courtesy of a goal from Aberdeen's Willie Miller. If Wales had won, they would only have needed to draw against Northern Ireland in their final game to become champions. Now Northern Ireland entered that game a point ahead and a draw might be enough to win the title, if England avoided defeat against Scotland in the final game.

The vital showdown was at Ninian Park in Cardiff on 23 May, three days after Northern Ireland's trip to Wembley. Once more it was an unchanged side, with Bingham keeping faith with the players who had performed so admirably in the first two games. Wales, on the other hand, were forced to make one significant change: Ian Walsh, who had caused England so many problems in their match, had been injured and was replaced by the young Ian Rush, who had just signed for Liverpool and was yet to play for them.

Only twelve thousand fans were there to see the final game, though this was the best attendance for many years in what was always the final game of the tournament for these particular two nations. Most seasons, the last match was a 'dead rubber' game with both teams just trying to avoid the so-called wooden spoon, but this year the reverse was true and both teams fancied their chances of becoming champions. As a result, more Irish fans than normal made the trip over in the hope of seeing history being made.

Northern Ireland started the game brightly and Armstrong hit a post while Brotherston got close with a header that he should perhaps have done better with. However, he soon made amends. In the twenty-second minute, Jimmy Nicholl made another trademark pressing run into the final third of the pitch on the right wing. He pushed the ball to Hamilton in the corner of the penalty area, and Hamilton passed the ball into the box and into Brotherston's path. Despite the ball bobbling up on the pitch, Brotherston brought it under control, twisted to send a Welsh defender the wrong way and placed it across Dai Davies and inside the far post to put the Irish 1–0 up.

Knowing that nothing less than a win would crown them champions, the Welsh pressed hard in the second half. Chris Nicholl was forced to head clear from under the bar following a Welsh corner, while Platt pulled off saves from Mickey Thomas, Terry Yorath and the substitute Carl Harris. It was a nail-biting game for Irish supporters but when the whistle was blown, Northern Ireland were champions. It no longer mattered what happened in the final match between England and Scotland.

Bingham ran on to the pitch and embraced Armstrong, and fans soon joined him in the rush to celebrate their first title in sixty-six years. John Motson in his television commentary phrased it as 'something of a minor miracle in Irish terms', and he was right. Northern Ireland had been 33/1 outsiders with the bookmakers when the tournament began – long odds indeed in a four-team tournament. Not only had Bingham managed to guide Northern Ireland to triumph just months after taking over but he had done so without all three of the important Arsenal contingent or his captain, Martin O'Neill. The team was not at full strength, yet through sheer hard work and determination they were now very deserving champions.

The *Daily Express* reported Bingham's praise for his players the following day. 'This team has done everything I have asked of them. They deserved their triumph and I am proud of them. If anyone had said at the start of the competition we would get three points, I would have been happy with that. To get five and play two of the games away is fantastic … This is Ireland's greatest achievement since we reached the World Cup finals in 1958.'

Stand-in captain Sammy McIlroy also voiced his appreciation of his team-mates: 'I'm overwhelmed. I can't tell you how I feel. It all happened because our defence is so good that, once we get in front, it's almost impossible to break us down.' These were perceptive words. This success had been built upon a solid foundation of defensive cohesion, one that was unrecognisable from what had been shown just twelve months earlier under Blanchflower.

Back in Belfast, the triumph was received rapturously by the press and public alike as a welcome distraction from the ongoing Troubles. The *Belfast Telegraph* devoted the front page to the victory, with a photograph taken in the dressing room and the headline, 'The Champagne Boys'. Alongside comments from local politicians eager to connect themselves to the story, there was a touching interview with Brotherston's father who described the family's joy as they gathered to watch the game, and the tears that had flowed when their son had scored.

Malcolm Brodie, so often the pessimist in his *Belfast Telegraph* columns, launched into an eloquent and quite heartfelt paean full of adulation for the conquering heroes and their fighting spirit. His particular praise, however, was reserved for Brotherston, the 'player of the tournament – of that there can be no doubt … His display was phenomenal. He created openings on the right flank, on the left, worked tirelessly in midfield, and came back to help that magnificent back four. To the Welsh, as to the English and the Scots, he posed a continuous threat.'

Absent captain, Martin O'Neill – who was preparing for the defence of Nottingham Forest's European Cup title against Hamburg at the Bernabéu Stadium in Madrid – reported his delight. 'I lived every minute of those games, particularly Friday's at Cardiff. I was filled with pride to see the lads do it, particularly after the stick and criticism they had got from some English writers. If I get another European Cup medal it will be consolation for missing out on it all.' O'Neill fulfilled this ambition a few days later as Forest won 1–0 in Kevin Keegan's final game for Hamburg before his move back to England with Southampton.

Looking back, even Bingham is surprised by how quickly fortunes turned around for Northern Ireland. 'I didn't expect to do it. I'm going to be truthful about that, but as we kept going forward and results went our way … that gave the team great confidence. It gave *me* great confidence.'

The atmosphere of new-found belief is also remembered by Jimmy Nicholl, 'When things are going well, everyone looks forward to coming to training every day … We were feeling it at international level. [We] started talking about winning games and possibly winning things.'

This was a feeling Billy Hamilton also recalls. 'You could almost sense the beginning of something. Getting that championship tucked under our belt we went with a confidence into everything and a belief that we were on the right track.'

The night of 23 May 1980 would live long in the annals of Irish footballing history, marking an incredible turnaround under the new manager – from last place in four consecutive competitions to champions. The *Belfast Telegraph* captured the celebrations of the team first hand and is worth quoting in full to demonstrate just what this victory meant to the team and those who followed them:

> The dressing room marked 'Visitors' was a scene of utter joy. In typical fashion of the friendly family that is the Northern Ireland international set-up, everybody was made welcome. There were no barriers placed. No stringent rules, no 'thou shalt not pass' edicts. It was an occasion for celebrating. Why not let everybody in? Photographers jostled with each other. Reporters pressed forward for the much-sought quote. Players, limp with exhaustion, somehow summoned more energy from their drained bodies. Bingham grasped me and said, 'We've written history – a huge page of it.' Champagne bottles were opened, sprayed like a hose, drenching everyone in that room. Nobody worried, nobody cared. The unbelievable had happened and Northern Ireland were champions. Some things become micro-filmed in the mind and for me the sight of those players languishing in the luxury of a hot bath singing 'When Irish Eyes are Smiling' and 'I'm Nobody's Child' will always be there – a lasting memory of a history-making event.

Northern Ireland, however, were not finished making history. In fact, they had only just begun.

CREST OF A WAVE

At this time, clubs and nations often held post-season tours to wind down a campaign (rather than the modern, more pragmatic, practice of pre-season tours, which build fitness up again ahead of a new campaign), so Northern Ireland's footballing calendar wasn't quite completed. In June 1980, to mark the centenary of the IFA, they toured Australia. Bingham had inherited this situation when he took over as manager, but he was happy to use it both to establish team bonding and to experiment in matches of little importance. One suggestion for the tour had been a four-team tournament with Chile and Hungary taking part but when they asked for a delay of one week to 16 June the IFA had to turn them down. The players were already eating into their limited rest time between seasons and losing another week would probably have reduced the numbers prepared to commit to the tour.

With the schedule now being three games against Australia in different cities and one against a representative Western Australia eleven, it appears a strange tour to undertake. However, most of the Irish players made themselves available – a sign of the confidence and goodwill in the squad under Bingham. Martin O'Neill, fresh from his European Cup success, was back as captain, although Sammy McIlroy and Mal Donaghy couldn't commit for domestic reasons. Of the rest, only the Arsenal trio, Jennings, Nelson and Rice, were forced to withdraw. They had endured a long and tiring season with their club. In the end Arsenal had collapsed in a devastating series of losses in the final fortnight of the season. Their defeats in the FA and European Cup Winners' Cup finals were compounded by losing their final league game, which meant that they missed out on qualification for the next season's UEFA Cup. If ever there were players who needed to recharge their batteries, they were Jennings, Nelson and Rice.

The IFA's Centenary Exhibition was officially opened in Belfast by FIFA boss João Havelange on Friday 6 June, and the team set off that Sunday for the arduous twenty-six-hour series of flights to Australia. They had the unenviable task of playing their first game in Sydney just twenty-four hours later as the IFA's request that it be pushed back a day had been refused on the grounds that it would then take place on a late shopping night and that might affect ticket sales. O'Neill wasn't prepared to use this as a defence, telling the press, 'I know there can be the excuse of jet lag. That doesn't count with us. We are all operating in a higher grade of football than the Australians. We simply have got to win and win well.' Bingham, meanwhile, warned his players about the eagerness of the opposition to impress. 'The Australians are hungry for success. They want to qualify for the World Cup. Our aim is to continue with our winning sequence. Cardiff last month was merely the springboard for better things to come. This is no holiday, no soft-touch tour.'

Bingham clearly meant what he said as his first team selection, barring the continuing absence of the Arsenal players, was the strongest he could field, minus McIlroy and Donaghy. Martin O'Neill was back into the midfield and John McClelland replaced Mal Donaghy at left back. The training regime was also no vacation, as Jimmy Nicholl recalls, 'As we flew into each city we were sent straight to our beds and all we did was train, play and sleep. We weren't allowed days off and a few of the boys, myself included, were less than happy. [Bingham] established what he wanted early on and no one argued with him.' Upon arrival, most of the Irish players slept for the day, then had a training session that night. As one anonymous player told the *Newsletter*, 'We thought it was to be just a loosener but he really made us sweat.'

The rigorous training paid off, however. In their first match, played on 11 June 1980 at the Sydney Cricket Ground, Northern Ireland took a 2–0 lead through a thirty-five-yard strike from defender Chris Nicholl, and a second-half goal from John O'Neill, who headed in a Gerry Armstrong lay-off almost on the line. Inevitably, though, the jet lag became a factor and Northern Ireland introduced four substitutes at various stages – including fringe players Derek Spence and the veteran Bryan Hamilton – and the very ordinary Australian side pulled a goal back towards the end. However, it was a satisfying performance for Bingham who declared, 'I asked the players at the start to give me everything they possessed. They certainly did. They fought from start to finish and I felt it was the championship all over again.' The *Newsletter*'s report made mention of how boring the game had been as a spectacle, but praised the Irish for sticking to the task in trying circumstances: 'The opposition was undoubtedly third-rate, but this must rank as one of Northern Ireland's greatest performances overseas – simply because they played the last thirty minutes from memory.'

From Sydney, Northern Ireland moved on to Melbourne Olympic Stadium. McCreery replaced Finney, his first start in the Bingham era, but otherwise it was the same team again against an Australian side who were arguably weaker. This was the Austrialian league season, played in the southern hemisphere's winter, so availability of players was limited. However, on a cold and windy night on 15 June, Northern Ireland fell behind after twenty minutes and during the first half were visibly the poorer team. It was a different story in the second half with constant Irish pressure, but it still took until just seven minutes from the finish for Northern Ireland to hide their blushes. The Australian keeper, Yakka Banovi, who would soon move to Derby County, slipped taking his goal kick and hit the ball straight to substitute Terry Cochrane. He played it through to Armstrong who flicked it to Martin O'Neill who shot it into the top corner from twenty yards. Humiliation was avoided, but only just.

Northern Ireland suffered a further fright in the third game, just three days later in Adelaide at the Hindmarsh Stadium. It was another familiar line-up, with only Cochrane coming into the side in place of McCreery, but they again fell behind thanks to an early goal, this time after just five minutes, when Peter Sharne scored for the third game in a row. Northern Ireland hit back in search of the equaliser and the second half in particular turned into something of a siege with the Australian keeper called into making a number of fine saves. Bingham brought on Bryan Hamilton to win his fiftieth cap, becoming only the seventh Northern Irishman to do so, and Colin McCurdy, top scorer in the Irish League that season for Linfield, was added to the goal-scoring threat upfront. Eventually Brotherston pulled the scores level in the seventieth minute with a twenty-yard shot and then, six minutes later, McCurdy made it a debut to remember when he headed in from a Gerry Armstrong cross for the winner. These were not the commanding wins Bingham would have wanted but at least he was maintaining his unbeaten start in charge of the team, which now extended to seven matches.

With the games against Australia finished, Northern Ireland

moved on to Perth for a non-international friendly against Western Australia at the WACA Stadium, and Bingham eased the regime slightly, allowing his players a day off to enjoy themselves. The match, however, was taken very seriously, and Bingham made only one change from the previous game, rewarding McCurdy with a start at Billy Hamilton's expense. Two goals in the first ten minutes from Armstrong and Cochrane against very weak opposition effectively ended the competition. Northern Ireland could take things slowly and pass skilfully around knowing that the opposing team had little with which to hit back. A third goal in the second half, scored again by Cochrane, reduced the game to almost walking pace and it was in the dying minutes that John O'Neill added the last in a 4–0 win, after Bingham had used all five subs allowed and given appearances to all those unused until then on the tour.

While the Australian tour may appear today as a meaningless series of games against opposition much weaker than Northern Ireland would encounter in their World Cup qualifiers, there is little doubt that Bingham, so short a time in the job at that stage, was able to use the matches to get to know his players and to allow them to gel them as a solid team. But there was also something far more important about the trip – it was a chance for the team to bond. Martin O'Neill explains, 'It came at the end of the season and you're thinking, "We should be on holiday," but once we got there it was an absolutely terrific time. Billy was thriving in the role and giving good guidance as well.'

Gerry Armstrong remembers it as time of great fun and friendship for the squad, 'The boys were great and the craic was fantastic. Only Irish people could understand it. We couldn't wait to get out and have a drink and have a laugh. Derek Spence was one of the funniest guys you'll ever meet and I loved him to bits, a real character. And Jimmy Nicholl's another one, Jimmy's so funny. You couldn't wait to meet up with them because you knew you would have a great time. Billy had said after one of the games, "Well done, lads. Go and enjoy yourselves but don't get into any trouble." He said there was an area there called King's Cross, a bad area, so don't be going down there. We went out and Derek Spence called out, "Five taxis, King's Cross, let's go." We all piled in, went down there and had a ball. It was a bonding thing for the players. We couldn't wait to meet up and have a bit of banter and Martin was so witty.'

On top of the spirit engendered by the tour, Bingham knew that the team could only get stronger once McIlroy, Donaghy and the Arsenal players were available again. All things considered, It was a worthwhile conclusion to a successful season, and confidence was high as the team took their summer rest and looked forward to their first home game of the World Cup campaign in October against Sweden.

A series of setbacks hit the team that autumn: John O'Neill was seriously injured playing for Leicester City and required an immediate cartilage operation (McClelland would take his place in the centre of defence); Jennings had not yet recovered from a foot injury that had recently kept him out of the Arsenal team; and both Pat Rice and Sammy Nelson lost their first team places and were therefore short of top-level match experience. Bingham left Rice out of the squad but kept Nelson (though he ultimately chose Donaghy in the left back position). He also kept faith with Gerry Armstrong who, apart from a goal in the unofficial Western Australian game, had so far failed to score in the Bingham era, and who was also behind Steve Archibald and Garth Crooks in the pecking order for a first team place at Spurs. While no one spoke of 'assists' in 1980, Armstrong's all-round work rate and contribution to the team counted just as much as goal tallies.

The mood in the Irish camp was, however, given a huge lift by the twin celebrations taking place, with a belated civic reception for the squad at Belfast City Hall to recognise their triumph in the British Championship, and the ongoing centenary festivities. In the lead up to the match, the *Belfast Telegraph* produced a large supplement looking back at the milestones of the last century and looking forward to the World Cup campaign. In the pull-out, Bingham spoke about what made his current period in charge of the team different to his previous reign. 'I have no Best, no Dougan this time and any manager would dearly love to have players of their calibre and stature at his disposal. And yet, despite that, I honestly feel that all-round this side is probably more solid. It is essentially a team rather than a collection of players and that is its strength. We have a nucleus of players; we are working on things as a team and I am very happy with it. The spirit in the squad is special and, as has been demonstrated, vital.'

Fortunately for Northern Ireland, the upswing in their collective team spirit came at precisely the same time that Swedish football was undergoing something of a crisis. Sweden had been to seven out of the previous eleven finals tournaments, including the last three successive World Cups; however, their recent form had been especially poor. Something of a malaise had set into the national team, despite Malmö FF reaching the European Cup Final just one year before. Sweden had been gifted an enviable start to the campaign with two home games, the first of which was against the weakest team in the group, Israel. However, a late equaliser for Israel in a 1–1 draw ensured that it was a bitterly disappointing beginning to qualifying. A drawn friendly with Iceland and a defeat in Hungary had followed before they returned to qualifying action against Scotland in September and recorded an even more upsetting result, losing 1–0 thanks to a Gordon Strachan winner in Stockholm. Although they had since registered a friendly win against Bulgaria, they were coming to Belfast with their dreams of going to Spain already in tatters, knowing that anything less than a win would administer the last rites to their chances in the group.

With the fortunes of the two nations in such sharp contrast the local press in Belfast were unusually optimistic. The *Newsletter* proclaimed, 'The Northern Ireland team is now on the crest of a wave which should sweep them to the World Championship finals in two years' time.' Bingham, too, was upbeat ahead of the game when he said, 'I look at it optimistically. I think we can qualify but we must take advantage of being at home. We must win, we must go at them.'

Go at them Northern Ireland did. In many ways the first half of the game, played in golden autumn sunshine on the afternoon of 15 October, represents some of the most attacking and swashbuckling football played during the entire Bingham era. After parading the British Championship trophy around the pitch before the game, the team swiftly got down to business and, almost straight from the kick off, Hamilton headed wide in an attack to set out the stall of Irish play. Hamilton and Armstrong used their strength to great effect and Northern Ireland comfortably won the key midfield battles, with Sweden content to soak up the pressure and defend the corners they were conceding.

It was in the twenty-fourth minute that Northern Ireland made the breakthrough. Hamilton won the ball and fed it through to Armstrong on the left-hand edge of the box. He centred the ball for McIlroy and, although his pass was a little scuffed and bouncing, it found its way into the path of the incoming Brotherston on the right who had time to pick a place and slot the ball beyond the advancing keeper.

Just four minutes later, Northern Ireland doubled their lead with some great determination from Armstrong down the right wing. He easily outmuscled the two taller Swedish players to dart between them and cross to the far post. There, McIlroy was waiting, with almost too much time on his hands. By the time the ball fell to him, he was in a nearly seated position inside the six-yard area when he might have jumped to meet the ball earlier if he had been under more pressure. Nevertheless, he made no mistake in guiding the ball over the line for 2–0 and Northern Ireland could now play some pressure-free football.

The home side still weren't finished their first-half business, however, and Jimmy Nicholl picked the ball up in the centre of the park, advanced to the thirty-yard mark and hit a rocket past the diving Jan Möller. It was a remarkable first goal to score for his country. In the end, it would be the only goal of his international career, so he reflects fondly upon it today, 'In the highlights that night they said, "What a brilliant bit of play by Nicholl," but I just hit it! ... It was a left foot half volley and what I was doing there I'll ever know! I didn't have to panic, there was nobody near me or anything. If you're only going to score the one you may as well make it a memorable one.'

Demonstrative of the confidence flowing through the side, Nicholl tried a similar effort shortly after, but the keeper managed to collect at the second attempt. The sides trooped in for the half-time interval, but by then it was clear that the contest was already over. As such, Northern Ireland could be forgiven for moving down a few gears in the second half, although McClelland did see a header hit the post. The reception from the press was hugely enthusiastic for such an emphatic victory and Malcolm Brodie led the way in the *Belfast Telegraph* with, 'Not for many moons has a Northern Ireland side looked so devastating. Here was a team moving as a team, the real underlying factor in its successful running sequence. Here was a team which at last could score goals.' Jimmy Dubois echoed this sentiment in the *Newsletter.* 'Bingham is to be congratulated for welding together a basically young team which is beginning to believe in itself. They were quicker in thought and deed and were very good value for their victory.'

Bingham described the performance as the best since he had taken over as manager, while Sweden manager Lars Arnesson lamented, 'Northern Ireland proved to be a much better team than we supposed and they fully deserved to win. They competed for every ball and had an urgency which we could not match.'

It was a game where everything had gone right for the home team, and while the players were thrilled by the result, McIlroy remembers that no one got too carried away: 'I wouldn't say we were going to qualify but there was definitely confidence throughout the squad. When you turn over the Sweden squad – and they were an experienced team, they'd been through all the competitions over the years – you begin to think we can make it difficult for anyone the way we were so close together, fighting and helping each other out on the park.'

For team captain O'Neill, it took a while for the success, and what it meant for Northern Ireland, to sink in, 'After you've played the game, generally speaking, you're flying off to your club again the following morning. There's not really that much time to discuss these things … but as you go back to your club, your own team-mates are saying, "That was a great result last night," and you start to think about it. Slowly you started thinking, we've got a chance.'

More good news was to follow. The Scotland home match against Portugal and the Israel match against Sweden in Tel Aviv both ended in 0–0 draws. Seeing Scotland and Portugal, their main group rivals, drop points did the Irish campaign no harm, but the Tel Aviv match was the final death knell for the Swedish team, and Bingham knew that, excepting unlikely turnarounds, his team was in a straight three-way fight with Scotland and Portugal for the two qualifying places on offer.

Bingham was further encouraged by the early return to fitness of John O'Neill, who made himself available in November for the trip to Portugal, and by Gerry Armstrong's return to first team football as he moved from Spurs to join the up-and-coming Watford Town in the Second Divison. The club had been surging up the English League system with two promotions in the previous three seasons under the managership of Graham Taylor, and regular first team football could only be beneficial to one of Bingham's key creative talents, even if it was at a slightly lower level. Unfortunately, there was still no return for Pat Jennings, who had ruled himself out of selection – he was back at Arsenal after his injury but was still unable to take his own goal kicks.

Attention had now turned to the task awaiting Northern Ireland in Lisbon. Portugal were, in many regards, something of a sleeping giant. Despite the country's passion for football and the reputation for classy and skilful players, they had failed to qualify for any tournament since the World Cup of 1966. Back then, a Eusebio-led team faced England for a place in the final and ended up winning the third place play-off. Since then, they had sometimes only narrowly lost out on qualifying, although there was a feeling that the current squad had the makings of a more successful team. Encouragingly, Northern Ireland's record against them was actually quite impressive. The two nations had played four times previously, all in World Cup qualifiers, and Northern Ireland had had one win and three draws. On the two occasions the Irish had travelled to Portugal they had returned home with important 1–1 draws. Bingham had famously played and scored in the first of these in 1957, en route to qualification for the World Cup, while O'Neill was a veteran of the 1973 game that had featured George Best. Northern Ireland were not heading into uncharted territory, therefore, and a hard-working and disciplined performance (from a side that had only conceded four goals in their nine-game unbeaten run of the last twelve months) would give their hopes of qualification a huge boost.

Still, the Portugal they now had to face was crafted entirely from the club giants of Benfica, Porto and Sporting Lisbon. Although captain Humberto Coelho was missing, Northern Ireland still had to contend with the forward pair of Rui Jordão and José Costa and clever playmaker, João Alves. As Martin O'Neill told the *Newsletter*, 'They are a bigger footballing nation than Northern Ireland, have many more players to choose from, and have style and skill. Right now, I would settle for a draw … In fact, I will be over the moon if we get one point.'

With the return of John O'Neill in defence the only change for the visitors, Northern Ireland began the game confidently, their back four easily able to keep the Portuguese at bay. In fact, during the first quarter of the game Northern Ireland made as many opportunities as the home team. Armstrong, Hamilton and Brotherston performed well up front and the Portuguese found it difficult to put their stamp on the game in any meaningful way. However, they slowly started to find their way and the half ended with Chris Nicholl twice being called into action to thwart chances. Tommy Cassidy was then forced out of the game during the break after two crunching tackles.

David McCreery took Cassidy's place for the second half, but this was now a more determined and slick Portuguese side. Jimmy Nicholl was required to kick the ball off his own line following a shot that Platt had been unable to hold on to, then, in the sixty-first minute, Fernando Chalana sent Jimmy Nicholl the wrong way and floated a cross over Platt to the far post. Alves cut the ball back to the waiting Jordão, who was presented with an unmissable chance, and the score was 1–0. Portugal eased off for the remainder of the match, satisfied with slowing the game down and keeping possession. Bingham introduced Terry Cochrane late in the game, but to no avail.

Northern Ireland now had to contemplate a very different group table. They were still top on goal difference, with three points from three games, but both Scotland and Portugal were level with them on points and each had a game in hand.

Still, the defeat was not a total disaster. The margin had been slim, preserving the Irish goal difference advantage in the group, and the spirit shown in chasing down their opponents couldn't be questioned. A draw had been a realistic target, so it meant that the defeat represented, psychologically at least, only one point dropped instead of two. Even Malcolm Brodie of the *Belfast Telegraph* was moved to say, 'Northern Ireland failed last night to scale a peak, but the summit of the World Cup mountain can still be attained. Qualification for Spain '82 is still very much a reality but losing to the Portuguese here last night before 60,000 in the Stadium of Light won't make life easier in the remaining five matches.'

Nevertheless, Billy Hamilton's recollections are of a slightly downbeat dressing room after the game – the players knew they had come close to picking up a precious away point. 'I remember in the dressing room a real sense of disappointment that we didn't get something out of that. A few years earlier it might have been, "Ach, we came close and that was it," but the guys were down and disappointed. It hurt, which is a good sign because it means your expectations are improving. It was also a very physical game. I came off the pitch with stud marks down my back. There was something put in the back of our minds along the lines of, wait until we get them back at Windsor Park. There's a few scores need evened here.'

Despite the defeat, Bingham remained upbeat after the game, telling the press, 'The group is tight, so tight, it may not take even ten points to win it,' and Scottish manager Jock Stein was full of praise, 'Most teams will find it difficult collecting even a point in Lisbon. The Irish played exceptionally well, but it was the skill of Alves in midfield which made all the difference. He is a player undoubtedly in world class.'

While the defeat was disappointing, it was the only blemish in what had been one of Northern Irish football's most successful years. It would be a long four months before Northern Ireland would play again and Bingham was already asking for extra training sessions with his squad. The press had questioned IFA secretary, Billy Drennan, about Northern Ireland's failure to arrange friendly fixtures, but worries over losing money by inviting another nation to Belfast were overriding the IFA's desire to help Bingham prepare his players. It was unquestionably a hindrance to have to wait until March of 1981 to assemble the team again while other nations in the group continued to play qualifiers.

The other games being played didn't go the way Northern Ireland had wished, although it was always a long shot that they would have. On 17 December 1980, Portugal defeated Israel 3–0 in Lisbon, the returning Coelho scoring two goals either side of a strike from Jordão. They now moved to the top of the table with five points from three games. In February 1981, Scotland beat Israel 1–0 in Tel Aviv, returning home with two points, courtesy of a second-half Kenny Dalglish goal, and putting Israel alongside Sweden in the ranks of hopeless causes with just three points out of a possible ten. Scotland moved to sit beside Portugal at the top of the table, both now two points ahead of Northern Ireland. There was no longer any room for failure. A defeat in their next match at Glasgow's Hampden Park would probably mean the end of the World Cup dream.

February 1981 also saw a significant transfer for one of Bingham's most important squad members. Martin O'Neill had grown dissatisfied with his role at Nottingham Forest under Brian Clough, craving the central midfield role from where he thought he could most influence a game, rather than being forced to play out wide. Forest had also been experiencing a somewhat underwhelming season following the high-water mark of the previous three campaigns, when they had won six trophies as well as the FA Charity Shield. O'Neill had seen triple disappointment as Forest's season collapsed on three fronts: they had failed to get far in their attempt to win the European Cup for the third successive season, crashing out in the first round to CSKA Sofia; the two legs of the UEFA Super Cup saw them relinquish another of their trophies as they lost to Valencia on away goals; and a trip to Tokyo to play in the Intercontinental Cup (the forerunner of the FIFA Club World Cup) saw them lose again to Nacional of Uruguay. Worse still, they were languishing in eighth position in the First Division with the very real threat that their nights of European adventure would be denied to them going forward, with even qualification for the UEFA Cup now an uphill struggle.

The transfer-listed O'Neill had been mentioned as a possible makeweight in Forest's pursuit of Norwich City's Justin Fashanu and, although this added further insult to injury, he was open to the idea of joining them. In fact, he had scheduled talks with them only to have to cancel when he was unexpectedly recalled to the Forest team for the home game against Arsenal on 21 February. It turned out to be a triumphant end to O'Neill's ten-year Forest career as he scored twice in a 3–1 victory and, with the fans aware that it could be his final game for the club, he was given an ovation as he raised his arms to them at the final whistle. He was obviously reluctant to leave but as he told the *Daily Express* after the game, 'The dispute has dragged on between the management and me for so long that I think it has gone too far. I had hoped Brian Clough or Peter Taylor might have made a move towards me. I had made my mind up beforehand that this would be my last match for Forest and I thoroughly enjoyed it.'

Nevertheless, Norwich had assumed the deal would now be off after O'Neill's excellent match-winning performance, and he had to reach out to them the next week and ask if they were still interested as no one from Forest had spoken to him. The deal then went through to bring the curtain down on a distinguished career for the European Champions.

Bingham managed to secure an extra training session, which took place in Birmingham a few weeks before the Scotland game, but there was bad news for the Irish manager. Tommy Cassidy, who had played in all nine games under Bingham, was forced out of the upcoming match by an ankle injury. Noel Brotherston also had to withdraw, thanks to a knee injury that required surgery and would see him out of action for some time. Finally, and much worse, the absolutely key midfield duo of Martin O'Neill and Sammy McIlroy were both considered doubtful. O'Neill had sustained an ankle injury in the weekend leading up to the midweek international and would not recover in time. Sammy McIlroy had been forced to sit out Manchester United's most recent game due to a bruised hamstring (though thankfully he would pass a late fitness test and still be able to play against Scotland).

One piece of good news was that Pat Jennings had recovered from his injury and, while Platt had performed admirably as his deputy, there was little doubt that Jennings would go straight back into the side when fully fit. Nevertheless, the odds were stacking up against Northern Ireland and three out of the four first-choice midfielders would be missing. After crafting a settled side for so long, Bingham would be forced to make radical changes in the centre of the park just as his team faced a game they dare not lose.

David McCreery, the ever-reliable midfield hustler, was drafted back into the centre alongside McIlroy; Terry Cochrane played in place of Brotherston; Sammy Nelson regained his place from Mal Donaghy, as Bingham believed that he could offer more attacking threat down the flank; and John McClelland, in a surprising decision from Bingham, played in midfield. The central defender had already been used as a makeshift striker and a left back, but this was a huge gamble in a position completely outside his normal operation and against a vastly experienced Scottish midfield.

The match was played on 25 March 1981 at Hampden Park, Glasgow, in front of a large contingent of Northern Ireland fans, who had taken the short trip across the Irish Sea to make their voices heard. The Scotland line-up had also suffered from withdrawals, and both Graeme Souness and Kenny Dalglish were injured playing for Liverpool in the League Cup Final.

However, Joe Jordan of Manchester United, who hadn't even been in the squad, was given a last-minute call-up to replace Dalglish, highlighting the strength in depth of the squad available to Jock Stein.

Despite the impressive line-up, Northern Ireland immediately showed their familiar combativeness. They were unfortunate not to be awarded an early penalty when McIlroy appeared to be fouled in the box by Alex McLeish, but the Scottish soon asserted themselves. While this was an away game in whichNorthern Ireland would be happy to draw, for the Scots it was a game in which they hoped to pick up two home points. They surged forward, looking for an early opportunity to relieve the pressure of expectation.

The first major worry for Northern Ireland came from an excellent effort by Steve Archibald. He received the ball from Danny McGrain on the right-hand corner of the box, swivelled, then squeezed the ball past two Irish defenders towards the far post. Jennings was beaten and desperately scurried back to his line as it passed him … and bounced off the post, before being scrambled to safety. Despite the Scottish possession, though, the Irish were solid in defence and, with McClelland playing as a deep midfielder, they essentially had an extra defender with which to extinguish any attacks before they got inside the box.

However, that didn't stop Scotland getting heart-stoppingly close again through Archibald. John Wark, on the right of midfield, planted a headed pass upfield with as much precision as any boot and it found Andy Gray scampering through into space on the right side of the box. John O'Neill raced over to cover the danger, but Gray turned him and squared the ball for Archibald, who was standing almost exactly on the penalty spot. Northern Ireland were lucky that the ball arrived at his feet, instead of invitingly in front of them as he would have wished, and he seemed to hesitate in deciding whether it was possible to hit the ball first time as Jennings started out to meet him. Instead, he trapped the ball with his right foot and was forced to pirouette and meet it again with his left. However, he would have been better advised to leave it for Wark, who was stampeding towards the ball and only inches from hitting what would surely have been an unstoppable shot.

In the event, Archibald still managed to skilfully place the ball past Jennings, but Northern Ireland were saved by Chris Nicholl, who had been prescient enough to run back and cover the goal line when he saw Jennings advance. It was this that saved the team as he threw himself across the line and headed Archibald's goal-bound shot to the left touchline. Nicholl had followed Bingham's preaching about covering up holes on the pitch when someone moved out of position and Scotland's breathtaking move, which had been worthy of a goal, was met by an equally commendable piece of defence.

Wark had hit thirty-two goals that season for Ipswich Town under Bobby Robson as they pressed for honours on three fronts – in the First Division, FA Cup and UEFA Cup – and his confidence was not in question. He was involved again before the break when he started a move with Tommy Burns, received the ball back inside the box and flashed it across the face of goal. However, Northern Ireland stood firm in the face of what the *Belfast Telegraph* later described as an 'onslaught' and, as things stood, were set to leave Hampden with a precious point.

Having weathered the first-half storm, Northern Ireland now began to create some chances of their own and were very unfortunate not to take the lead in a move that had evolved from a Sammy Nelson throw-in on the left wing. After the ball had popped around the box for a time, it was fed out left for McIlroy who played it back to Nelson for another attempt to find a target in the penalty area. His high-looping ball caused all sorts of trouble for the Scottish defence as Alan Rough took a step towards it then retreated to his goal line. At the far post, Billy Hamilton used his body strength to hold off the attention of McLeish as he backed away and waited for it to drop. When it did, it was awkward to get to, slightly behind him, but he got his head to it and used whatever power he could to guide it towards the top right corner. Agonisingly, it hit the post and McLeish, from a sitting position, was able to hook it away for a corner. The commentator erroneously showered praise on Alan Rough for getting a hand to the ball to guide it on to the post, even after the replay conclusively proved he had done no such thing. Hamilton had deserved the goal but even though Northern Ireland were dismayed by the miss, they had been shown a way in which Scotland could be beaten.

Wark had another chance when he smacked a powerful shot from the edge of the area, but it was straight at Jennings who was able to pat it down and gather it on the bounce. The match then turned in the seventieth minute. In a familiar play, Nelson ran over the ball from a free kick on the left flank and left it for Sammy McIlroy to float into the box. Incredibly, despite the threat that Hamilton obviously posed from such set-piece plays, no one picked him up as he moved through the box and on to the six-yard line, where he found himself completely unmarked. With the simplest of headers, he guided the ball into the net on the far post side. Once again, Rough came out for the ball only to find himself flat-footed and unable to move as Hamilton seized the opportunity.

However, it took Wark just five minutes to gain the goal his performance deserved and spoil Northern Ireland's dreams of finishing the smash and grab exercise with two points. Captain Archie Gemmill took a short free kick inside the centre circle to Willie Miller who advanced down the pitch and executed a perfect pass. It cut diagonally through the Irish defence to the incoming Wark who calmly slotted underneath Jennings, and the scores were level once more.

Wark had a header go over from six yards and Archibald had a very nonchalant half volley saved by Jennings from a corner but

Northern Ireland comfortably saw the remainder of the game out from this point, resolute in their defence. A 1–1 draw was a fair result for both teams, rewarding both the Scottish desire epitomised by Wark, and the steadfastness of the Irish defensive lines. However, when the final whistle blew, it was Sammy Nelson who raised his arms in triumph to show that this was a better result for Northern Ireland than it had been for Scotland in the overall context of the group.

The *Belfast Telegraph* report also saw the result this way and waxed lyrical about the performance, 'Northern Ireland, the midfield fragmented by injury, played magnificently. They did us proud in ninety minutes of sheer non-stop action. Every ounce of energy was drained from their bodies as they battled in the downpour, defending resolutely and breaking with devastating speed and effect.'

Of course, the draw gained Northern Ireland no ground on Scotland in the table but Bingham could now look forward to three home games out of the four remaining fixtures. All games that they had to win, of course, but the advantage of being at home meant that fortune was in Northern Ireland's favour. Scotland would not relish having to come to Belfast, where they had lost the previous year, in search of points, and while Portugal were a point ahead of Northern Ireland with a game in hand, there was always the potential to undo that advantage when the Portuguese visited Windsor Park in April.

In the end, what would unfold over the next eight months would test the nerves of even the most stout-hearted Irish fans as fortunes veered one way and then the other, while explosive political events in Northern Ireland were about to impact upon both the national team and the future of the British Championship.

'PLAYERS WITH FIRE'

The early 1980s were a grim time in Northern Ireland that often saw reports of funerals overlapping with the news of another unfolding tragedy. Army Saracen vehicles patrolled the streets, and Belfast shoppers were stopped and searched for bomb materials at the 'Ring of Steel' (a series of security fences erected around the city centre), and then searched again at almost every shop. Buses would stop at search points to allow security guards to check for bombs, and every forgotten or unattended shopping bag could lock down a street for hours. Meanwhile, Belfast city centre crumbled and fell into disrepair. Quite apart from the many buildings being blown apart or set on fire, the once grand Victorian buildings of old were left to decay, with almost no one prepared to take the risk of investing in a city centre on the front lines of a decade-long war.

And things were about to get worse. On 1 March 1981, Republican prisoners in the H-Blocks of the Maze Prison organised a hunger strike, demanding the reintroduction of their political status. The British government refused to accede to the demands, resulting in a stand-off that led to further frightening bouts of civil unrest.

Convincing the Portuguese that it was safe to come to Belfast was a problem, but the IFA worked strenuously behind the scenes throughout April to make sure that the game went ahead as scheduled and to assure the Portuguese FA that there were no security worries about staging the game. Even the Irish team, the majority of whom were returning from their homes in England, would have been all too aware of the threat posed by the current situation. By the time the Portuguese team arrived in late April 1981, Bobby Sands, the first of the hunger strikers, had been without food for almost sixty days, and Northern Ireland was a powder keg of rioting, violence and death.

Such was the background against which the players were expected to perform, and against which Bingham had to select his team for qualification.

Cassidy and Brotherston were still out with injuries, but Bingham was at least able to welcome back his influential captain, Martin O'Neill, and the only other injury worry, John O'Neill, passed a late fitness test. Bingham also saw off an attempt from his old club Luton Town to get Mal Donaghy freed from international duty to play in their promotion push at the top end of the Second Division. With such a crucial game ahead of him, Bingham was having none of it.

Meanwhile, news from the group was not promising. As expected, Scotland had made easy work of Israel at Hampden Park, winning 3–1 to move three points clear at the top of the group. It was looking increasingly likely that Scotland would qualify and leave a straight fight between Portugal and Northern Ireland for the remaining place. One point was therefore of little value to Bingham and his team. The Portuguese had shown when they had travelled to Scotland the previous year that they weren't afraid to throw almost every man behind the ball and defend for the whole game. If they were to employ the same tactics in Belfast, then a point would almost certainly carry them onwards to qualification. This was a must-win game.

The Portuguese coach, Júlio Cernadas Pereira, known as Juca, knew exactly what to expect from the Irish at home and was full of praise for their recent efforts. 'There is plenty of fire in the Irish team. I was most impressed with them in Glasgow. The Irish team are well disciplined and were much better than Scotland over the ninety minutes. They have spirit and we are expecting an onslaught from them. Northern Ireland have many good players – players with fire.'

Returning captain Martin O'Neill summed it up perfectly: 'We're having to fight hard for everything we get. When you achieve something like that it is very satisfying. Portugal are capable of winning tomorrow but with three of our last four games at home, we have the chance to qualify for Spain next year without relying on favours from anyone else … if you aim for the stars you can win the moon. If you think you can do something, you always have a chance.'

On 29 April 1981, Northern Ireland and Portugal took to the pitch, each hoping to shape their own destinies in the group. It was a largely uneventful first half with the Portuguese doing what was expected and sitting very deep in defence, content to run the ball on the break when they got a chance. At one point there was what looked like a clear handball from Rui Jordão, who was hit in the shoulder by the ball and then allowed it to run down the length of his arm to guide it back to his feet, but the Norwegian referee, Svein-Inge Thime, was on the other side of the box behind a forest of players and probably hadn't seen it. After thirty minutes, from another corner the ball fell to Hamilton, just a few yards from goal, but he seemed to be caught unawares and it bounced off his thigh, just wide. It was the only chance to speak of during the first half as the Portuguese defence did its job impeccably well.

During the second half, however, with so much at stake, Northern Ireland significantly upped the pressure. Nelson, playing high up the left wing, swung the ball invitingly into the box for Hamilton, but the Burnley man headed it directly to the Portuguese keeper, Manuel Bento. A Terry Cochrane corner fizzed into the box at the near post where it was flicked on by Martin O'Neill. Armstrong controlled it, spun and unleashed a shot from six yards, which was blocked and deflected wide by a defender on the post. From the resulting corner, the ball looked as though it would fall to Chris Nicholl near the penalty spot, but Bento charged out, only to knock the ball further towards his own goal. When the ball fell, it pinged around the box, affording Jimmy Nicholl a shooting chance, but it sailed harmlessly over the bar.

Nicholl was also involved in the next chance, though – he pumped a long free kick into the box, and Hamilton outjumped Bento to win the ball, but he just couldn't angle it into the net and it went narrowly wide. Shortly after, a Cochrane cross saw McIlroy and Bento collide while going for the ball; the keeper then bravely recovered to gather as Hamilton menaced the rebound, and Bento collected an accidental foot to the head for his efforts.

Soon after, at the other end of the pitch, the ball was cleverly flicked through for António Oliveira who found himself unmarked in the box and with time to shoot. Attempting to lob Jennings, however, his effort bounced off the top of the bar and out of play. It was a let-off for the Irish following a rare Portuguese attack, and they heeded the warning and struck back – they were inching closer and closer to breaching the Portuguese lines.

Yet all their efforts were almost undone by a prolonged period of utter stupidity from a small section of local hooligans in the Spion Kop stand. Just after half-time, a bottle landed near Bento at the post. He showed it to Thime, who made Bingham aware that the match could be abandoned if the disturbance continued, but another bottle was soon lobbed over the wire fence along with a shower of coins. Thime discussed the matter with one of the linesmen and showed Bingham the evidence of the bombardment. Having already received a warning, it looked as though this could be the end of the match, and of Northern Ireland's qualifying campaign, but Thime instead allowed the match to continue, presumably issuing a final warning.

Combined with the sectarian unrest that undermined Northern Irish society at this time, the hooliganism running rampant throughout soccer in the United Kingdom formed a lethal cocktail in Northern Ireland at club level – particularly between teams closely associated with one or other section of the community. Unlike England and Scotland, however, whose games remained a nightmare of policing – particularly against each other, culminating in the Scottish pitch invasion of Wembley in 1977 – Northern Ireland had enjoyed a fairly good reputation at international level and the IFA was content that its fans had not, at least until this point, been involved in disturbances within stadiums.

Just then, events on the pitch took a dramatic turn. A Sammy Nelson free kick, almost from the line on the left wing, had been delayed for several minutes by the most recent of the stoppages for crowd trouble. When the game was eventually restarted, Nelson floated the ball to the far side of the box. Chris Nicholl had beaten a number of surrounding Portuguese players to win the ball, but had only been able to head it away from goal towards the byline. However, it was at this point that Terry Cochrane performed one of the most inspired ball chases in Irish football history. He scrambled after it and, just before it went out of play, managed to trap it under his foot, right on the line. The Portuguese had probably felt that the ball was heading out for a goal kick and by the time they were alert to the danger it was too late to regroup.

Cochrane's momentum had taken him over the now stationary ball, but he turned round and ran back to whip the ball in before any Portuguese player could react. His cross was perfection itself, falling to the six-yard line where any one of three Northern Irish players were waiting to pounce. The central of these, and best placed, was Armstrong, and he guided the ball past Bento for an absolutely priceless goal. He immediately took off towards the Irish bench in celebration and, after being mobbed by various team-mates, sought out Cochrane whose running had made the goal. Cochrane leaped into his arms while punching the air in triumph. It was a moment to remember.

The next was a moment to forget. The team were doing Northern Ireland proud in a time of unbelievable national anxiety, but from the crowd came another barrage of missiles. With bottles strewn behind the Portuguese net, Bingham, who had just been celebrating the priceless goal, sprinted to the Spion Kop end, lifted a bottle, smashed it back to the ground and began yelling at the crowd. As Malcolm Brodie theorised in his column the following day, Bingham seemed to be saying, 'You bloody fools! Is this your way to show support to players who have given everything for you?' It was a remarkable intervention from Bingham who had acted similarly nine years earlier at the same ground during his time as Linfield manager. It had worked then and it worked now.

Portugal, having played defensively for so long, now had no meaningful response, and it was Northern Ireland who looked the more likely to score in the closing stages. From a free kick twenty-five yards out, Sammy McIlroy ran over the ball and left it for Martin O'Neill who was following behind him. O'Neill cheekily back-heeled the ball to Jimmy Nicholl in a pre-arranged move but the set play looked set to falter with the arrival on the scene of a Portuguese player who looked suspiciously as though he had set off on his run long before O'Neill's touch of the ball. Nicholl, however, simply sidestepped him and then struck a ferocious shot, which shook the frame of the goal when it hit the left-hand intersection of post and crossbar. It would have put his effort against Sweden in the shade if it had sneaked in.

In the ninetieth minute, Cochrane and Armstrong combined again with the Watford striker meeting another cross, only for Bento to save and put the ball out for a corner. Bingham was on his feet, urging his men forward for the corner kick and ordering them to show no mercy – their opponents were on the ropes and goal difference might yet be a factor in the final outcome of the group. The match finished 1–0, though, and Northern Ireland could take pride from a magnificent result. Group leaders Scotland had found it impossible to break down the Portuguese defence, but Northern Ireland, through dogged tenacity, had kept their hopes of qualification alive by finding a way through.

Martin O'Neill was justifiably proud of those around him. 'I don't know where we rank on the world scale, but I have never seen a side play with so much enthusiasm, commitment and sheer gutsy determination. And when Gerry scored, I could have married him on the spot.' Armstrong's goal was a deserved reward for his tireless work for the team over the last year and his selfless setting up of others.

Of course, while the Northern Irish press received the result rapturously, Malcolm Brodie pulled no punches in his damning attack of the mindless hooligans who threatened to derail the team they purported to support. 'The dream of making it to España 1982 may still be realised but how near it all came to disaster last night by the crass stupidity of those fans, the folly of the few.'

Fortunately, while admitting that the lengthy stoppage just before the Northern Ireland goal had perhaps unsettled his team, Portuguese coach Juca didn't seek to capitalise upon it or use it as an excuse. Instead, he sought to play down the bottle throwing, 'It is difficult to avoid this kind of thing in football. It happens all the time at games throughout the world.' Of course, Thime and the match observer prepared a report on the incident for FIFA, which would have been the source of some nervous anticipation in the halls of the IFA. However, no sanction was forthcoming and Northern Ireland breathed a sigh of relief.

The two points the team had won transformed the standings in the group. Northern Ireland, now on six points, moved up into second place. They were two behind Scotland, having played the same number of games, but one ahead of Portugal, having played a game more. In theory, this game in hand gave Portugal the advantage in the race for the second qualifying position (with Scotland now likely to qualify in first place). However, as games start to run out in any qualifying campaign, points on the board often count for far more than theoretical points from games in hand. Northern Ireland, who were to play their next game, away against Sweden, several weeks before Portugal returned to action, now had a chance to apply some pressure to the Portuguese. Two more points against a team who had long given up any hope of qualifying, and Portugal would need to win both of their resulting games in hand to overhaul the Irish.

Unfortunately, on the same *Belfast Telegraph* back page that carried the news of the team's important victory over Portugal came the darkening clouds of a gathering storm that was about to overtake sport in Northern Ireland. While Portugal had been persuaded to go ahead with their World Cup qualifying game, the political situation in Northern Ireland was deteriorating daily and a large number of sporting occasions were being cancelled, including a junior international football match between Northern Ireland and Wales. This would soon impact upon the national football team.

The final away game of the qualifying campaign was set for early June, so Bingham's focus turned to defending Northern

Ireland's crown in the British Championship. Three games were scheduled for late May and two of these were to be played at home, which was ideal in the lead up to the Sweden match.

Preparations went ahead as normal. The squad was named, and permission even obtained for David McCreery, who had been signed to the Tulsa Roughnecks only a week before the qualifier against Scotland, to travel across the Atlantic, despite his contract only stipulating release for World Cup qualifiers. Tommy Cassidy had recovered from injury but wasn't deemed fully match fit, so Trevor Anderson, at one time of Manchester United but now playing for Linfield, was recalled in search of his first cap since the Blanchflower era.

The political situation in Northern Ireland changed for the worse, however, on 5 May 1981 when Bobby Sands became the first of the hunger strikers to die. Anger and violence spilled on to the streets and the Football Association decided to withdraw England from the game in Belfast.

The English withdrawal was not well received by the IFA who had been working closely with the FA to reassure it that the match could go ahead. However, FA Secretary Ted Croker explained the decision, 'We felt enough young men over there had their lives at risk and we were not prepared to add to this. We had no alternative but to pull out.' His Irish counterpart, Billy Drennan, was reported as saying, 'We're terribly disappointed. We work closely with the security authorities and they, like ourselves, were quite satisfied that they could have seen the match through without any difficulty.'

Clearly, the IFA was very unhappy with the FA for ignoring the advice of both the Royal Ulster Constabulary (RUC) and the British government, especially as the cancellation of the match now left them with a large financial shortfall. Tickets would have to be refunded and the costs of programme publication written off. Bingham's reaction was understandable: 'It is a sad day for Irish sport. I'm surprised the FA have not attempted to rearrange the match because it means the championship series is now kaput. I would have been happy for the team to have played in England if it would have saved the match.'

It is this failure to reschedule that perhaps indicates the FA's real reasons for pulling out. While the British Championship generated significant income for the Irish and Welsh FAs, England and Scotland had, for several years, viewed it as little more than a chore, often complaining about the fixture congestion it caused them each year. It had already been agreed that the 1981 tournament was to be the last in which all the games were played over just one week and, for the next season, games would be spread out, beginning in February.

Of course, fixture congestion didn't seem insurmountable when there was money to be made, as England were scheduled to play a glamour friendly against Brazil just four days before the British Championship game against Northern Ireland. So, as the FA collected the Wembley gate receipts, the IFA was left to calculate the financial impact of the loss of a game it always relied on for a big attendance.

If the FA thought that there would be a begrudging acceptance of their reasoning for the withdrawal and that any minor unhappiness would soon blow over, it was much mistaken. The *Belfast Telegraph* responded the next day with a front-page editorial castigating the FA: 'They have shown discourtesy to the Irish FA by simply withdrawing at virtually the last minute. And they have not helped the morale of all those in Northern Ireland who have worked so hard to keep football alive in the past twelve terrible years. The English in one move, and not without arrogance, have torpedoed the British Championship … It is a sad episode revealing a total lack of backbone.'

Even more telling was the revelation by England goalkeeper Ray Clemence that the FA had not consulted the players about the decision, and that they had been quite prepared to travel to Belfast as normal. The sympathies of the English press lay squarely with Northern Ireland, as shown by David Miller in the *Daily Express* who wrote: 'The FA's lamentable decision to pull out of Saturday's match against Northern Ireland has been done in such a way as to give maximum offence and discourtesy to the maximum number of people.'

Jock Stein was particularly insightful. 'It would suit England not to have to play the likes of Northern Ireland. They are getting too big for that and would rather face teams like Brazil. England have too much on their plate at the moment. They didn't think Liverpool and Ipswich would reach the European finals and complicate team selection.' Stein did have a point. Even in their lucrative friendly with Brazil, which they had squeezed into the calendar, England were without the services of all the players from those two teams. Liverpool were up against Real Madrid, seeking a third European Cup triumph, while Ipswich were attempting to make up for narrowly coming second to Aston Villa in the First Division by taking the UEFA Cup against AZ Alkmaar. The annual slog against Northern Ireland without their best team to select from was something England seemed grateful to avoid.

More bad news was on the horizon for the IFA. It had been assumed that the Football Association of Wales (FAW) was keen for its own match with Northern Ireland to go ahead as relations between the two smaller football associations had always been very good, particularly of late as they both fought to preserve the integrity of the competition. But soon came the announcement that several Welsh players had reported doubts about the fixture, and a number of them refused to travel. The FAW had guaranteed any dissenters anonymity and therefore could not replace them (it would have been immediately obvious who had pulled out when the new squad was named), so the FAW had no choice but to follow England's lead and opt out of travelling to Belfast. Although in their case at least, the decision was clearly made with genuine reluctance and was driven by the players.

Once more, the decision flew in the face of all official advice from the security forces in Northern Ireland and left the IFA now facing an enormous deficit with no home games in the tournament. It also made something of a mockery of that year's competition. Northern Ireland's trip to Scotland would still go ahead, as would all other games between England, Scotland and Wales, but as only Scotland would be able to complete all three games, the tournament was declared null and void.

On 16 May in Swansea's Vetch Field, in the first game of the now truncated and meaningless fixtures, Wales beat Scotland 2–0. But this wasn't the most interesting development that day. Discussing the FA and FAW withdrawals on television that evening were *Match of the Day* presenter and chairman of Coventry City Jimmy Hill and Manchester United's Scottish international Lou Macari. They proposed that some sort of match should go ahead in Belfast with an International XI – a team of players who would travel to Windsor Park and play the full Northern Ireland international team to make up some of the financial shortfall for the IFA. Immediately after the programme, both men, along with Mike Murphy, an editor on *Match of the Day*, started putting their words into action, contacting players and seeking the IFA's approval. Hill told the press, 'We are determined to get this sorted out. We want to help Northern Ireland – to give their public something after England's withdrawal.'

It was a generous offer and was received warmly by the IFA who said it would consider it quickly once the final details were presented. Billy Bingham was particularly eager to see it go ahead. 'It would be a match to keep faith with those back home. What motivation players would get appearing again at Windsor after England and Wales saying no. The response from the public would be enormous.'

With the collapse of the Welsh game, Bingham had planned to keep his squad in Glasgow following the upcoming match against Scotland on Tuesday 19 May. A behind-closed-doors game against Rangers had already been arranged. However, a home game was always preferable, and as he told the *Belfast Telegraph*, it was an opportunity to 'throw egg in the face of the English and the Welsh'. Belfast's famous Europa Hotel had even offered to accommodate the potential International XI and all that seemed required for the game to go ahead was the cutting of some red tape.

However, it was the red tape that proved to be an increasing problem. The international team needed to obtain the permission from the players' clubs and from the English FA. The latter, however, informed the IFA that such matches were usually only organised for charitable purposes, which was obviously not the case in this instance. A decision on the matter was forthcoming. The IFA, while promising to swing into action and organise a game as soon as FA approval came through, was also clearly worried about rocking the boat too much. IFA president Harry Cavan announced to the press, 'We cannot subject our relationships with the other British Associations to any further stress. We must act with diplomacy here. We await their verdict; the situation has arisen because of them.'

And as the IFA waited patiently on the verdict from FA headquarters, there was still the matter of a match to be played. Jock Stein had been none too happy with his side's capitulation against the Welsh a few days before and he responded by making seven changes to the team. He was also very wary of the threat posed by the Irish and told the press, 'Northern Ireland obviously must be so determined, so anxious to get a result. They proved in the World Cup tie with us in March that they are players with pattern, skill, organisation and physical aggression.' However, it would not prove to be a night for Bingham and his squad to remember.

Since John McClelland's surprise use as a defensive midfielder had worked so well against Scotland two months before,

Bingham opted to play him there again in a starting eleven that, apart from having Martin O'Neill available in midfield, was otherwise unchanged from that game. However, after just five minutes, things went wrong for Northern Ireland owing to some uncharacteristically poor defending. From a Tommy Burns free kick, the ball was pulled back to just outside the box and the defender Ray Stewart thumped it past Jennings into the bottom left-hand corner of the net. Having been caught cold at the start of the first half, Northern Ireland fell victim again early in the second half when a Scottish break, just four minutes after the restart, saw Asa Hartford play a wonderful diagonal through ball to Steve Archibald, who slotted past Jennings under pressure from Jimmy Nicholl; though matters could have been worse if Archibald had scored from an earlier header that hit the bar. However, the game petered out and the only man in a green shirt who was able to take anything positive from the evening was John McClelland, who had put in another solid performance and then clinched a transfer to Rangers immediately after leaving the dressing room.

It had been a long time since the knives had been out for the Irish team in the local press, given that their only previous defeat in the last fourteen months had been on the tough away trip to Portugal. However, out they came now, the headline in the *Belfast Telegraph* reading, 'From champagne to flat beer – forget Spain on this performance.' Harsh words indeed considering the ripping up of their schedule and preparation ahead of the game and all the controversy that had gone with it. Brodie's report was scathing – 'Unquestionably the poorest display since [Bingham] took over … unable to put it together, appeared out of their class' – and he concluded with, 'A result which numbed the team like a cold shower and made them realise that a repetition of this embarrassing sub-standard play in the June 3 World Cup match with Sweden could only spell disaster.'

It had been a chastening night for Northern Ireland and

things got worse the next day. Having decided to abandon the game against Rangers and return to Belfast, regardless of the outcome of the International XI game discussions, the team were met with the news that the game – in theory, just two days away – would now definitely not be taking place. Word from the FA had been expected the previous afternoon, ahead of the clash with Scotland. Twenty-four hours later, the FA – despite the overriding urgency of the matter – had still not responded with permission. The IFA was left with no choice but to abandon plans for the game, as committing to it at that stage would have left it open to further financial disaster if the FA were then to pull the plug.

It was a devastating blow for the IFA, and it was not difficult to read between the lines of Harry Cavan's carefully worded statement about the matter: 'Strenuous efforts have been made by Mr Hill and the Association to obtain the necessary permission. Unfortunately, on returning to Belfast this morning, it was learned the FA has not given permission and time is running out. The task of promoting a match at such short notice and other circumstances make it now impossible to proceed.' He went on to thank Hill for his efforts and to apologise to the fans in Northern Ireland, leaving it abundantly clear where the blame for the abandonment of the game lay.

It was a final act of cowardice from the English FA. It was clear to most observers that they didn't want the match to be played but, instead of making a judgement, they procrastinated until the IFA had no choice but to cancel the match. The decision became that of the IFA and not the FA. In many regards, this was even worse than telling the IFA up front that it didn't want the game to go ahead and merely served to rub salt into the wounds already inflicted upon the smallest of the four home associations.

That night England recorded a dismal 0–0 draw with Wales, and three days later suffered a 1–0 home defeat against Scotland. The abandoned tournament finished with Scotland on four points from three games and Wales just behind them with three points from two games. England had only one point and would surely have been in danger of finishing bottom of the table if Northern Ireland had been able to play their two home fixtures.

As for Wales, who had been enjoying a great tournament, they were left to lament that, if only their players had been prepared to come to Belfast for the final game, they could have clinched their first British Championship for forty-three years.

It was a miserable month in Northern Ireland, with a deteriorating socio-political scene and no world of sport to offer respite from the horror of the nightly news. Bingham's plans to use the British Championship matches to prepare for the crunch game away against Sweden in two weeks' time were also up in smoke. From being on top of the world a year earlier and riding the crest of an exciting qualifying campaign, things now suddenly looked a lot grimmer for Northern Ireland.

They were about to get even worse.

THE DREAM IS DEAD ...
AND ALIVE AGAIN

Billy Bingham's preparation for the trip to Sweden had been greatly upset by the events surrounding the British Championship. Instead of a morale-boosting final game at home to Wales, all the team had to think back on was the lambasting they had taken from the local press for the defeat in Scotland. Though, as Gerry Armstrong told the press, 'Hampden really meant nothing to us. We were deflated. I think you'll find it will be much different – very much different – in Stockholm.'

Bingham instructed his squad to keep training over the next few weeks, despite it being the summer off-season. He was keen to point out that, though they had beaten the Swedes 3–0 the previous year, Swedish manager Lars Arnesson had axed many of the players who had failed in Belfast and this would be a drastically different side. As he told the press, 'The Swedes may be in the depths of despair, maybe going through a difficult phase, but that's when they can be most troublesome. They need a result to lift morale. Arnesson requires a victory to save his job.'

Arnesson, meanwhile, was confident that his side could deliver. 'I have watched that Windsor Park game half a dozen times on video. I still find it difficult to believe my eyes. We had a day when absolutely nothing worked. I don't think a recurrence is humanly possible. Now we seem to have found new enthusiasm. I certainly have not given up hope of qualifying for Spain. A victory over Northern Ireland and another over Portugal three weeks later would make the group much more interesting.' It was a hope that wasn't widely shared among his countrymen who could point to the group table where they were currently languishing in last place.

Bingham made only one change to the line-up that had played Scotland – putting David McCreery in midfield in place of John McClelland – confident his settled team could bounce back from their recent disappointment. Martin O'Neill's excitement was palpable as he spoke to the *Belfast Telegraph*, 'If you cannot get turned on for a World Cup tie you may as well forget about football. This is it – the big one. Whoever remembers a country winning the British Championship? It's an honour, a great honour, but everybody in Northern Ireland still talks about the 1958 World Cup series. We want to make them look at 1982 as another glory era.'

However, it was to be another day of anguish.

Things did not start well when, after just a few minutes, Terry Cochrane and Jimmy Nicholl became embroiled in a dispute with each other on the pitch. It prompted Bingham to leave his seat and vent his anger at the pair, forcing them to concentrate on their duties.

By all accounts the game never really kicked into gear and Northern Ireland found it difficult to find their rhythm. Most of the Irish players had ended their season nearly a month earlier, and they were playing a team that had been picked from a league in full flow, and who played summer football every year. The wisdom of the IFA in agreeing to schedule the game for this date had to be questioned but it still didn't excuse the fact that Northern Ireland suffered 'one of those days' as the afternoon slid from bad to worse.

Jimmy Nicholl made a very uncharacteristic error when a back pass of his almost resulted in Thomas Sjöberg lobbing into the net - thankfully, Jennings pulled off a fine save. The Swedish keeper, Thomas Ravelli, was called into action when, with his leg, he luckily saved a goal-bound header from Armstrong, but there appeared to be a general lack of urgency in the Irish play. Nevertheless, with the score still deadlocked 0–0 at half-time it had hardly been disastrous. Unfortunately, the second half was one to forget for Northern Ireland. Jimmy Nicholl brought down Jan Svensson in the box in the forty-ninth minute and it was an easy decision for the referee to award a penalty. Hasse Borg stepped up to coolly dispatch past Jennings for a 1–0 lead. Five minutes later, Terry Cochrane and Borg had a run-in and Borg ended up on the ground. Cochrane was sent off and Borg received a second yellow card, so was also forced to leave the field. Northern Ireland could find no more gears to move into and they finished the game rather tamely as they registered a second successive defeat for the first time under Bingham.

It was a bitter disappointment, especially when, as Jock Stein said afterwards, 'You should have hammered Sweden. We all know they were due to do something after such a dismal series but Northern Ireland should never have lost this one. They just didn't compete.'

Portugal manager, Juca, was even more forthright as he celebrated the result that seemed to have handed him qualification on a plate, 'Two bad teams but a good result for Portugal and Scotland.' There was no arguing with that assessment.

Northern Ireland were still a point ahead of Portugal, but the

Portuguese now had two games in hand – and both of them were against the unimpressive Swedes. It seemed inevitable that they would overtake Northern Ireland and ease into the qualification berths. Northern Ireland's fate had slipped out of their own hands. Portugal needed to lose two of their remaining four fixtures for Northern Ireland to have a chance, and since three of those fixtures were against the bottom two teams in the group, that looked very unlikely – it seemed that dreams of going to Spain were over. 'We just didn't play, it was as simple as that,' was the stark reaction from Bingham who also read the riot act to Nicholl and Cochrane after the game for their on-field argument.

Gerry Armstrong remembers the lack of discipline shown on the pitch that day – highly unusual during the Bingham era. 'Terry Cochrane played in front of Jimmy Nicholl and Terry was a nightmare for not keeping his mouth shut. Jimmy was losing it and ended up giving the penalty away … we had to pull them apart at half-time because Jimmy was going to bang him one. [Terry] was a cheeky wee sod but he had great fire, you know. I booted him up the arse at Windsor Park one day, we were playing England [in a British Championship game in May 1979] under Danny Blanchflower. Me and Cochy ran into each other and he says, "Get out of my fucking way, you big bastard," and I just went *boot* and says, "Shut your wee mouth." The referee didn't know what to do. He saw it and thought, what do I do? Nowadays they'd send both of us off.'

The local press were quick to launch into histrionics, and Malcolm Brodie's piece in the *Belfast Telegraph* was particularly savage as he called the players and their performance 'simply appalling … beyond comprehension … the nadir in mediocrity … a humiliation … players who let everyone down.' Under the banner of 'It's adios to Spain', he proclaimed that the game represented the 'graveyard' of Northern Ireland football: 'It hurts me to say it but this must rank as one of the most abysmal performances ever from an Irish side.' No team can win every game, but it seemed that any defeat at all – even to a team of Sweden's ability – was to be noted as a national shame. Brodie had been a journalist when Northern Ireland were conceding eight and nine goals in the British Championship to England and Scotland and yet a narrow 1–0 defeat away from home during the off-season was now somehow considered worse. Most remarkable of all was the claim that there could be no excuses for the performance. This was from the same journalist who had, just three days earlier, written an article detailing five specific reasons why Northern Ireland were at a disadvantage going into the game.

While the Swedish papers were no less cruel, they at least put some of the blame at the doors of the IFA, with the daily *Dagens Nyheter* announcing, 'We humbly thank the Irish FA for staging this match in June, a month ahead of the English league season. That was kind of our guests.'

The real blame for the Swedish defeat lay with those within the IFA who had agreed to the date. The players could not be faulted for not being sharp enough for a one-off match a month after they'd last played for their clubs. Put simply, it had been an act of footballing self-sabotage by the administrators of the IFA to agree to the match in June. As Gerry Armstrong remembers, they also had previous form on this front. 'They'd done it before. The Iceland game in 1977. We'd been to the British Championships and then been on holiday and a week later we were called back. It was the twelfth of June, Pat Jennings' birthday, that's how I remember it. We went to Iceland and we were shit. Who would organise a game at that time in June, knowing that the Home Internationals finish at the end of May? Then we had a two-week break. It was ridiculous. But they did things like that.'

It was even worse than Armstrong remembers. There was also an excursion to Denmark in 1979, as Northern Ireland notched up three June trips in five seasons. Unsurprisingly, they lost all three games. On each occasion, they played against a Scandinavian team who played their domestic football over the summer. As Jock Stein remarked after this most recent summer excursion, 'Football in June may be very nice for the legislators, but it is no good for the players.'

Regardless of where the fault lay, it was clear that Northern Ireland had played at a level beneath their capability and there was huge disappointment within the squad. Armstrong recalls, 'I didn't even go out that night. I sat in with Pat Jennings and had a drink at the bar. The lads always used to go out afterwards but I wouldn't even go out. I was so pissed off because I thought we'd blown it.' John McClelland went out with some of the Swedish players after the game, despite being crestfallen, and he recalls one particular conversation from the evening, 'They said, "Don't worry, we'll beat Portugal." "Why should you beat Portugal?" I asked. "You can't qualify for the World Cup. Why should you go and beat Portugal?" But they kept saying, "We'll beat them."'

McClelland paid little heed to these words of bravado at the time but Martin O'Neill had confidence in Sweden's ability. 'Sweden got off to a poor start in the tournament, but I knew that Sweden were not as bad as people were making them out to be. On the way back Pat was very down … I said, "Pat, Sweden will beat Portugal." They were going to play eight or nine days later, and Sweden were up for it now. They were quite physical, Sweden, very strong, and now that they'd got that win under their belt, they felt this was their chance.'

Two weeks later, Portugal took their turn to visit Sweden. The Portuguese league season finished later than that in England – the end of May rather than early May – but, even for the Benfica and Porto players in the squad who had contested the Taça de Portugal final in the first week of June, it had been two and a half weeks since they had played competitive football. Once more, Sweden, in the full swing of their summer domestic season, took advantage of their opponents' generous scheduling and put the visitors to the sword, running out 3–0 winners. It certainly served to put Northern Ireland's narrow 1–0 defeat in context but, more than that, it dramatically changed everything in the group.

Scotland's place at the World Cup was now virtually guaranteed – the last two games in the group had worked in their favour in a way they could only have dreamed of and they sat at the top with eight points from five matches. Northern Ireland were still second, with six points from six matches. Just behind them now on goal difference were Sweden who, out of nowhere, had breathed life back into a campaign which had seemed dead almost from the start, amassing six points from six games. Portugal had now slipped to fourth place, but their five points from five games still made them slight favourites for the second qualifying spot. They just needed to recover from their two consecutive defeats and beat Sweden in Lisbon when they played again in October. Although the group had seemed all but over at the start of June, it had suddenly become an exciting four-horse race as the finishing line came into view.

Martin O'Neill, meanwhile, moved on from his short stint at Norwich City. This followed their relegation to the Second Division after coming agonisingly close to saving themselves at the end of the season. Manchester City boss John Bond made O'Neill an immediate target, giving the Northern Ireland captain a lifeline back into the First Division. O'Neill had only signed a three-month contract at Norwich to take him up to the end of the season, but these were very different times in football, before the rulings that brought greater freedom of movement for the players. A fee still had to be negotiated between the two clubs, even though O'Neill was a free agent and Norwich wanted to make sure they got back every penny of the £300,000 they had paid Forest for him a few months earlier.

In September 1981, Scotland welcomed the resurgent

Sweden to Hampden Park for the next qualifying match in the group. The Swedes had everything to play for as a victory could elevate them to the top of the group on goal difference, albeit having played a game more than the hosts. However, the unlikely turnaround of bottom place to first faltered in Glasgow as Scotland comfortably grabbed the vital two points on offer with a 2–0 win, and Sweden's chances of qualifying now hung by a thread. They needed to beat Portugal away in their final game and hope that both Northern Ireland and Portugal could drop points along the way.

Scotland, meanwhile, were almost home and dry and could start planning their preparations for Spain the following summer. Four points clear at the top, and with the best goal difference in the group, the only way they would fail to qualify was if they lost their two final games by large margins, and Northern Ireland and Portugal hoovered up maximum points. A victory, or even a draw, in their match against Northern Ireland in Belfast the following month would make their qualification official and confirm their place among the twenty-four nations in the next World Cup. And, despite the turbulent situation in Belfast, it looked as though the Windsor Park match would go ahead. The city had been on a knife's edge throughout the summer of 1981. Ten of the hunger strikers had died, with each death followed by rioting, killing and violence on the streets. But the start of October brought an end to the protest, and a degree of normality started to return. The match was sanctioned by FIFA, who had threatened Scotland with loss of points if they refused to travel.

Bingham's focus at that time was on choosing the twenty-two player squad for the crunch match. With only a small pool of players operating at a decent standard of football, the same familiar faces would make up the list, with the occasional amateur Irish League player rounding out the numbers. As a match drew closer, that list would be whittled down to a final sixteen. Bingham's squads were usually very predictable – he knew his player's strengths and how well they worked together, so there tended to be very few surprises. On this occasion, however, his twenty-two-man list had one headline-grabbing inclusion – George Best.

Best was now thirty-five years old, but playing international football at that age certainly wasn't out of the question (after all, Pat Jennings was a year older, although, unlike Best, he had maintained himself at the peak of physical fitness throughout his career). He was playing for the San Jose Earthquakes in the US and appeared to have, at least temporarily, turned a corner in his battle with alcohol. He looked lean and healthy once more and in July 1981 had scored what is considered one of the greatest goals ever seen in the North American Soccer League.

Playing against Fort Lauderdale Strikers, he took the ball up twenty-five yards from goal in a central position. Evading one player and leaving him for dead, he moved into the box where three more opposing players converged on him. He shifted off to the left to leave one of them flat-footed behind him while the other two followed. He held one of them off with his body and, as that player committed himself to the tackle, Best simply shifted back to the right and left him in his wake. At this point, with just one player left in front of him, the second player to have been left behind came back into play as Best turned towards him. Best then twisted left again to remove both of these players from the equation. As a fifth player came charging in from the left to tackle him, Best was now just eight yards from goal and slotted home. Best's footballing intellect had tied his opponents in knots. He still had it.

San Jose Earthquakes had come to play a series of games in the UK where Best was already present on a promotional tour for his autobiography, *Where Do I Go from Here?*. They were preparing to play against Best's previous team, Hibernian, in an October friendly, and it presented the perfect opportunity for Bingham to scrutinise the wayward star at close quarters. As he told the press, 'I'll assess his performance. Best is like any other player – he must prove his match fitness. His ability isn't questioned. Fitness is the key.'

Best had been so impressive that September, when he had turned out as a guest player for Middlesbrough against Sunderland (in a testimonial for his old international team-mate, Jim Platt) that the Middlesbrough manager, Bobby Murdoch, had tried in vain to sign him afterwards. Best had only charged for his airfare to Newcastle and went back to his hotel while the rest of the players had gone out drinking afterwards. Enjoying his football again, fit and fighting back against the alcohol, Best looked like he could still do a job on the pitch, his passing and vision making up for any loss of pace.

'I've scored eighteen goals in the US this season, have been training since I came to England and my weight is almost the same as in the First Division,' remarked Best. It was certainly no pipe dream that this legend of the past could once more represent his country. It is a possibility that has been slightly lost in the mists of time but, back in 1981, Best's ambitions were even grander than helping out with the Irish cause once more – he wanted to play again for Manchester United.

Again, this was no fantasy at the time nor a romantic rewriting of history from today's viewpoint. Ron Atkinson was looking to make big changes at United in his first season in charge and he had just spent £600,000 on bringing the midfielder Remi Moses from his old club, West Bromwich Albion, in September. Best had left United seven years earlier following his personality clash with manager, Tommy Docherty. The more defensively minded years under the guidance of his successor, Dave Sexton, would never have appealed to a player of Best's swashbuckling style, but Atkinson represented a sea change at the club where there was now a possibility of flair and attack being back in fashion.

Matters seemed to reach a crescendo when United travelled to play Arsenal for a league fixture on 26 September. Best was in the stands to watch them play and the United supporters chanted his name and left it in no doubt that they would like to see him pulling on the famous red shirt once more. The club chairman, Martin Edwards, faced BBC cameras to talk over the issue, admitting their interest. 'The club position is that George Best has expressed a wish to come back to Manchester United and Ron Atkinson is sufficiently interested to want to talk to him. I've spoken to the manager about him and I've said, obviously, the club would want to be satisfied on one or two things. One, of course, would be his fitness and whether he'd be up to the rigours of First Division football at the age of thirty-five now. If he is, and he proves his fitness, then he can take a chance with the other players in the squad.'

Whatever happened, the rumours disappeared altogether when Atkinson recruited another of his young and highly promising West Brom protégées, Bryan Robson (United broke the British transfer record in paying £1.5 million for him). Any talk of recruiting a thirty-five-year-old player with suspect fitness at the end of his career now melted away with United having just bought two young and hungry midfielders.

One player who would have cause to worry about Robson's arrival was Sammy McIlroy who operated in the same position for the club. However, his immediate response was to score a hat trick against Wolverhampton Wanderers on 3 October, the day Robson famously signed his United contract at a table set up on the pitch. It would ensure that McIlroy kept his place, with Atkinson accommodating him in the team as part of a mouth-watering midfield alongside Robson, Moses and Ray Wilkins.

San Jose played their friendly against Hibernian, losing 3–1 in a drab affair played at walking pace. It wasn't the kind of game Best needed if he was to impress the watching Billy Bingham. Two days later the Earthquakes played Linfield at Windsor Park in Belfast. That game finished 1–1 and was probably a better showcase for Best, but the appraisal in the next day's *Belfast Telegraph* from Malcolm Brodie was that, sadly, his time was up. It had been only the second match Best had played in six weeks, and then he had had to play two within the space of forty-eight hours, so any comments on him being off the pace in the match report seem to rather miss the point. Best had been training by himself while in England, promoting his book before meeting up with the Earthquakes, and he had not for one second expected to receive the call-up to the initial squad for the Scotland game. As Best himself was quoted as saying, 'If I had, then I could have got down to some serious preparation.' Probably weighing far more against Best was the fact that his contractual obligations with the San Jose side meant that he would probably not be available on the arranged date, and it's likely that this was the ultimate deciding factor in Bingham omitting him from the final squad for the qualifier.

Also missing from the squad were Terry Cochrane, suspended after his sending off against Sweden, and Sammy Nelson (now transferred from Arsenal to Brighton and Hove Albion), who was recovering from an injury. Thankfully, the important trio of Chris Nicholl, Billy Hamilton and Gerry Armstrong had passed late fitness tests, and Noel Brotherston had recovered from his operation over the summer. Jimmy Nicholl was still in the squad, though since he had lost his place at Manchester United (Ron Atkinson preferred new signing John Gidman) he would be making his first senior level start of the season against Scotland.

There was no denying that the Scottish side looked better on paper than the home team. They had a strong spine from defence, through midfield, to attack with the Liverpool trio of Alan Hansen, Graeme Souness and Kenny Dalglish. The Irish players would have been all too aware of the task before them, and they could not afford a repeat of the lethargy shown in their last game.

Victory in this match was essential. Portugal would be playing a home game later that evening and any hope of the Swedes repeating their shock win must have been very slim indeed, away from home where they hadn't scored a single goal in the group so far. If Northern Ireland could beat Scotland, they would move to eight points. Portugal were expected to beat both Sweden and Israel and move to nine points. So if, in their final game, Northern Ireland beat Israel and finished on ten points, and *if* Scotland could either beat or draw with Portugal in Lisbon, then the Irish goal difference would still be better.

John McClelland, now at Rangers and with an inside knowledge of Scottish football, was confident his team–mates were up to the challenge. 'It's going to be a blood and thunder game with a cup final atmosphere, but we can win. We have proved in the past that we can disrupt the Scots. They don't like our style and are uneasy against big strikers like Gerry Armstrong and Billy Hamilton.'

With the British leagues now in full swing again and with a raucous crowd at their backs, this would be a Northern Ireland team who would either grab hold of the result it required or go down fighting. Bingham was quoted in the *Daily Express* as saying, 'I have to calm my players down rather than psyche them up. They are pretty high.'

Pre-match motivation was, surprisingly, given to the Irish squad by the visiting manager, Jock Stein. The normally diplomatic legend of the game perhaps unwisely suggested to the press, 'I think we should be good enough to beat Northern Ireland who, in my opinion, are not as good as they were two years ago.' It's easy to imagine Bingham making much of these words in the dressing room.

Taking to the pitch before an extremely vocal Windsor Park crowd, both teams were eager to attack. Scotland clearly saw winning the game as being the surest method of collecting the single point they required to guarantee qualification. Northern

Ireland were aggrieved not to be awarded a penalty in the early stage. Brotherston had played the ball into a dangerous area of the box for Hamilton to attack but, as the replays showed, Willie Miller shoved Hamilton in the back and forced him to the ground. The ball was then collected by Hansen.

Shots from distance tended to be the story of the first half as both sides tried their luck without being able to carve out the simpler chances they craved. Strachan for Scotland and Brotherston for the Irish saw chances go wide from the edge of the box, and Souness shot over the bar from forty yards and again from twenty-five. Strachan then went on a weaving run from midfield but, again, was forced into shooting from just outside the box. This time, however, Jennings was at least forced into going to ground and making a save.

The Scots were undoubtedly creating more chances at this stage and they fashioned their best of the match so far when Robertson played a ball into the left corner of the box for Steve Archibald. The striker found himself unmarked and was able to turn and loft the ball towards the far corner of the net, only to see it go too high and out of play. Something needed to change for Northern Ireland to get a grip on the game, and Bingham decided to swap Brotherston on to the left flank. This immediately created problems for Scotland, and Brotherston was soon on the end of a cross from Armstrong, although his shot from the edge of the penalty area sailed safely over the target. He was involved again, starting an attack that finished with Armstrong rushing into the six-yard box. Keeper Alan Rough came off his line and took Armstrong out, but he had managed to get to the ball first to fist it away and avoid conceding a penalty.

As half-time approached, Dalglish did very well on the left-hand side of the box and sent a low and dangerous ball across the six-yard line. Jennings attempted to save with Archibald looking ready to tap into the net, but, uncharacteristically, Jennings fumbled, and the ball squirmed through his hands and out the other side of the box, fortunately avoiding any other Scottish players.

It was to be Northern Ireland, however, who enjoyed the final and best chance of the first half, following some tenacious work by Jimmy Nicholl down the right wing. When the ball came into the box it bobbled about in the air between Armstrong, O'Neill, Hamilton and Brotherston, with the Scottish defence momentarily looking confused and unable to clear. The ball eventually fell for a shooting chance to McIlroy near the penalty spot, but he sliced it narrowly wide.

It had been a fairly even first forty-five minutes but the second half was a different story. Scotland may have wanted to win the game but, as things stood, they were still qualifying for a third successive World Cup. Northern Ireland, on the other hand, absolutely had to score, and they launched into all-out attack upon the visitors. An early taste of what was to come saw Jimmy Nicholl cross the ball high to the centre of the box where Hamilton outjumped his marker, only to aim the header straight into Rough's waiting arms.

From a throw-in, Martin O'Neill managed to evade both Strachan and the pursuing Souness to dart into the box and shoot – Rough was forced to save at his near post. There was a slight moment of concern for Northern Ireland when Donaghy slipped while chasing Strachan and the ball fell for Archibald who attempted to chip it into the far corner of the net. The backtracking Jennings was relieved to see it go over the bar and the Irish were soon on the attack. Hamilton and Armstrong combined on the byline to hold off the Scottish defence and Hamilton lifted the ball to the far post, only for Chris Nicholl's header to be off target and wide.

If it seemed like Northern Ireland were knocking on the door of the Scottish goal, they were soon taking a battering ram to it … but Scottish defences remained steadfast. From a corner, the ball fell to Martin O'Neill just nine yards from the goal line and he cracked his shot with force, Rough's momentum taking him the wrong way as he dived. Fortunately for Scotland, Rough was able to save it with his flailing foot, but the ball bounced straight to the waiting Armstrong who was standing on the six-yard line. Instinctively, he lashed it to the side of the floored Rough, only to find the Scottish captain, Asa Hartford, standing on the line and the ball deflected off him to safety.

Andy Gray came on for the visitors, and Billy Hamilton attempted the spectacular with an overhead kick from just inside the penalty box. However, it drifted narrowly wide and Rough was not forced into action.

Donaghy then tussled with Gray right beside Russian referee, Valeri Butenko, but the ball had been kicked forwards and diverted Butenko's attention, so he didn't notice Donaghy kick Gray just before he scampered onwards to collect the ball. The referee was probably the only person inside the stadium unable to see the foul, so it was perhaps fortunate for him that Northern Ireland failed to score – Rough saved the shot that Donaghy unleashed from the edge of the box.

Scotland were by this stage hanging on for dear life. They wanted their qualification guaranteed without having to seek a point in their final game in Portugal. That probably explains the professional foul by Kenny Dalglish with just over a minute of the game to go. Brotherston had taken control of the ball just inside his own half and cut inside from the left flank to leave Dalglish in his wake – but the Liverpool striker stuck out a leg and caught him in the midriff to concede a free kick and end the dangerous break. The Scottish defending became even more frantic and Brotherston was again the victim inside the final minute as Asa Hartford made a wild lunge against him on the left-hand touchline. He managed to sidestep it coolly to get his cross in and from the resulting passage of play, Armstrong received the ball inside the box. Sensing danger in these final seconds, Souness slid in to make the tackle but appeared to take

Armstrong first before clearing the ball. The fans bayed for a penalty, but the clock was ticking and Armstrong jumped to his feet to chase after the ball again. It wasn't quite the final action, though.

With the referee checking his watch and the commentator suggesting that Scotland could start booking their tickets to Spain, Jennings hoisted the ball up field. It landed just outside the Scottish box and bounced high in the air, but Armstrong leapt up and headed it down towards the byline. McIlroy chased after it and desperately crossed the ball for one last effort on goal. It was met in front of the near post by Billy Hamilton who angled it perfectly goalwards, only for Rough to reach up and make the save. With Chris Nicholl following in to pounce on any drop or rebound, Rough then gathered the ball as it fell into his arms and the game was over.

'We did everything we could that night against Scotland but they defended brilliantly,' remembers Jennings. 'It was disappointing, but we couldn't have given anything more.' No one could dispute that. There could be no possible reproach for them after this performance, despite failing to gain the two points they required.

However, there was also no doubting the fact, as they trooped off the pitch and watched the Scottish players celebrate qualification, that their own hopes had ended. Bingham had nothing but praise for his brave players when he said, 'They were magnificent – every one of them. Some of our players are fretting but I have told them how proud I am of all of them. It was one of the best performances we have ever given in Belfast and Scotland had a lot of good fortune … I am delighted for Scotland and I would still like to see Wales, England and the Republic get through as well.'

For Jock Stein the nervous discomfort he had endured in the second half was at an end. 'I'm pleased and relieved. We may not have deserved a point tonight, but we have qualified by coming here with ten points beforehand.' For Northern Ireland he had the following words, 'If your team had played like that throughout, they would be in Spain now – not us.'

All the compliments in the world, however, could not change the simple fact that it was the end of the road for the team's hopes of qualification. There was now only a meaningless game against Israel to look forward to the following month. The mood in the dressing room was one of despondency and Bingham had to work hard to lift their spirits, telling them that it was not over yet. 'I thought we'd blown it,' recalls Armstrong. 'We went back to the hotel and we were really down, we had no chance now.'

Martin O'Neill, however, still clung to hope, 'I'd never really given up on it. Northern Ireland don't qualify for too many World Cups and this was going to be my big chance as I was twenty-nine at the time. You do have to believe, even if it's sometimes crazy. But I knew this group was so, so tight that matches could go in our direction.' Portugal would be playing their home game against Sweden later that evening and, while the chance that the Swedes could repeat their shock win was very slim, O'Neill still decided to listen to the match on the radio.

Following games from other countries, especially low-profile games, wasn't as easy in 1981 as it is today. Die-hard fans would have had to tune in to foreign long-wave radio stations if they were interested, and it's unlikely that even the BBC Ceefax service would have carried the latest updates from Portugal. Yet it was a match that would change everything.

Portugal had taken to the pitch looking to avenge their defeat by the Swedes a few months earlier. However, the seventy-five thousand fans inside the stadium were stunned when Sweden managed to score their first away goal of the campaign and hold on to it for a half-time lead. Halfway through the second half, though, the Portuguese equalised and it's possible that even the most optimistic of Northern Ireland fans turned off their radios. A draw would have been enough to pull Portugal up the table, to sit just a single point behind Northern Ireland, and they expected to beat Israel (and so move ahead of the Irish) going into the final game. As the final whistle approached, things seemed to be sewn up ... until Sweden attacked in the final minute, scored and won the game, 2–1.

Armstrong recalls O'Neill's delight as he delivered the final score to the rest of the team: 'We partied after that when we found out the result. Martin then said, "All we have to do is beat Israel in our last game and we're there and nobody will be able to do anything about it."'

Everything had changed for Northern Ireland in the space of a minute. Portugal had been favourites to qualify right up to the second Sweden scored. Now, their position suddenly looked desperate and Northern Ireland had become the more likely to go to Spain. Portugal still had a game in hand with which they could draw level on points, but the Irish goal difference was superior by three, giving them a slight edge. Bingham had been right when he tried to tell his players it wasn't over yet, while the Swedish promise made to John McClelland at the bar back in June had been fulfilled not just once, but twice.

The next day's late edition of the *Belfast Telegraph* included a front-page story on how the official World Cup travel agent was considering opening a branch in Belfast to deal with the expected demand for trips to Spain, while the back page outlined the potential financial windfall the IFA stood to make from qualification.

Bingham's assessment of the team's chances was also covered by the press: 'I'd say the odds were never better. Certainly, more so than in 1958 when we last qualified. Let's take it calmly. I'm confident we can do it but let's not count the chickens yet.'

The Portuguese press, meanwhile, went into instant mourning. The *Diário de Notícias* reported, 'Portugal needs a combination of favourable conditions which are theoretically possible but, in reality, unlikely. Having seen last night's poor performance, this demonstration of the inability to gain results, why should the bounce of the ball give Portugal two victories in the remaining games and, more than that, a surprise win for Israel in Ireland?' The Portuguese team seemed shellshocked. They had sailed through the first three games of qualifying without conceding a goal and, even after the defeat in Belfast, their manager had been able to allow himself a large smile when he watched Sweden beating Northern Ireland. Now, Portugal had collapsed in three straight defeats and things were about to get even worse for them.

Two weeks later, Portugal made the trip to Tel Aviv. Israel had only scored two goals in their first six games in the group and hadn't won a single match, struggling to notch up three points in the table via three draws and three defeats. But that evening they hit Portugal with a salvo of goals and beat them 4–1. With five points, they now moved level with Portugal, but were ahead of them on goal difference. In a final ignominy, Portugal were sent to the bottom of the group. Two weeks earlier they had been only a few seconds from almost certain qualification, yet now it was impossible. Unlikely as it seemed, Sweden, who had finished their schedule of matches and had a total of eight points, now represented the only barrier to Northern Ireland qualifying. However, even a draw for Northern Ireland at home to Israel would be enough for the Irish to qualify on goal difference, and the country now blazed with World Cup fever.

Bingham, however, remained cautious. He knew his team had a golden opportunity to qualify, but there was still a job to be done and the game needed to be approached in the right frame of mind. Nevertheless, the mood among the fans was buoyant and ticket sales for the final game were phenomenal, with everyone wanting to be there on the historic night Northern Ireland gained their first World Cup qualification in a generation.

The all-important match was set for just three weeks after

Portugal's capitulation in Israel. The Israeli team spent a number of days in advance of the match training at Bisham Abbey in England, and manager Jack Mansell made it clear to the press that they wouldn't be overawed by the occasion or Northern Ireland's desire to qualify. 'It doesn't make any difference to us that we shall not be going to Spain. We are going to Belfast to win, and after what we achieved against Portugal we believe it is possible. I don't care whether Ireland or Sweden qualify – that is their look-out. My main concern is that we play well.' One spy in their camp was David McCreery who had watched them play a practice game against Coventry City. 'There were fists flying everywhere and it was the Israelis who were mostly dishing it out … It wasn't their strongest team, though I saw enough to convince me they will be a physical side.'

To add to the pressure, there was mixed news for Bingham. Sammy Nelson had recovered from his injury and had returned (though Mal Donaghy would retain the left back position) and Sammy McIlroy, who had sustained a damaged knee ligament in the match against Scotland, was thankfully deemed able to play. Tommy Cassidy had also finally been declared fully match fit, which was fortunate as, in his first international appearance in over a year, he would have to stand in for Martin O'Neill. The Northern Ireland captain had picked up a hamstring injury playing for Manchester City in the League Cup. He had received a lot of treatment, but was not fully recovered and Bingham decided not to risk him in such a crucial match. O'Neill was very downbeat about his failure to make the team, telling the *Belfast Telegraph*, 'I've thought about nothing else now for a month. I wanted so much to play – to be part of it all.'

The captaincy would now revert once more to Sammy McIlroy who had led the side to Home International triumph the year before. 'The British title win was an unforgettable experience,' he told the press, 'but suddenly I've been given the chance to lead the boys to the World Cup finals. It looked impossible for us to win the British Championship, but we did it, and now we have the chance to do what many claimed was impossible by winning tonight.'

On 18 November 1981, Northern Ireland took to the field for a night of destiny as a capacity crowd of forty thousand fans urged them on. As Jimmy Nicholl recalls, 'At Windsor Park it was always hard for people, for the foreign players, coming to Belfast and thinking about the Troubles, and the firecrackers seemed like little bombs going off. It probably intimidated people without us realising it. Our record at home was great for a long time.'

Sammy McIlroy also recalls the benefits of playing at Windsor, 'The crowd was absolutely fantastic … it was like a goal start sometimes with the atmosphere they created. I'd seen some big teams coming to Windsor Park and thinking "Aye, I don't fancy this," especially if it was a cold, wet, blustery Northern Ireland night. We could sense this, and the crowd got right behind us.'

Bingham had masterfully guided his team to the brink of qualification through his rousing speeches, in addition to his tactical knowledge, and he also remembers the crowd and how he reminded his players of the fans. 'It was something I used in my speeches to them. I said, "This is a fortress boys. Nobody's going to pierce us," – giving them confidence. The way we were playing it would take a very good team to get through us. One of the strong things that we had behind us besides the fact that we were playing well was the fact that the crowd was so for us. They could see the team was better and their expectations were that much higher.' The Windsor Effect was something borne out by the evidence. Under Billy Bingham, Northern Ireland hadn't even conceded a single goal at home, let alone lost a game.

Israel may well have promised not to come and defend, while making claims about wanting to win the game, but the Irish pressing play early in the game gave Israel little choice other than to sit back and hope they could hold out as the home team went in search of the much-needed goal that would eliminate any nerves about qualification. Armstrong had a header that flashed wide and Tommy Cassidy couldn't find the target with a couple of shots, but in the twenty-seventh minute came the moment the home fans had been waiting for.

Noel Brotherston had won Northern Ireland a free kick on the right wing. He ran over the ball to leave the kick to Jimmy Nicholl, who floated it to the centre of the box where Billy Hamilton, easily outjumping his marker, won the header. He nodded it down perfectly into the path of the unmarked Armstrong and the Watford player spun to hit it on the volley before it could even touch the grass. There was no chance for the despairing Israeli goalkeeper, and Northern Ireland had one foot on the plane to Spain.

It was a momentous goal, though the set-up had caused some confusion on the pitch. 'Billy had us well prepared for that game,' recalls Hamilton. 'We [had done] a lot of preparation for set pieces and one of them paid off ... Jimmy was supposed to put a hand up for the near post or two hands up for the far post.' But in the heat of the match, Nicholl's instructions were unclear. 'He put one hand up first,' adds Armstrong. 'Then he put two hands up ... We hadn't a clue. I thought it was a crossover so I blocked Billy's man off as he made his run to the far post, so Billy had a yard or two of space. The ball went right to the far post and I just looked at Billy's shape and I had an idea of roughly where I thought he would plant it. He put it straight into where I thought he would, and I hit it on the volley straight into the back of the net from about eight or nine yards out. That was the only goal and there weren't many chances, but I never really felt under pressure. I thought we were very comfortable.'

There was pandemonium among the ecstatic supporters, but it's fair to say that the rest of the game was something of a disappointment. The precious goal had been attained with over an hour of playing still to go against a team that didn't seem to be in the mood to attack. If the referee had blown the final whistle there and then, the fans and the teams would probably have been more than happy to wrap matters up early.

Armstrong, Hamilton, Brotherston and Cassidy all had chances they failed to convert but the result never seemed in doubt, apart from a late scare when the Israeli captain, Gideon Damti, headed at the Irish goal in a rare attack. If he had scored, then it might have made for a nervous last few minutes but when the referee blew the whistle for full-time, Windsor Park was re-energised once more in celebration.

The crowd all stayed behind to sing and chant long after the game had ended; the Spanish referee asked Armstrong to swap shirts; and the Northern Ireland players made a slow procession around the edge of the pitch to acknowledge the fans and the part they always played in bolstering the team's morale.

Two of the older players in the squad, Chris Nicholl and Sammy Nelson, thirty-six and thirty-two respectively, summed up what qualifying meant to them. 'We have done something that can never be taken away from us,' said Nicholl. 'This was my last chance and I'm delighted.' Nelson agreed, 'This is something I've waited a long time for.'

Interviewed by BBC Northern Ireland after the game, Bingham revealed, 'I'm ecstatic. So proud to take a team to the World Cup and emulate the feat of 1958 and my then-manager Peter Doherty ... I'm thrilled and the players are equally thrilled. Tension wastes energy and you could see it in their play, it was a bit staccato, they spluttered a wee bit. And yet, through it all, we had all the pressure and we had four chances we could easily have put away.' When the BBC presented him with a bottle of champagne, he broke into a smile and joked, 'You're giving me this because I'm taking you to Spain!'

Northern Ireland's campaign had been an up and down affair in which morale-boosting victories had been followed by the despair of defeat, played out against a soul-destroying background of killing and conflict. In the end, teamwork, Bingham's guidance, and a superb home record combined to deliver a memorable evening. Now, the players, the fans and the population could all look forward to a summer celebration of football at the World Cup.

All would not be plain sailing but, for now, the smallest nation ever to qualify for the tournament could revel in having done it again.

THE DRAW

The next morning, as the players basked in the glory of their achievement, fans started making phone calls to travel agents. A representative of Hamilton Travel told the *Belfast Telegraph*, 'We've hardly had time to draw breath. Our switchboard has been choc-a-bloc with calls from supporters asking if we are providing special package deals to Spain.'

It is telling, not to mention an indication of the troubles ahead, that no congratulations appeared in the press from the IFA; the only statements were of the financial reward it looked set to reap. 'It is impossible to assess the figure until the finals are over but, taking Argentina 1978 as the guideline, it could be in the region of £200,000 or more,' was what IFA secretary Billy Drennan had to tell the press. This was slightly more conservative than the figure quoted by the president, Harry Cavan, who had calculated the figures as soon as Portugal lost to Sweden the previous month. Back then he had told the press, 'The formula of the World Cup tournament cash hand out depends on the number of matches you play. Say you qualify for the quarter-finals, the amount you earn would be much greater than if knocked out earlier. However, at a guess we could collect around a quarter of a million.'

IFA top brass repeatedly told the press that they hoped to build a new modern stand at Windsor Park, and the British government indicated that they would at least match the funding put forward by the association, while those who had actually made these dreams possible wondered, not unreasonably, if they would be rewarded. After all, it had been Bingham's management and the footballing skills of his players that had led to this windfall. Cavan told the press, 'Martin O'Neill and I had discussions on this before the series started and, after discussions with the manager, we left it in abeyance until we saw the outcome. Our players will be looked after properly but, to be honest, I've always found that cash is not the main consideration with them.'

That cash was not the driving motivation of the players was never in question. If ever a team had shown what spirit and heart could achieve it was this group of players. However, there had clearly been an understanding that if the players came through on the pitch the IFA would give them a share of the spoils. The tournament in Spain was, in many ways, the first modern World Cup, where TV money and sponsorship became ever more important. The IFA would get a slice of this cake and it was only natural that the squad would expect their own payments to be formalised as quickly as possible and their governing body to share the riches. Martin O'Neill and the players had acted without any sense of greed in their dealings with the IFA, trusting that it would be honourable. Sadly, their faith was entirely misplaced.

For the most part, players of other nations had set out their own terms before qualifying even began. Not so with the Irish squad. They had simply got on with the job and collectively said, 'We'll sort all that out later.' Money was never a priority for them. This is best illustrated by their reaction to an offer the IFA made instantly after the final game against Israel in the form of a one-off payment as a token gesture for winning the crucial match. But as Martin O'Neill told the *Daily Express*, 'We turned down the £300 because it was unfair on players who figured in the earlier World Cup games.' Excluding a player who had missed the final game through injury or deselection seemed unfair to the squad and none of them accepted the bonus for that game.

However, the question of how players would be paid for the World Cup the following summer was a legitimate one, and the local press covered the financial implications of qualification extensively. In the weeks following the victory over Israel, an IFA spokesperson told *Ireland's Saturday Night*, 'We are hoping to have this cleared up soon – certainly before the draw in Madrid on 16 January.' Little did the players know that they would still be fighting to get a fair deal from the IFA six months later, on the eve of the World Cup.

Bingham, too, was embroiled in salary negotiations. The management position was part-time, paid on the same terms as those of his predecessors, Terry Neill, Dave Clements and Danny Blanchflower. However, the three previous managers had other incomes from playing or journalism. Bingham's only footballing income was his present part-time job. More importantly, the previous regimes had all ended in relative failure. Bingham had brought success back to the IFA by devoting himself to the job full-time, in a way his predecessors, however well meaning, could not. The IFA had already let him down when it denied his request to be made full-time after the success at the British Championship, despite the fact that he could easily have managed another team to trade on his success. He had already turned down several other jobs as that wasn't what interested him. He wanted success for Northern Ireland and he knew he had to devote himself solely to that cause, yet his contract was due to run out in February, and the IFA had already left negotiations perilously late. As he told the *Daily Express*, 'I don't want to be left wondering about my future now with the World Cup coming up. It's a full-time job and it's up to the Irish FA to organise something with me, and in their wisdom I'm sure they will.'

Bingham's annual salary at the time was estimated to be £11,000. Allowing for inflation, that is equivalent to £43,000 today, but is still an incredibly small sum compared with the wage demands of modern managers. For some context, it is estimated that Michael O'Neill commanded a wage in excess of £500,000 per year before leaving the post in 2020. Even taking into account the differences in the world of football in the early 1980s compared to today, Bingham's services were being acquired on the cheap.

Bingham knew he had a strong hand of cards to play. Although the IFA had not responded with a better offer after the British Championship victory, World Cup qualification was an entirely different matter. By guiding the team to this achievement, Bingham had made himself one of the most popular men in the country. Therefore, with the IFA having loudly trumpeted to every journalist who had asked, and many who hadn't, how much money they hoped to reap as a reward for participation the next summer, the feeling was that now was the time to reward the man who had made this possible.

As the highly influential Castlereagh Glentoran Supporters Club stated in the *Belfast Telegraph* on 25 November 1981: 'Emotional pleas to the IFA should be unnecessary in the face of hard facts of which we are all aware. Bingham has the dedication, motivation and the charisma to continue his amazing run of successes.'

Bingham had the upper hand and even the notoriously frugal IFA would have to bow to his demands or face a public backlash. On 17 December, the *Belfast Telegraph* was able to report that the IFA was still insisting on the job being carried out on a part-time basis, but Bingham's pay would now be more in line with that of a full-time post throughout the new three-year deal. Whatever semantics the IFA insisted upon to save face, it was clear that Bingham was the winner. Bingham told the press, 'I've got a good agreement and I'm happy. It didn't cost them the Bank of Monte Carlo, but it is a fair deal.'

The IFA acceded to another of Bingham's demands that day. If Northern Ireland were to stand any chance of qualifying for the second phase, he argued, then their preparations would have to be thoroughly professional and well-staffed. Bingham wanted a number of assistants to help him on the road to Spain and, along with some junior backroom roles, he was now able to name an assistant manager (Martin Harvey, who was almost appointed to the role back in 1980) and an assistant who would assess the opposition. For this role he immediately appointed his old Glentoran and Northern Ireland team-mate, and former Northern Ireland manager, Bertie Peacock. 'I'm delighted to accept the job – delighted I can be of some assistance,' Peacock told the press. 'I was going to Spain anyway on one of the trips. Now I won't have to wonder what match I'll attend.'

But while Bingham's negotiations had now publicly been put to bed, little was done behind the scenes to appease the players. The acknowledgement behind the IFA's closed doors was that Bingham would bring in more money through success than he would cost. However, dealings with the players were conducted with an entirely different mindset. Players couldn't walk away and take their services elsewhere. They were proud to play for their country and sought at every turn to increase their number of caps. Playing in the World Cup would be the crowning glory of their careers. It was the IFA who held the upper hand, and it didn't consider the matter to be immediately urgent. This was an attitude that would come back to haunt the IFA in the months ahead.

★

One important footnote to these last weeks of 1981 was that, with qualification now assured, George Best suddenly became focused on playing for his country on the greatest stage of all. Middlesbrough manager Bobby Murdoch had reached out about a possible return to the First Division and Best quickly showed his interest – this could provide the platform and the level of football to show Bingham he was worth his place in the squad.

As Murdoch told the *Belfast Telegraph* on 1 December, 'His desire to return to England and play top-class soccer again is fuelled by the fact that he still has one burning ambition left – to play in the World Cup. I've been quoted as saying I didn't think he could come back but it's different now. The World Cup is the difference. That in itself is a great incentive for him to do well here and prove to Billy Bingham that he should go to Spain ... That means he'll be trying all-out. His experience, too, can be invaluable to us, and Northern Ireland.'

Bingham himself was immediately alert to the developments and told the paper, 'George will have to play consistently good performances for an English club and prove himself fit to come under the international microscope. If he doesn't achieve the standards, then he just won't make it to Spain. I'll be watching the situation closely.'

It wasn't just the fans and management team at Middlesbrough who were becoming increasingly excited by the possibility of Best returning to English football. George's old Manchester United and international team-mate, Sammy McIlroy, was also enthusiastic. 'If Billy Bingham selects him it will be because he is fit and playing well,' McIlroy told *Ireland's Saturday Night*. 'There is no way that the manager would have him in under any other circumstances. And who wouldn't want a fit George Best in their side? It could only do us good and our qualification is a great incentive for George to get back with Middlesbrough in the First Division.'

When the story broke, it appeared as though the transfer was a fait accompli. Best's agent, Bill McMurdo, seemed confident that the star would be in England within a matter of days and confidently announced to the press, 'If we can get him over in time, he could play on Saturday.' There was more from McMurdo the following day when he explained the situation with the San Jose Earthquakes. 'George has an excellent relationship with the club, and he will be going back after the finals in Spain. They are releasing him now because they accept it's his last chance to play in a World Cup.'

Nine days later, however, Best had still not signed a contract with Boro, let alone pulled on their red top in competitive action. 'There's still a lot of talking to be done before we can name a date for me to play for Middlesbrough,' Best explained. 'While I have been given the go-ahead to talk to Boro in England, the negotiations are far from complete. San Jose want some assurances and I hope to get them this weekend.' It seemed that his American club, while sympathising entirely with his desire to play at the World Cup, still wanted to retain his services for the future. George Best was box office in the US and while they had no objection to him signing for an English club outside of their season, they wanted him back for their first match of a new campaign in early April.

Boro had apparently agreed to these conditions and it was difficult to see what could go wrong with the proposed signing. Best was quoted the next day, 14 December, in upbeat mood, 'I'm determined to make it. I want to get back in the Irish side. Who wouldn't want to play in the World Cup finals?' And yet, the very next day, the *Belfast Telegraph* carried the story that it was all off.

Best's former international team-mate, Jim Platt, was clearly devastated: 'It's hard to put into words how disappointed I am … all the players were excited by the prospect of working with him today and playing with him on Saturday. People have been stopping me in the street since the news first broke asking if he'd really be coming, and I was always confident.'

Terry Cochrane, another Northern Ireland international at Ayresome Park, was equally dismayed by the collapse of the deal. 'It's a big let-down for me personally and, of course, everyone else at the club. But he has made his own decision, and he must have had good reasons … I'm sure once he started playing, and [got] to know the lads, he would have been able to settle. But I suppose he's thirty-five now, been such a great player, that he was feeling the pressures of people expecting so much of him.'

While these pressures were given as the reason the signing did not go ahead, it's hard to imagine that Best, determined to fulfil his World Cup dream, would have opened negotiations only to pull out at the last second. His skill was still there, he appeared to be in good physical shape, his desire wasn't in question and all that needed to be done was to sharpen his match fitness. Whatever the reasons for the disintegration of the deal – some thought the change in lifestyle for his family, from the warm luxury of the West Coast of the USA to the cold winter of industrial north east England, was a factor – it seemed that Best's hopes of going to Spain had similarly collapsed. As he caught the plane back to San Jose he must have known in his heart of hearts that he was leaving behind his greatest unfulfilled ambition.

A bumper crop of teams from the British Isles had qualified for the 1982 World Cup. Not since 1958, when all four UK teams qualified for the only time, had more than one national side made the journey to the finals. England had been the lone representative in 1962, 1966 and 1970 but had then endured twelve years in the wilderness, with Scotland being the only British side in West Germany in 1974 and Argentina in 1978. However, it was very nearly a British Isles full house for 1982. Wales had been cruising nicely towards qualification with maximum points after four games, only to stumble badly in the final stages – unable to win any of their final four games. They endured an agonising couple of weeks waiting for the final game in their group to be played – Czechoslovakia and the Soviet Union – but in the end, the Czechs gained the point they needed to qualify ahead of Wales on goal difference.

The Republic of Ireland suffered a similarly heartbreaking situation. Drawn in a nightmarish group with the Netherlands (runners-up in the two previous World Cups), Belgium (runners-up at the 1980 European Championship) and the highly-fancied France, they finished ahead of the Dutch, but still failed to qualify. Like the Welsh, they also had to wait anxiously for the final game to be played after their own fixtures had been completed. They had beaten France 3–2 in their final game in October, but the French played two further games in November and December to catch up on points and squeeze past them on goal difference.

Nevertheless, with three teams present, interest in the World Cup and its expanded format of twenty-four teams was high, especially with the media juggernaut of the English press covering an England team at the finals again after such a long absence. All attention was now focused on the draw, which was held on Saturday 16 January in Madrid. Bingham, Cavan and Drennan travelled to the event to represent the IFA.

The system used to determine the groups will seem arcane to followers of modern World Cups. Whatever might be said about the merits of the FIFA world rankings, at least its method of determining the seedings for tournaments is clear and understandable. Not so in 1982, when England were selected as a top seed at the host nation's request.

Other nations questioned the seeding and the benefit to England of avoiding all the other top nations. France and Belgium lodged official complaints, unimpressed by the award to a team who hadn't been at the last two World Cups and who had only narrowly qualified for this one. However, FIFA executive Hermann Neuberger told the press, 'The Spanish want England to play in Bilbao for security reasons.' England, with their reputation for hooliganism preceding them, would be playing their three games in the security-heavy area of the Basque region to allay some of Spain's policing fears.

The knock-on effect of this seeding, however, was that the British teams might now be drawn against each other, and the Scottish contingent were far from happy about this. Ernie Walker, the SFA secretary unhappily told reporters, 'It is utterly absurd if this is what happens after all the planning. The South Americans and the East Europeans are kept apart. Why not the British teams? If it meant not seeding England, then let them not be seeded.'

The draw itself proceeded in a farcical manner. While there was now a chance the British teams would play each other, FIFA maintained the stipulation that no countries from South America should be drawn in the same group. There were only four teams from South America, but two of them – Brazil and Argentina – were among the top seeds. It meant that the groups with those two nations would need to be ring-fenced from any further South American teams.

The solution, as FIFA explained to the press, was that they would initially exclude the balls containing both Chile and Peru from the draw for the teams in Pot B. With the other four Pot B teams, including both Scotland and Northern Ireland, all being European, the first two teams drawn out would go into Argentina's group first and then into Brazil's. Once this had been accomplished, Peru and Chile could be safely added to the draw.

Future FIFA president Sepp Blatter, in his role as acting general secretary, oversaw the draw. First of all, Chile and Peru were not removed. Fortunately for FIFA, the first two teams drawn were Belgium and Scotland. However, Belgium weren't placed beside Argentina, as they should have been, and were instead installed in Italy's group. With no one realising the mistake, Scotland were drawn next and paired with Argentina instead of Brazil. At that point, someone realised what a mess it was and, after several minutes of confusion, parts of the draw were redone to place Belgium and Scotland into the correct position within the groups. The cages used to jumble the balls then broke down and one ball even split open inside after several attempts to fix the machinery.

The IFA's Harry Cavan, in his role as FIFA vice president, was part of the World Cup organising committee. He pulled no punches in his assessment of the Spanish organisation when he told Malcolm Brodie, 'It was embarrassing. A case of too many cooks spoiling the broth and a draw being far too complicated. Worst of all was when the balls became entangled in the cage and had to be pushed out. Their planning is so slipshod in its execution. They just don't seem capable of operating with twenty-four teams – and I don't think any nation [is].' Nevertheless, personal incompetence and worldwide humiliation proved to be no bar to future progress for Blatter.

When things were running smoothly again, the two South American teams were drawn out of the cage leaving just France and Northern Ireland, with the next team drawn due to be in England's group. Back in the BBC studios in London, player representatives of the three nations were gathered to watch the draw and there was visible light-hearted relief displayed between Kevin Keegan and Pat Jennings when France were the next team announced and the prospect of two British teams facing off against each other had been avoided. However, Northern Ireland now knew they would be placed in the only remaining group – that of the host nation, Spain.

Also in Northern Ireland's group were Yugoslavia and Honduras. Yugoslavia would represent formidable opposition. Their club sides were well respected in European competitions and they had breezed through qualification with an impressive goal difference to top the group ahead of Italy. Little was known about Honduras in European footballing circles, but they had topped the Central American Zone of the Confederation of North, Central America and Caribbean Association Football (CONCACAF) qualifying. They progressed to the final round with representatives of the North American and Caribbean Zones, as well as El Salvador from Central America. Controversially, in those days the final round was played in one country over a few weeks (though this was the final year it would happen). Honduras had been the host nation for this round and maximised their home advantage to once more top the group ahead of El Salvador, their draw with Mexico in the final game causing the CONCACAF's most successful nation to miss out on qualification. Although they had qualified from a traditionally weak federation there was no doubting that Honduras weren't quite the no-hopers some had thought. They were the best the region had to offer and would be used to the heat of the Spanish summer into the bargain.

Now that Northern Ireland knew who their opponents were, and in which stadiums they would be playing their matches, the immediate task was to pick a base that would best suit their needs and that had adequate amenities for both training and relaxation. As Bingham had told *Ireland's Saturday Night*, 'It is important we get this right. Proper billeting for such a prolonged period is vital to the psychological build-up of a team.'

Bingham had been one of the players who in 1958 had benefited when Northern Ireland found an excellent location for their base – one that had allowed them to train and unwind in attractive surroundings – so he had first-hand experience of how a team could thrive in the right environment. Worryingly, the IFA hadn't yet started checking accommodation. Of course, until the draw was made, Northern Ireland wouldn't have been aware that their games were going to be played in Zaragoza and Valencia, but other nations had already been scouting around to be first out of the blocks once match venues were known.

Fortunately, Jock Stein had already undertaken a lot of hotel inspections and he promised to share his information with Bingham and the IFA.

With the opponents now known, managers, players and pundits could speculate about the possible paths to glory in the tournament. Bingham immediately and astutely saw what needed to be done when he told the press, 'We have to win or at least draw against Yugoslavia in the opening game because I expect Spain to beat Honduras. Yugoslavia then play Spain while we hope to beat Honduras. I hope Spain beat the Yugoslavs because they might not need an extra point against us – and our game in Valencia would then be quite relaxed. In those circumstances, I would fancy us to take something out of it.' The need to get points in the first two games was paramount as Spain not only had the home advantage but had beaten England 2–1 at Wembley the year before.

Spain's manager, José Santamaria, was alert to the potential for the Irish to cause an upset, 'Despite what everyone says, this is not an easy draw for us. Northern Ireland hold the key to it. If they beat Yugoslavia in the opening match, and that's a distinct possibility, then the entire group remains wide open. Northern Ireland could be the dark horse here, particularly with two teams qualifying for the quarter-final.'

The other British managers present at the draw were positive about Northern Ireland's chances and offered Bingham hope. 'Spain are settled now,' Ron Greenwood offered, 'but if you beat the Yugoslavs you could go through.' Bingham reacted mercurially, 'Sure we'll do it. Maybe we'll meet England in the quarter-finals at Barcelona.'

Meanwhile, Jim Gracey of the *Belfast Telegraph* spoke to key members of the squad back in the UK to gain their reactions. Billy Hamilton suggested, 'There's no doubt that [Spain] is the big one. I just hope we get a good, firm referee. We don't want anyone who will be influenced by the crowd and scared to give us anything. I am pleased though that we have late-evening kick offs. By the time we play it will be quite cool and we won't suffer in the way we would under a blazing sun.'

Sammy McIlroy was very upbeat about their chances and told Gracey, 'After this draw I am convinced we can be World Cup dark horses and surprise everyone. Even being in the same group as Spain may turn out to be a bonus. I know the records say the host country always seem to do well, but Spain have not been too hot in the past. With their crowds expecting so much of them they could crack under the pressure.'

The IFA, in the meantime, had been keen to make the most of World Cup fever, off the pitch as well as on the field of play. As Harry Cavan explained, 'We intend to make sure that everything is properly marketed. It's a wonderful opportunity to sell Northern Ireland – and the Irish FA.' To this end they hired Clive, Allen and Stewart, the consultants who handled Scotland's promotion and commercial activities, to devise both a mascot and an official emblem to represent the association. Team mascots could be exploited commercially, and were nothing new. In 1966, English mascot World Cup Willie, a football-playing lion, even had his own comic strip within the pages of *TV Comic*; while the overall mascot for the tournament was already Spain's Naranjito, an orange decked out in the Spanish kit, who became one of the most fondly remembered World Cup mascots of all. A successful mascot could take on a whole marketing life of its own and be applied across a wide range of merchandise, and Northern Ireland weren't slow in realising the potential in this area.

On 25 November, Cavan told the *Belfast Telegraph*, 'We have got something which is not divisive in nature – something acceptable to the community. I had thought about the name "Yer Man" and a character similar to Andy Capp with the duncher and the green jersey. We'll see how it all develops.' Renowned local artist Rowel Friers was commissioned and by 7 December the mascot was officially unveiled to the press. 'Yer Man is someone everybody in Northern Ireland knows,' explained Cavan. 'He is someone who could not be identified but yet everybody knows him.'

The IFA's choice of Yer Man was certainly novel. It eschewed the tendency towards anthropomorphic animals dressed in national football colours. Instead, Yer Man was a flat-capped working man sporting a green and white scarf and rosette and clutching a suitcase with 'España '82' written on the side. So far, so good. Unfortunately, Yer Man also had a lit cigarette hanging from the corner of his mouth, which, even at the time, raised some eyebrows. Still, despite the questionable health endorsements, it was at least a more memorable mascot than those produced by the other home nations that year: England's Bulldog Bobby fell lazily into the stereotype of such designs, and the less said about Scotland's anatomically ludicrous Sandy, the better.

A limited amount of embroidered clothing was made featuring Yer Man but it's unlikely that it became the money spinner that had been hoped for. Then, in January 1982, came the announcement of an official Northern Ireland World Cup song that would feature lyrics celebrating the mascot.

Official squad songs were another World Cup tradition, dating back to England's famous 'Back Home' in the lead-up to the 1970 Mexico tournament. In the 1980s – long before New Order would reinvent the wheel in 1990 for England's 'World in Motion', or the jaunty singability of The Lightning Seeds' 'Three Lions' perfected the art form of the football song – the public thirst for footballers drearily sleepwalking their way through the lines of a novelty song had reached something of a zenith. These were the days of a squad lined up, as if at gunpoint, and forced to recite the words from shared lyric sheets while awkwardly swaying from side to side for the accompanying video.

Nevertheless, Tottenham Hotspur had teamed up with cockney singing duo Chas and Dave to great effect for a Top Five hit ahead of the 1981 FA Cup Final, and 'Ossie's Dream' would soon be followed by another hit ahead of the 1982 final. While it was not unknown for clubs to release entire albums of their players singing football chant standards in this period (Jimmy Nicholl and Sammy McIlroy had featured on the 1979 album by Manchester United, *Onward Sexton's Soldiers*), a team-up with an established chart act usually yielded more success – Scotland had reached number four in the charts in 1978 with Rod Stewart – so Northern Ireland sought their own local star with UK-wide appeal.

Various artists came forward with suggestions for the team song but the one selected was written by Eurovision-winning starlet Dana and her brother Gerry Brown. Graeme Grant, the person in charge of the players' commercial pool, told the *Belfast Telegraph*: 'We had a large number of offers to write the song but we've selected this one. I think the public will like it. Dana is taking no royalties from the record. It's her contribution to the team's achievement in reaching Spain.'

Martin O'Neill, Pat Jennings, Gerry Armstrong and Billy Hamilton were among the ten members of the squad to feature alongside Derry's finest songstress and the end result was 'Yer Man', an inoffensively catchy little number that disgraced no one. Despite Grant's lofty assertion that the record would be distributed throughout South America and Europe, as well as the UK and Ireland, it sank without trace upon release and failed to chart. It was a sad fate for the single that was more memorable than Scotland's funereal 'We Have a Dream', which somehow reached number five in the UK charts, or England's 'This Time (We'll Get it Right)', which was only kept off the top spot by Paul McCartney and Stevie Wonder's 'Ebony and Ivory'.

The collaboration with Dana, however, was not the only Northern Ireland World Cup single to be released that year.

Local comedian Sammy Mackie, a veteran of the working men's club circuit, gained a fair amount of publicity by dressing as Yer Man and recording his song, 'I'm Yer Man', a throaty exhortation with an infuriatingly catchy chorus, which defied its musical deficiencies. And it didn't end there. Another local comedian, Gene Fitzpatrick, released a single called 'Viva Ireland!' with 'Bingham's Back Again' as the B-side. Barbara Allen released 'Northern Ireland are Magic' (set to the tune of 'Una Paloma Blanca'), and even John Watt, the Singing Farmer, got in on the act with the Irish country tune, 'Three Cheers for Billy Bingham and His Boys'.

With such jovial distractions, the team could not have foreseen the sequence of disasters set to befall them in the months ahead. The high tide of optimism would soon be replaced by serious worries and doubts about their ability to compete in the tournament, and their first match of the British Championship, in February 1982 against England, was unquestionably where it all started to go wrong.

IT ALL GOES WRONG

On 23 February 1982, Northern Ireland would play their first match since qualification, a British Championship game at Wembley against England. But a lot had changed for some of the players. Jimmy Nicholl, after losing his place at Manchester United, had agreed to a loan deal at Sunderland. He had hoped it would lead to a permanent move but the North East club could not afford the appearance money due to United for each first team game he took part in. Struggling to afford United's estimation of £250,000 for a permanent move, they reluctantly allowed him to return to Manchester, much to Nicholl's dismay: 'I don't expect I'll even get into the Old Trafford reserve side. It's a sickener, especially with my ambitions to go to Spain with Northern Ireland next June. It was a blow to me when I was told the deal was off. At the moment my future doesn't look too bright. If there is no place for me at Old Trafford, I hope it won't be too long before someone comes in for me.'

Two other key Northern Ireland players, Sammy McIlroy and Martin O'Neill, had also changed clubs in the weeks leading up to the England game. McIlroy had left Manchester United, a team he had been with since the 1960s, for First Division Stoke City as they could offer him a regular berth in which to keep his game sharp ahead of the World Cup. As he explained to *Ireland's Saturday Night*, 'I had thirteen magnificent years there and never realised how much of a wrench it would be to leave. But when the time came, I knew deep down I had to move on. I was in and out of the side and realised that a prolonged period out of the First Division limelight wouldn't do either my form or my chances of playing for Northern Ireland in Spain any good. In a way, Stoke's interest came at an ideal time. They're a smashing little club with a great set of lads and I'm thoroughly enjoying my football with them.'

O'Neill, meanwhile, had not had a happy time at Manchester City, and he was quoted by the *Scotsman* as saying, 'John Bond bought me and could not wait to get rid of me.' Norwich City had not wanted him to leave at the end of the previous season and they rescued him from City, paying only half of the fee they had sold him for. Of course, this meant returning to the Second Division where Norwich City were a struggling club, but O'Neill believed that they could turn their form around and push for promotion. As with McIlroy at Stoke, it was more important to be somewhere he was valued in the final months of build-up to a World Cup.

While training at the Irish base in St Alban's, Tommy Cassidy was diagnosed with a medial ligament injury and was instantly ruled out of the British Championship game. Added to this news was the realisation that David McCreery would not be able to take his place in the heart of midfield. McCreery's only recent football had been the less demanding American indoor season and that, combined with jetlag, led Bingham to the disappointing conclusion that he wouldn't be up to the rigours of playing on

Wembley's wide and heavy pitch. Instead, Mal Donaghy would be drafted into the midfield from defence.

Thankfully, Pat Jennings, who had been out of action for seven weeks with a groin injury sustained in an FA Cup derby game against Tottenham Hotspur, would be able to earn his ninetieth cap. He came through a fitness test on the day of the game and, despite not having played first team football in 1982, was a welcome bolster to the Irish lines – after all, he had more experience of playing in this stadium than many of the players in the experimental English line-up.

Northern Ireland were still technically the British Champions going into the game, following the cancellation of the 1981 event, but their hopes of retaining the title were dealt a hammer blow after just forty-five seconds. From the kick off, Mal Donaghy had conceded a free kick after a tackle on Glenn Hoddle. Hoddle passed to Viv Anderson on the right flank who released the ball to Trevor Francis, who powered his way past Sammy Nelson. He crossed into the Northern Irish box where Bryan Robson turned the low ball past Jennings. Northern Ireland hadn't touched the ball once.

Despite the horrific start, Northern Ireland rallied and found their way back to a steadier footing, and managed to avoid being swept away. However, they were unable to create any real danger in the final third with England playing a rather defensive formation that saw Ray Wilkins employed as a sweeper for the evening. In fact, such was the lack of attacking thrust from both sides that the Wembley crowd booed the players off the pitch at half-time with the match having remained goalless since the opening minute. In many ways, this was good news for Northern Ireland – an angry crowd agitating an unfamiliar line-up of players would play into Irish hands, leaving the team open to snatching an equaliser at some stage in the second half. Unfortunately, it was to play out a different way.

Only four minutes after the restart, Trevor Francis sent a cross over Chris Nicholl's head, which was met with precision by Kevin Keegan, and the game now looked beyond the Irish. With the game practically won, and Northern Ireland unable to find any way back, Ron Greenwood rang further changes, bringing on Tony Woodcock for Tony Morley and handing a first cap to West Brom's Cyrille Regis in place of Francis. In the final stages, England added two more goals, the first from Wilkins following a blocked shot from Dave Watson, which then took a wicked deflection off Sammy Nelson, and the second a simple tap-in from Glenn Hoddle following a Jennings save. It certainly hadn't been reflective of the game as a whole, but it did demonstrate that England possessed a more ruthless streak in front of goal when it mattered. One thing that was certain was that the 4–0 loss had started Northern Ireland's preparations for Spain in somewhat disheartening fashion.

Reaction to the wide margin of defeat fortunately wasn't entirely negative in terms of the headlines. Even the *Belfast Telegraph* led with 'Defeat could be blessing in disguise' across its back page the following day. However, the article itself fell into the familiar trap of heavily criticising individuals and making sweeping statements. Just the day before, the spearhead of Armstrong and Hamilton had been commended. Post-match, Hamilton was now considered to have 'struggled throughout and appeared out of his depth.' Worse criticism was meted out to Donaghy, playing out of position in midfield, who was noted as having 'neither the mobility nor the creative skills for such a role'. Jimmy Dubois, perhaps more accurately, summed up the performance in his report for the *Newsletter* when he wrote, 'Northern Ireland promised much with some neat, controlled build-ups but the killer punch was missing when it was needed.' Nevertheless, any player would have been crestfallen to read the *Belfast Telegraph*'s downbeat assessment: 'Now everyone knows how much work has to be done, on a group of players with limited talent, to avoid embarrassment in Spain next summer.'

One other concern to take away from the match had been the relatively low attendance. The crowd of almost fifty-five thousand was actually one of the better turn-outs for this bi-annual Wembley fixture but, as Harry Cavan pointed out to *Ireland's Saturday Night*, 'Here we had two World Cup teams in action but the stadium was only half full. England may well take the view in future that it would be more profitable for them to play a foreign side than the British Championship.' There was little doubt that both the IFA and FAW were nervously looking over their shoulders. The relentless whispering in football circles concerned England's loss of enthusiasm for the series and the IFA couldn't countenance a world in which the guaranteed annual television revenue from the matches was removed from its budget.

Watching in the crowd that night in London were the managers of both Spain and Yugoslavia, eager to view at first hand the style of play they would encounter four months later. Yugoslavia's Miljan Miljanić had announced the previous month that he would watch all of Northern Ireland's build-up matches as he saw the game against them as the crucial one in the group. 'I see Northern Ireland as an obstacle. We just have to win this game if we are to reach the second phase. The Irish can be resolute and tough. They are a big challenge.' Having now watched them play, however, he summed up his views by saying, 'Plenty of promise and threats, but nothing in the goal area.' Spain's José Santamaria was equally unimpressed, concluding, 'There is no scoring power in the Irish team.'

Bingham's own views were more upbeat and he tried to conceal his disappointment, 'Losing out to England will make players realise how hard it is at this level. The other games should have a similar lesson. There is a mountain to be climbed before June. It won't be easy reaching the summit and defeat won't do us any harm … So long as we can peak around May or June, I'll be happy.'

Bingham's old Glentoran and 1958 international colleague-turned-football-writer, Jimmy McIlroy, warned, 'You can have a team shattered by defeats and morale low before the real goal is reached. The schedule could, perhaps, have the opposite effect to that intended.' However, Bingham himself believed that the best approach was to get as much experience playing against high-ranking teams as possible, 'Playing formidable sides is the correct approach. You don't therefore go into the finals with any false or grandiose ideas. You know what to expect.' It was fortunate for Bingham, then, that the IFA had accepted a request from France to play a friendly that March.

As is often the case before major tournaments, teams drawn against England would look to arrange a friendly with one of the other home nations to give themselves a work-out against the 'British style' of play. England had already lined up a prestige friendly against France for March, but when the two were put in the same group in the World Cup draw, the two nations decided to cancel – neither wanted to give their soon-to-be opponents any hints about their strengths and weaknesses. France approached Northern Ireland to fill this void in their schedule, and would also add a game against Wales in June.

Preparing a team with the right friendlies was, of course, an important task. For England, Scotland and Northern Ireland, the British Championship that year acted as both a help and a hindrance. On the one hand, three warm-up fixtures were already slotted into the calendar. On the other, the games weren't perhaps the most diverse in terms of opposition. England would probably have been secretly dismayed at having to use up two games against Wales and Northern Ireland, whom they viewed as weaker opponents, when they really wanted to test themselves for the summer. Even Northern Ireland hoped they could find continental opposition, or someone with a similar style to the Hondurans. Bingham had spoken at the draw about the need for a programme of friendlies, telling *Ireland's Saturday Night*, 'I want a game in Belfast in May, a sort of farewell tribute from the fans, and then one abroad in a hot climate in June.' Unfortunately, he would find himself frustrated in these plans. They struck lucky with the March friendly against France but apart from accepting that game, nothing more was forthcoming from the IFA administrators. It's difficult to understand the logic behind that inaction – preparation for the tournament was of supreme importance and yet they did little to try and organise it.

As far back as mid-December it was reported that Israel had offered themselves as opponents to the IFA. Good relations had been forged with the Israeli authorities during the qualifying campaign and they were exactly the kind of opposition Bingham was searching for – not too difficult, not too easy, and used to playing in a warm climate. The IFA could even reuse the facilities and arrangements from their previous trip in 1980. And yet for reasons unknown the match failed to happen. There were also rumours about matches against the United States, Iraq, Hong Kong and Switzerland, though they too failed to materialise – and even if they had, these were not really the types of teams Bingham required. Both Iraq and Hong Kong fell short of the standard required and Switzerland could not provide a comparable climate to that of Spain.

Harry Cavan already seemed to be downplaying expectations for the friendlies when he told the press, 'Altogether we want around five matches before the World Cup, but agreement has yet to be reached with these countries and, most important of all, players have to be released by English League clubs which could be difficult due to the heavy backlog.'

It had been one of the severest winters in recent memory, with fixtures postponed for weeks on end under snow-covered pitches, so there was indeed the potential for fixture congestion. Nevertheless, the tone seemed remarkably defeatist. It was also at odds with what the manager was telling the same journalist at the same event, with Bingham again firmly setting out his stall:

'It is essential we have continuity with a match almost every month before we kick off in Spain.'

With the British Championship game against England in February, a trip to Paris in March, a game against Scotland in April, and another against Wales in May, all the IFA had to do to meet Bingham's minimum expectations of 'a match almost every month before we kick off in Spain' was to schedule one friendly. And Bingham was adamant that the final game should be in a warm climate. For a while, the press speculated that Greece were a possibility, and by early March they had suggested Morocco as candidates, but no direct quotes from officials ever backed up this press conjecture.

By late March, as Northern Ireland prepared to meet France in Paris, it now seemed certain that another of Bingham's ideas – that of a game played in Belfast as a rousing sending off for the tournament in front of the home fans – was now mooted to be unlikely, with it being deemed financially unattractive to the IFA to bring in a 'lesser' nation for such a game. With time to organise any games beyond the British Championship now beginning to run out, Bingham accepted that the Windsor Park friendly wouldn't happen but told the *Belfast Telegraph*, 'I must, however, press my claim for a match in a warm climate just before our June 13 arrival in Spain. We need to get acclimatised. I don't want to play a club team if at all possible. I would prefer an international side but, in the end, I might have to accept a compromise. It is, however, essential to have players realising just what it is like to toil in the heat.'

Bingham could not have been more explicit about how vital such a game was to their preparation and the very next day it was mentioned that a game in Portugal, possibly against a club side, was on the cards. Bingham wasn't thrilled, but it was clear that he was now desperate when he said, 'There are a lot of dangers in such a fixture, but we may be forced to take it. There aren't too many options open to us.'

For now Bingham's focus shifted to the match against France. Jennings was unavailable again owing to a recurrence of his groin injury, but Bingham was able to bring Billy Caskey into the squad as the midfielder had been holidaying in England with his Tulsa Roughnecks team-mate, David McCreery. Also added to the squad for a closer look was a young twenty-year-old winger named Ian Stewart who had been showing encouraging signs as part of Terry Venables' successful Queens Park Rangers squad.

Just days earlier, the Triple Crown-winning Irish rugby team had floundered in Paris, failing to add the Grand Slam to their honours in taking that year's Five Nations trophy. It was to be a sorry visit for Northern Ireland as well, even with the home team missing their talismanic star player, Michel Platini, through injury.

The game had started very brightly for the visitors, and Brotherston in particular seemed confident in his ability to run at the French defence. In just the fourth minute he broke down the right flank to cross for Sammy McIlroy. Taking the ball on the edge of the box, McIlroy ghosted past two French defenders and then shot across goal on the diagonal, only to see the ball slip inches past the far post. Just a few minutes later, Brotherston received the ball deep in his own half and slalomed his way at great speed up the centre of the pitch, beating no fewer than four French players as he did so. When he reached the edge of the penalty area, he blazed his shot high over the bar. Nevertheless, it was an incredible start to the game for Northern Ireland.

The Irishmen continued to look comfortable but after twenty-five minutes Bingham was forced to bring off Terry Cochrane, who had picked up a hamstring injury, and give the young Ian Stewart his international debut. After thirty-one minutes the increasing French pressure paid off when an Alain Giresse cross found Bernard Zénier unmarked at the far post for an easy header into the net for the first goal. The Irish gamely tried to respond but France now began to ooze confidence and

Platt was twice forced into saves. Almost at the end of the first half he was called upon to make another stop from Zénier, but Alain Couriol was waiting to pounce on the spilled ball for a simple tap in and Northern Ireland trudged off the pitch at the break two goals down.

The second half brought more hardship for the Irish and while it was far from being one-way traffic, there always appeared to be a greater threat from the French attacks. When Brotherston gave the ball away badly in the fifty-seventh minute it was latched on to by Jean-François Larios who ran unimpeded through the heart of the Irish defence in clear space. Platt faced him down brilliantly and pulled off a good save, but when the ball fell to Bruno Bellone, he had little choice but to bring him down and Larios made no mistake with the resulting penalty. Still, the Irish kept doing their best and Bingham injected some extra pace halfway through the second half when he introduced Billy Caskey and Derek Spence for McCreery and McIlroy.

Stewart soon had an excellent angled shot well saved for a corner and only a goalmouth scramble saved France from conceding in the set piece that followed. The result was never in doubt though, and in the eightieth minute the French substitute, Gerard Soler, led Chris Nicholl a merry dance down the wing and crossed the ball perfectly to an unmarked Bernard Genghini who found the net from a few yards out. Even missing several stars this French side looked deadly as they completed their 4–0 victory.

The local press response to the defeat was predictably brutal, with Malcolm Brodie mercilessly stating, 'Northern Ireland have no mission in the World Cup finals this summer. The ultimate achievement was simply to qualify. To assume otherwise would be a delusion and, looking at the prospects now, defeat by Yugoslavia and host nation Spain seem inevitable with the only success likely against Honduras, and I would not even bet on that ... There were times when the Irish looked a

Northern Ireland's 1980 British champions.
Back, L–R: Tommy Cassidy, Billy Hamilton, Noel Brotherston, Mal Donaghy,
Chris Nicholl, John McClelland.
Front: Jim Platt, Jimmy Nicholl, Sammy McIlroy, Martin O'Neill
and Gerry Armstrong.

Sammy McIlroy scores with a header in a 3–0 victory over Sweden,
Windsor Park, 15 October 1980.

The three captains, Martin O'Neill (left), Kevin Keegan (middle) and Danny McGrain (right), at Heathrow Airport before travelling to the World Cup finals in Spain, 25 April 1982.

L–R: The Scotland, Northern Ireland and England managers – Jock Stein, Billy Bingham and Ron Greenwood respectively – at the World Cup draw, 16 January 1982.

L–R: Pat Jennings, Jimmy Nicholl, Gerry Armstrong, Sammy McIlroy and Martin O'Neill with Dana, recording 'Yer Man', Willesden recording studio, 21 February 1982.

© Alamy/ Mirrorpix

Pat Jennings (front) and Gerry Armstrong at the training camp, 1 July 1982.

© Alamy/PA Images

Northern Ireland v Yugoslavia (0–0), La Romareda, Zaragoza,
17 June 1982. Norman Whiteside takes on Velimir Zajec.

Northern Ireland v Spain (1–0), Estadio de Mestalla, Valencia, 25 June 1982. Gerry Armstrong scores against Spanish goalkeeper Luis Arconada.

Gerry Armstrong celebrates with Sammy McIlroy and Norman Whiteside.

Gerry Armstrong hugs Billy Bingham after the Spain match.

Northern Ireland v Austria (2–2), Estadio Vicente Calderón, 1 July 1982.
Billy Hamilton celebrates one of his two goals in the match.

The team prior to the start of the match against France, 4 July 1982.
Back, L–R: Chris Nicholl, Norman Whiteside, Mal Donaghy, John McClelland
and Billy Hamilton. Front: Pat Jennings, Jimmy Nicholl, Gerry Armstrong,
David McCreery, Sammy McIlroy and Martin O'Neill.

Martin O'Neill exchanges pennants with French captain, Michel Platini,
Estadio Vicente Calderón, 4 July 1982.

Billy Bingham and the Northern Ireland team make a triumphant return to Belfast in an open-topped bus parade, November 1982.

soccer embarrassment.'

Bingham, however, refused to be entirely downhearted and suggested that this was something they could learn from. 'We cannot hide the players from the quality they will be up against in Spain. We didn't have to play France but now my players have seen what it is like. It is better this way.'

However, one added setback from this defeat was the one dealt to Bingham's friendly plans. Malcolm Brodie reported in the *Belfast Telegraph* on 25 March, 'After the humiliation at Wembley was re-emphasised here in Paris, Irish FA officials are to cut back on the build-up programme. There will be no farewell match in Belfast, simply because the opposition of sufficient crowd-pulling appeal cannot be obtained.' He went on to say that the odds of securing Bingham's hot-climate game had also lengthened somewhat and that the only remaining matches would now be the British Championship games against Scotland and Wales, which had been planned long before qualification.

It seems that the IFA wasn't willing to organise opposition for friendlies, even though it meant sending the team underprepared to the World Cup. As was so often the case, the reasons were financial. The IFA feared that the only kind of nation it could attract to Windsor Park would be less than glamorous and that it would therefore suffer a financial hit. With an income of a quarter of a million pounds seemingly guaranteed from the World Cup, it was an unusual stance to take as a small loss on a friendly would be more than compensated for, even with a group stage exit in the summer. And if the friendly could in some way help Northern Ireland with their preparations and aid their qualification for the second phase, then any loss would be recouped many times over.

Sadly, it seems that the IFA lost its heart for friendlies only after the France game and the second successive 4–0 drubbing as right up until the Paris game the *Belfast Telegraph* had reported daily suggestions regarding possible friendly opponents.

Immediately following the match, the paper was able to report that the IFA considered the British Championship games 'sufficient preparation'. Going to the World Cup, picking up the cheque for £250,000 and coming home now appeared to be the limit of the IFA ambitions and it didn't seem to want to gamble a single penny on progressing further and reaping an even bigger financial windfall.

This was even more frustrating in light of the other home nations and their build-up for the tournament. England went to Spain for an unofficial game against the Basque region's top club side, Athletic Bilbao, familiarising themselves with the stadium they would be playing in. England also played full international ties against the Netherlands, Iceland and Finland. Scotland also managed to play a game in Spain against the host nation, and another against the Dutch. Even Wales, who weren't going to the World Cup, managed to play more friendlies than Northern Ireland. Before their own match with France, they too provided the Spanish with some practice against British opposition. Meanwhile, Northern Ireland's World Cup opponents Honduras notched up six friendlies in just over two months before heading to Spain. In comparison, Northern Ireland's preparations were decidedly lacking. By the time they returned to British Championship action a month later at the end of April, Bingham had come to accept that there were to be no further games scheduled.

With games running out, Bingham needed to use the British Championship match against Scotland in Belfast as a testing ground for any fringe players beyond the automatic choices for the squad. Northern Ireland had only managed to score one goal – against Israel – in the previous six games, and just four in their last nine. It was clear that goal-scoring had become something of a problem and Bingham now looked to expand his options in attack. Having already given substitute appearances to Ian Stewart and Southend United's Derek Spence, a player on the

168

edges of the squad throughout Bingham's tenure, he now cast his net wider. For the game against Scotland he looked both to the Irish League and to the lower reaches of the English League, with Fourth Division Brentford's Bobby Campbell making an unlikely return to the international set-up.

Even as a teenager, Bobby Campbell was already earning the 'wild man' reputation that travelled with him wherever he played. When he was just eighteen, and already on the books at Aston Villa, he was chosen to represent Northern Ireland at youth level in an away trip against Switzerland in 1975. After the game he, along with team-mate Bertie McMinn, stole and crashed a car, and McMinn was sent to the hospital. Campbell initially denied any wrongdoing, but confessed when told the IFA would pay the damages and that he would still be able to play in a game against England a few days later. Instead, he was promptly sent home.

Campbell's foolishness was unlikely to have gone down well with even the most lenient of coaches, but the youth team manager at the time was 'Iron Man' Tommy Casey, a veteran of the 1958 World Cup team and an FA Cup winner at Newcastle United, who froze Campbell out of the team. When the IFA met in due course to discuss the matter, both Campbell and McMinn were handed down life bans. Campbell later recalled that at first he wasn't too concerned, 'They banned me for life. I thought I could live with that. I said to myself, "I'm too old to play for the youth team now." I didn't realise that the ban meant the whole lot.'

For many years, the ban appeared almost academic as there was little chance of Campbell ever playing for the senior Northern Ireland squad. He failed to make any meaningful breakthrough at Villa and spun from one club to another in a trail of transfers that took in spells in both Canada and Australia before he landed at Bradford City in England's Fourth Division. It was here that Campbell finally seemed to find a level and a club that suited him and his performances and goal tallies improved enough to catch Bingham's attention. By the end of the 1980/81 season he had found the net twenty-two times in all competitions and he had already improved upon that by April the following season. Bingham had been searching for attacking options, not only for the squad to play against Scotland, but to take to the World Cup itself.

Of course, there was the not inconsiderable hurdle of the lifetime ban to be overcome, and there had already been representations on his behalf to have the ban overturned on the basis that a player's whole future shouldn't be determined by the exuberant folly of youth. It could well be argued that Campbell wasn't all that much of a reformed character, with a reputation for hard living that he seemed rather proud of. But there were certainly those who took the more pragmatic view that the IFA shouldn't cut off its nose to spite its face with regard to Campbell, given that he could perhaps be the man to solve their goal drought problems. Nevertheless, the Youth Committee initially remained steadfast, seemingly resenting the intrusion from outside bodies into their internal disciplinary processes. A month later, however, the IFA Council stepped in and formally requested that it overturn the bans for both Campbell and Distillery's McMinn, and this time it relented.

Campbell was overjoyed to be selected for the Scotland game. 'Now I'm in the squad I want to win a place in the team. My life's ambition has always been to play for my country. Now there is the added incentive of the World Cup Finals.' However, while Bingham now had new options up front, he had headaches in other areas of the field. Cassidy and Cochrane were both still out injured, Jennings was still playing reserve team football while recovering from his groin strain, and Chris Nicholl was ruled out due to a chipped ankle. Jimmy Nicholl had been transferred from Manchester United to Toronto Blizzard in Canada. However, he had yet to play a game for his new team after picking up a toe injury just before the game against France. Meanwhile, both Gerry Armstrong and David McCreery were unavailable due to club matches. While Bingham was probably already planning on using this final home game before Spain to experiment, it seemed that he now had no choice.

One piece of good news was that John McClelland was now fit and available again, having been out injured for several months after suffering a horrific dislocated ankle early in the year, while Campbell was certainly showing some commitment to the cause. Expected as a late arrival to the training camp, Campbell, fresh from scoring a winning goal the night before for Bradford, boarded a 7 a.m. flight and managed to meet his new international team-mates for breakfast. He was assured of a place in the starting line-up by Bingham who told the press, 'I took him aside and told him I was not concerned with what happened in the past. It's what he does in the future. I think he'll make it for us.'

Also named in the squad for this match were five well-regarded Irish League players Bingham wanted to have a closer look at. George Dunlop, the Linfield goalkeeper, had already played on the Australian tour against a non-international side, and his centre half team-mate, Roy Walsh, was now brought into the squad. There were also two representatives from Glentoran, Jim Cleary and Johnny Jameson. It is almost impossible to imagine today but in the early 1980s the top English sides frequently came over to Belfast to play friendlies against Irish League sides. Even more implausibly these weren't pre-season kickarounds, but actually took place during the season itself and with first-choice teams put out. Manchester United and Liverpool were regular visitors, but teams such as Spurs, Arsenal and others also made the trips. Liverpool had just made one such visit to The Oval to play Glentoran, and Jameson in particular had shone during the game, which almost certainly played a part in his selection for the international squad.

The local contingent was completed by Felix Healy of Coleraine, who had just scored in the Irish Cup Final and been crowned Ulster Player of the Year. Healy and Cleary were given the nod to start the game alongside Campbell.

Another injury struck the team late in the day with Billy Hamilton forced out through a groin strain in training. Gerry Armstrong, who had just played and scored for Watford the night before, loyally responded by jumping on a plane and making himself available for his second game in twenty-four hours, albeit via the bench. Armstrong would not be required during the match and his unavailability for the starting line-up meant that the Irish were missing a total of eight regular first team players. Such a weakened squad faced the real possibility of adding to the team's recent woes, especially with a number of untried local players facing up to a strong and experienced Scottish side.

Bingham told the *Irish News*, 'A home defeat would obviously seriously damage morale. But this gives me the chance to be fair to everyone before I have to name my final twenty-two for Spain. Now I feel that I have covered every possible player who had a claim to a place and who knows, it has happened before that players have come in and grabbed the limelight just before the finals.'

The match itself, played in front of twenty thousand fans on 28 April, acted as a means for Northern Ireland to restore their pride after the recent heavy defeats, and they applied themselves well throughout the ninety minutes. The Irish performed better in the opening exchanges with a number of chances, and almost forced Scottish defender Alan Evans into an own goal when he headed against his crossbar under pressure. Another effort from Bobby Campbell was kicked off the line by Asa Hartford. However, when Scotland took a first-half lead, the home fans might have been forgiven for thinking it would lead to another night of pain. A great pass forward from Kenny Dalglish in midfield found Alan Brazil on the edge of the box and he lashed a shot at goal, which Platt did well to block. Unfortunately, John Wark was waiting to head in the easy rebound chance and the teams went in at half-time with the visitors in the lead.

Northern Ireland's equaliser, seven minutes into the second half, was a beautifully worked goal. Mal Donaghy took possession of the ball in his own half and managed to carefully work his way through three Scottish players in close formation before passing to Brotherston. The Blackburn winger weaved past two Scottish players then played an exquisitely weighted ball into the box for Sammy McIlroy to latch on to. McIlroy let it run in front of him before he turned and deftly aimed it across the goal and into the net.

The final 1–1 scoreline against the team who had topped their World Cup qualifying group was definitely a morale booster. Many Irishmen had shone on the night, with O'Neill and McIlroy judged to have put in good shifts in midfield while McClelland and Donaghy had been outstanding in defence. Bingham was pleased. As he told the press, 'I'm satisfied with the performance, particularly of the new boys. Every game enlightens me a bit more about my final World Cup twenty-two. This match answered more questions than usual. I have used a wide variety of players and, though we still have a small panel, the situation certainly isn't as depressing as it was a month ago. Now I hope I can go away and come up with the right selectorial decisions.'

Following the Scotland game, Bingham's next task was to announce the initial forty-man squad for the World Cup. This was released in the press on Saturday 8 May and contained many points to raise eyebrows. Famously, Northern Ireland had only taken a squad of seventeen to Sweden in 1958, five short of the number they were allowed. It was said that they only had that number of players of a sufficient standard, although it seemed more likely, going by some of the omissions, that they chose instead to save money on a smaller squad. While other nations also failed to take a full complement, it was noticeable that the IFA didn't call up a replacement when its main striker was injured before the tournament even began. It was certainly the case in 1982, though, that the pool of players available to Bingham was somewhat limited. He had an exceptionally reliable core of players making up the first team and the immediate fringes, but beyond that there was a sharp drop-off in quality. Filling out an initial submission of forty players to FIFA must have involved picking players who Bingham knew had absolutely no chance of ever boarding the plane in the summer. So, it followed that many on this list must have been surprised at their inclusion, which made the absence of one player all the more difficult to rationalise.

Announcing the squad in the *Belfast Telegraph*, Malcolm Brodie described it as no surprise that George Best's name was missing. Certainly, the signs had been there for all to see and the word circulating around footballing quarters was that he wouldn't be picked. Apart from anything else, his last-minute pull-out from the Middlesbrough deal meant that Bingham was unable to watch him play in person. Yet Best's omission must still be interpreted as a somewhat baffling decision. Unsurprising? Yes. Logical? No. Best had probably seen the decision coming himself, but what must have rubbed salt into the wounds of his disappointment was the inclusion of a number of other Northern Irish footballers from the North American soccer scene. There were certainly no issues with including Jimmy Nicholl of Toronto Blizzard or David McCreery of Tulsa Roughnecks. They were loyal and dependable campaigners who had already proved themselves with Manchester United as winners at the highest level. However, the decision to include both Vic Moreland and Billy Caskey of Tulsa Roughnecks seemed unfair on Best. While he could look down the list, which included nine Irish League players and five players from the lower English divisions who had never been capped, and surmise that, at thirty-five, he was still a better player than any of them, he would have been stung to see two players from his own league who he was clearly much superior to. Bingham would have had no opportunity to watch Moreland and Caskey play club football and, until Caskey had come on as a second-half sub in the Paris disaster in March, both of them had been capped a mere six times in the 1970s under Danny Blanchflower.

Gerry Armstrong remained friends with George Best until his death and he maintains that the wayward star should have been picked. 'He could still have given something, even at the age of thirty-five. Just the lift he would have given the squad to have him with us in Spain. It didn't seem to make sense and George thought that the matter was down to Bingham just not liking him.'

Best himself reflected on the matter in an interview with *FourFourTwo* magazine in 2001, 'I wouldn't have expected to play every game, but I wished he had just taken me as a member of the squad and thrown me on for fifteen minutes, only so I could have played in the World Cup.'

John McClelland, however, takes a more dispassionate view, 'I think Billy realised that George would be the focus and it would all be on George rather than the team unit ... George had a talent, but we were playing against teams better than us and we had to defend a lot and run a lot and it might not have worked.' Bingham had to make the decision with his head, rather than his heart, and he muses today that the off-the-pitch problems ultimately did play a part in the star's exclusion: 'It wasn't because he was too old. I just thought that he wasn't as good as he was before ... he'd lost a lot of his pace. Now, George had a life outside of football as you well know, and I wasn't sure what he was doing, but that was an influence towards his selection, an influence that wasn't good for him.'

But while Best's omission had not come as a surprise, the

inclusion in the squad of Norman Whiteside, a boy who had only turned seventeen the day before, and who had only made his debut for his club a mere two weeks earlier, was a real shock.

There had been a steady increase in the mentions of Norman Whiteside in the local press the preceding year, with his goals at schoolboy international level attracting some attention. In March 1982, the *Belfast Telegraph* mentioned him as a possible substitute as Manchester United visited Linfield for a mid-season friendly. Although Whiteside ultimately took no part in that game, the next month he was included in the United squad playing Brighton in the league. Aged just sixteen, he came on as a late substitute.

Alongside a young Mark Hughes, he was part of the impressive Manchester United youth side that made it to that year's FA Youth Cup Final against Watford. Though the Hornets won the match 7–6 on aggregate, Whiteside's performance had been so impressive that, two days later, he was in the initial Northern Ireland squad for the World Cup and gaining headlines for his inclusion.

With the good performance against Scotland and the job of picking the squad for the finals now in process, Bingham could have been forgiven for thinking that the recent troubles of the team were behind him. However, the next month would bring fresh disasters and threaten to destroy the morale of the team on the very eve of travelling to Spain.

FALLOUT

Almost six months had passed since qualification in November and the issue of the players' bonus payments and World Cup appearance money had still not been resolved. With the players growing increasingly angry, a situation that should have been professionally and dispassionately administered soon festered into a headline-grabbing public argument.

There were two matters to be considered: the bonus for qualifying for the tournament in the first place, and the appearance money for the World Cup itself. Clearly, if the IFA was set to make the kind of money they had consistently boasted of in public, then the players should receive a fair cut. As Harry Cavan spelt out a week after the Israel match, 'Players are seeking around £5,000 for qualification. In fact, the total amount concerned will be around £80k. Then there will be further sums sought for the matches in Spain.'

At first, things seemed promising. On 25 November 1981, the

Belfast Telegraph included a quote from an unnamed IFA delegate who said, 'We have no intention of going to Spain and facing problems like that which confronted Scotland in Argentina … I'm hopeful within the next two weeks this aspect of the planning will have been finalised.' Four years earlier, Scotland had qualified for the World Cup, but the SFA had dragged their heels about confirming player bonuses, and the players had to force the issue just days before their first match. They were then told that they would earn less for reaching the second phase than they had been offered for qualifying for the tournament in the first place. It had made for a combustible atmosphere and everyone seemed to be keen that Northern Ireland do things differently.

The players appointed captain Martin O'Neill, Sammy Nelson and Chris Nicholl as their official representatives and, on 9 December, Cavan told the press, 'We have drawn up a blueprint of what we can pay out but that's as far as we've got. The other parties must be consulted and no doubt we must compromise.' A week later an IFA spokesman declared, 'We are anxious to have the financial aspects cleared up as soon as possible.' However, when Bingham's new contract was agreed that evening there was no tandem negotiation with the players as expected and, instead, the IFA expressed the hope that it would be sorted out before the draw in January.

As the New Year arrived, Bingham was as anxious as the players to see the matter resolved – he wanted a settled and focused team – and on 5 January he was quoted as saying, 'I think you'll find an early compromise reached. There is not a big gap and, hopefully, it can all be fixed up before the draw in Madrid on Saturday week.'

Over the coming days it emerged that the players wanted a total of £95,000 in bonus payments for qualification, a fraction more than the £90,000 the SFA had offered the Scottish squad. The IFA, however, were prepared to pay only £60,000 and, despite both Martin O'Neill and Harry Cavan assuring the press that the matter would be resolved within the week, the World Cup draw passed without face-to-face talks even being scheduled.

Over a month later, as the players grouped together in preparation for the game against England, there was still no sign of a deal, although O'Neill reported to the press that a compromise of £75,000 offered by the IFA was acceptable and he was looking forward to finalising it.

However, yet another month went by and still no agreement was reached. It was now late March and the players had gathered together for the game against France. Finally, a meeting was held between Cavan and the three player representatives, with an IFA spokesman stating beforehand that the final offer was £77,500 and that, 'We won't be going beyond that for that's our economic limit.' Nevertheless, O'Neill perhaps felt that there was room for further manoeuvre and was still hoping that the original objective of £90,000 was obtainable. 'I don't think we will have too much argument over the additional £12,500 – the difference between what we want and what was offered. I don't expect any hassle.'

In the end, there was no hassle, but the players blinked first and accepted the IFA offer with Cavan reporting the next day, 'Everything has been settled amicably.' The cheque was to be forwarded to the players' pool within the next month and they could look forward to a further 25 per cent cut from the estimated £250,000 the IFA hoped to pocket for playing in the tournament.

However, instead of formalising the agreement for the summer match fees at the same time as sorting out the qualifying bonus, the IFA once more needlessly prevaricated, attracting a lot of unwelcome articles in the back pages of the Northern Irish press.

Most of April passed without any further attempt at

negotiation and it was the day after the Scotland game, 29 April, that the *Belfast Telegraph* outlined the players' expectations. Based upon the IFA's anticipated, and oft-quoted, figure of £250,000, and a suggestion from Harry Cavan that they would receive a quarter of this, the players had opted to ask for £66,000 for the first phase, rounding up the amount to £1,000 for all twenty-two players for each of the three games, rather than the awkward figure of £946 that would have been the true 25 per cent share. The players had not plucked this figure from the air. They had been privately told by Cavan himself that the IFA hoped to make this amount and that they could have a quarter of it.

Incredibly, there was still no progress almost a month later – the IFA appeared to be in no rush to settle the matter. It was only the gathering of the squad in Wrexham that May, for the British Championship match against Wales, that seemed to put the matter on the agenda again and set off another flurry of back-page stories. The IFA's reluctance to negotiate began to paint it in a poor light. With the squad clearly unhappy on the issue and gathered in one place, the coverage in the papers increased and briefings were given out by both sides on a daily basis.

On 24 May, the IFA International Committee met to discuss the issue, but Cavan had already given his opinion to the *Belfast Telegraph*, 'I've heard it said they are looking £1,000 per match. There is no way they can get that. In fact, I understand Scotland are paying £600. What sum we'll agree on I cannot say.' Despite Cavan's willingness to bandy figures around in the press, the players themselves were still in the dark. Martin O'Neill told the *Newsletter*, 'We have still received no firm offer from the Irish FA, but we are certainly looking for about a quarter of the pot in overall incentive. We are not trying to be unreasonable, just realistic, and we are eager to come to terms with the Association.' However, the *Belfast Telegraph* believed that £600, to match the Scottish squad, was what the Irish players would be offered.

When these terms were presented to the team, as part of the information package on travelling to Spain, they were swiftly rejected. Harry Cavan told the press that the figure was based on what the other nations were paying: 'Normally we are regarded a bit below the financial level of Scotland, but we have offered our players the same terms. Remember, next Saturday the Scots will pull in around £500,000 from their game with England, whereas the average gate for us at Windsor Park is around £45,000. It's quite a difference.' It was also a slightly disingenuous remark to compare Scotland's most profitable game of the year with a rather conservative figure for a game at Windsor Park when they wouldn't be playing top-class opposition.

On 27 May, the day of the game against Wales, an all-out war of words broke in the press with Martin O'Neill openly voicing his displeasure with Cavan and the IFA. 'We were given a verbal promise of 25 per cent of £250,000 by President Harry Cavan – and that has been broken.' He then stated that the players would not be signing a contract 'even if it meant no World Cup for them'. The cards were now firmly on the table. The players felt so strongly about the issue that they were prepared to walk away from negotiations altogether and leave the country with no experienced players to pick from.

Cavan now denied that he had made the team any promises. 'There was never any agreement. I would say that's our final offer. The committee were unanimous in the offer which is similar to that offered to Scotland. Our revenue and resources are limited. We have already had to apply to FIFA for a cash advance to go to Spain.'

The players were understandably aggrieved that a deal far below what they had been given cause to expect was being foisted on them at the last possible second. The IFA's many months of stalling seemed like a deliberate tactic, hoping the players would have no choice but to accept much reduced terms at the last minute. It was now just four days from the naming of the final twenty-two-man squad and five days from departure to the World Cup training camp. The promise to learn from the mistakes made by Scotland in 1978 had been a hollow one, and the current situation threatened to eclipse even that disagreement.

The players released an official statement that pulled no punches: 'We, the members of the international squad, in March 1982, had discussions with Mr Harry Cavan in which we were promised 25 per cent of between £250,000 and £260,000. We thought this would work out at over £60,000. Yesterday we received documents which included news about World Cup bonuses from the Irish FA. This shows that the offers promised had been halved. Harry Cavan denied making the original offer. But as far as the players' committee present at that meeting are concerned, we witnessed everything. Throughout these negotiations we have conducted ourselves with honesty and integrity. We expected the same in return and have been grossly let down.'

Sammy Nelson assured the footballing public that greed was not their motivation. 'We don't want hassle. We don't want to be looked upon as mercenary. We are proud to be playing in the World Cup for our country, but a promise was made before witnesses and, so far, has not been kept.'

Again Cavan countered: 'When I spoke to the players originally, I said it would be difficult to set a bonus payment until we knew exactly how much would be made from Spain. I told them I was confident, however, the association would act with fairness and generosity. Players asked what that meant, and I said it could be 25 per cent of profits made in Spain. Players felt that was not specific enough, rejected the suggestion and said they would prefer a fee. The International Committee decided it would be more appropriate also to have a specific figure so that's what we have done. Players won't accept this but are assuming there will be a £250,000 profit and looking for the 25% of this.

We have given the players the same terms as Scotland. I don't think they have been grossly let down. The figures speak for themselves. We want to avoid confrontation for it is damaging to the team and to the Association.'

This statement would have done little to quell the anger of the players and contains much that was contradicted by earlier statements. The IFA had explicitly stated back in November that they wanted to sort out the payment issue quickly, but setting match fees based on 25 per cent of profits would mean that fees couldn't be set until after the tournament; Cavan claimed that the players were wrong that an offer of 25 per cent had been made, but confessed now that it actually had been. He attempted to reconcile this difference by suggesting to the *Irish News* that it wasn't really a concrete offer but just an idea: 'At no time did I promise. My comments were made off the top of my head and were pie in the sky figures.'

But if that were the case, surely it was somewhat irresponsible for the President of the IFA to have given 'pie in the sky figures' to the players, and then not correct them about the misunderstanding in the months that followed. It was hard to see how the players' demands could now be considered 'unreasonable' by the person who had suggested the figure to them in the first place.

For Billy Bingham, the chaos created by the IFA reneging on the deal with the players can only have caused dismay on the day of their final game before the World Cup. Diplomatically, he informed the press, 'There has to be a compromise. Players want to appear in the World Cup. The Irish FA need the money from the competition. Let's get it sorted out quickly.' Even Malcolm Brodie, who would have been close to the IFA's inner circle, spoke out about the harm being done: 'For such a wrangle to have developed almost on the eve of the World Cup is extremely damaging to morale, clouds preparations and is not helping the image of the Irish FA. The International Committee must stand condemned for not resolving the issue immediately upon qualification. When that £77,500 fee for reaching Spain was agreed – and what an interminable battle existed over that – the match fee should have been negotiated and not left until now with the disagreement given international publicity.'

With such storms hanging over the Irish camp, the mood going into the Welsh game would have been downbeat, but it was not the only threat to the players' participation in the World Cup. In the weeks leading up to the game came the very real threat that the three British teams would be forced to boycott the tournament.

On 2 April 1982, one week after it had landed marines on the nearby island of South Georgia, Argentina launched its invasion of the Falkland Islands – both British Overseas Territories. A large British naval taskforce was hurriedly launched in case peaceful negotiations failed, and the story dominated the British news over the following months.

At first, it seems that little serious attention was paid to how this might impact upon the World Cup but, as the weeks went by and the taskforce arrived in the southern reaches of the Atlantic, the thought of a tournament in which three participating nations were at war with another competitor – the reigning champions, no less – began to cause unease in some quarters, particularly within Margaret Thatcher's government.

By the end of April, a possible World Cup boycott was reported in the press, although not too much alarm was raised at this point. For instance, a report in *Ireland's Saturday Night* on 24 April suggested that the Sports Minister, Neil MacFarlane, would not discourage meetings with Argentina at international level. Harry Cavan was quoted as saying, 'We expect the minister to make his position clear at the meeting on the World Cup.' However, the fact that this meeting wasn't due to take place until 13 May in London was demonstrative of the lack of concern from all quarters at this stage.

As the weeks passed, however, the government must have known that it would have to address the matter more seriously and urgently. It was one thing to delay dealing with the issue while the taskforce was on its way, but quite another once actual fighting began. So far, any conflict had been limited, and only a small British force was required to land on South Georgia and force the surrender of an equally small Argentinian outpost on 26 April, but larger and bloodier battles lay ahead. The government would have known that these would be fought well ahead of the 13 May meeting.

Bombing of the airfields around the capital of Port Stanley started on 1 May and there then followed a steep escalation in the conflict when, the very next day, a British submarine sank the Argentinian cruiser, *General Belgrano*. Two days later the Argentine air force responded by hitting HMS *Sheffield*, which would sink in the days that followed. As the BBC News reported, this was now a 'shooting war.'

Predictably, this situation changed the opinions of some people about whether the British teams should attend the World Cup, particularly as the draw made it possible for Scotland and Argentina to meet in a three-team group in the second round. With casualties mounting rapidly within the war zone, it was thought inappropriate for the nations to meet in sporting engagement.

Rather surprisingly, the call for a boycott was led by representatives of the player unions in both England and Scotland. Harry Lawrie of the Scottish PFA not only supported a boycott but seemed to be actively seeking one. On 6 May he was reported in the *Belfast Telegraph* as saying, 'I have proposed to the English PFA that we send a joint letter to Mrs Thatcher indicating the position and asking her to tell the associations of England, Scotland and Northern Ireland not to go to Spain.' Incredibly, it can be inferred from his statement that the English and Scottish PFAs would, in effect, determine the fate of Northern Ireland with no consultation with the equivalent local body.

Alan Gowling of the English PFA indicated that he would support a government boycott and added, 'It would be difficult to justify playing against a country responsible for the deaths of English lads.' The Scottish FA said it intended to sit on the fence at present but would be guided in their actions by the government.

The PFAs seemed determined not to go and the associations appeared unwilling to commit either way. Only Northern Ireland, through the IFA to its credit, were prepared to speak out against the boycott, although it's possible that they feared the economic ramifications as much as letting down the players. Billy Drennan was quoted in the *Belfast Telegraph* as saying, 'England, Scotland and Northern Ireland have signed contracts committing them to taking part in the World Cup. If we do not fulfil our obligations heavy fines and sanctions are certain to be imposed. Under the rules, FIFA can ban us from the next World Cup. With this in mind Northern Ireland intend going to Spain. Although I cannot speak for England and Scotland, I do not envisage any disruption at this moment.'

This was the age of the sporting boycott. South Africa had been ostracised from the sporting community since the 1960s in response to apartheid; in 1980, sixty-five nations boycotted the Moscow Olympics, ostensibly due to the USSR's invasion of Afghanistan in 1979; and in 1984 the USSR and fourteen other Eastern Bloc nations staged a reciprocal boycott of the Los Angeles Olympics. This was a period in which politics and sport mixed frequently, and the threat to Northern Ireland's participation in the World Cup was a very real one.

FIFA, meanwhile, took a dim view of the speculation. It had made clear that boycotts at this stage would be met with bans and fines, but it was also clear that contingency plans existed for any withdrawal of British sides. *Ireland's Saturday Night* quoted

Raimundo Saporta, the president of the organising committee, who said, 'There will be a World Cup and it will be played with twenty-four teams as planned. FIFA will decide which teams replace any country not competing because of the Falklands dispute.'

As expected, there was no talk of withdrawal from the defending champions, with the Argentinian FA stating, 'Our planning goes ahead as normal. We'll not be altering course.'

The following week brought no further major casualties in the conflict on either side as diplomatic efforts continued in the background. However, the chances of a boycott suddenly became very real indeed when, on 11 May, the British government abruptly cancelled a meeting with the three football associations. The meeting had been intended for the launch of documents outlining travel advice and how British fans should behave in Spain and was something the government had been keen to push for some time, with the backing of high-profile players from each nation. Ominously, the reason given for this last-minute cancellation was 'the realistic possibility' of British teams withdrawing. Desmond McCartan reported on the front page of the *Belfast Telegraph* that, 'According to official sources, it was felt premature to issue any guidance to British fans at this stage, when the possibility of withdrawal was still in mind. According to Whitehall the decision was made, "because of the fluidity of the situation".'

Although the government's policy hadn't technically changed, and there was still no requirement for the teams to boycott, they must have been aware that their cancellation of the travel advice to the fans and associations would reverberate internationally. Fans were also panicked – they had signed up for expensive package deals and now faced the prospect of travelling to a tournament without a team to support.

On 12 May, the *Irish News* quoted Alfonso Senior, head of the Columbian Soccer Federation, who told the press that

FIFA 'neither permits nor accepts that political, race or religion problems interfere with football. Mechanisms exist to impose drastic sanctions. All FIFA members know well what they would be liable to ... Soccer is soccer and politics is politics and one thing has nothing to do with the other.'

For all the commotion the British government had caused, it still appeared reluctant to commit to either attending or boycotting the tournament, and, on 13 May, Sepp Blatter stated, 'We've had no communication from the British countries about withdrawal and we don't expect any. They should be competing as normal. Argentina will be taking part – and I reckon England, Scotland and Northern Ireland will too.'

Two days later in *Ireland's Saturday Night*, Harry Cavan informed the paper that he believed it was the government's wish for the teams to fly to Spain. However, he added, 'Obviously if there was large-scale war activities and thousands of deaths we would have to think again. We are not saying we are going regardless. At this time there is no reason why the British teams should withdraw. We've done nothing wrong. If the government asks us to withdraw – and I don't see that happening – then they would have to accept the necessity of financial compensation.' Again, throwing in a mention of the sums of money involved was a canny move from the cash-conscious IFA. If it was to be forced out, then it was making sure that the onus was on the British government to foot the bill.

The *Belfast Telegraph* reported on the matter again on Monday 24 May, just days before the game against Wales, under the headline, 'Government thumbs up – FA officials left to decide.' Over the course of the weekend British forces had made amphibious landings on East Falkland and there was now no doubt that the ground fighting between the two opposing sides was about to begin and that casualties would soon be mounting. Despite this, the government seemed to have quietly given up any plan for a boycott at exactly the moment when the conflict was escalating. Harry Cavan was quoted in the article as saying, 'I had talks with the Minister for Sport, Neil Macfarlane, at the FA Cup Final on Saturday when I got the clear indication that the government would not be acting. His view is that it is a matter for the Football Association officials of England and Scotland to say they are going, and I see no reason why we shouldn't go either.'

Without ever making a public statement to outline their final position, the government now accepted that the home nations would be going to Spain as planned. For one month, press speculation had been allowed to run wild. Now, just as a number of British ships were being sunk and the conflict entered a more serious phase, they abdicated responsibility by handing the decision to the respective associations. Interestingly, documents released to the National Archives under the thirty-year rule reveal a report drawn up by Michael Heseltine, Secretary of State for the Environment, who had ultimate responsibility for sport. It confirms not only that the government were prepared to wait and see what happened, but that they feared the financial consequences: 'The Scottish and Northern Ireland Football Associations could be bankrupted … while there might be no legal obligations on Her Majesty's Government for compensation, there could be a moral one.' In the end, money won out.

As the boycott threat and the appearance money disagreement played out on the back pages of the press, Bingham concentrated on selecting his side for the final British Championship game of the season. He had selected Norman Whiteside for his forty-man squad for the World Cup while he was still an apprentice, but since then the Belfast boy had signed professional terms for Manchester United – just a few days after his seventeenth birthday. After making his debut against Brighton on 24 April he had played no further part on the pitch in the four games since. However, with United guaranteed to finish in third place, win, lose or draw in their final league game, Ron Atkinson decided to hand the teenager a place in the starting line-up against Stoke City for his first game in front of the Old Trafford faithful. Although it was a meaningless game for United, for Sammy McIlroy's Stoke it was a crucial contest as they were locked in a four-way battle for the final relegation place and needed points to guarantee their safety. It turned out to be a dream game for Whiteside who scored with a header before half-time to add to Bryan Robson's opener. Fortunately for McIlroy, Stoke were able to beat West Brom in their final game and survive for another year in the First Division.

The end of the league campaign brought further good news for several Northern Ireland stalwarts. Mal Donaghy was finally heading to the level his skills belonged, as Luton Town were crowned champions of the Second Division. Watford had clinched their third promotion in five seasons under Graham Taylor in a remarkable rise from Fourth Division to First, putting Gerry Armstrong back once more in the nation's top division. Taking up the third spot for promotion were Norwich City where Martin O'Neill had led a resurgence since his return to the club in mid-season; they managed to bounce back to the top flight immediately following their relegation. Billy Hamilton and Tommy Cassidy at Burnley had won promotion from the Third Division to the Second as champions and Bobby Campbell's Bradford City were also moving up a tier after finishing second in the Fourth Division.

Balanced against this good fortune was Middlesbrough's relegation from the First Division, which was bad news for Jim Platt and Terry Cochrane, but Pat Jennings and Chris Nicholl had both qualified for the following season's UEFA Cup with Arsenal and Southampton, and Sammy Nelson's Brighton had achieved a very respectable mid-table position in the top flight.

When Bingham named his squad for the trip to Wales on 19 May there was no place for the young Whiteside, who was on tour with United, but it was heartening that several players missing from action against Scotland were now available. Jennings appeared to have finally overcome the groin injury that had plagued him so far and was playing in an end of season tour for Arsenal in the Caribbean. Jimmy Nicholl was fit again and was set to cross the Atlantic with David McCreery, as both had been made available from then until the World Cup by their North American clubs. The new caps, Bobby Campbell, Jim Cleary and Felix Healy, were all retained for another close look, while Chris Nicholl and Billy Hamilton were also fit again.

The only bad news was that Terry Cochrane had not yet recovered from the injury he sustained playing in Paris back in March. He announced his intention to withdraw from consideration for both the forthcoming game and the summer tournament, quietly closing the curtain on his World Cup dream: 'I've had to make a heartbreaking decision. It would be unfair on the rest of the players for me to go to Spain.' As he reflected in his autobiography, 'It was definitely the lowest ebb of my footballing career and I found it very difficult to overcome, not only my physical injury, but more so my distress and frustration.'

Bingham did what he could for the stricken player, and in a wonderful act of compassion, 'He kindly arranged for me to receive the exact same money as the rest of the team had earned whilst in Spain. I thought this clearly demonstrated his affection for, and his trust in, me.' Cochrane's equaliser against England at Wembley, which paved their way to becoming British Champions, and his incredible byline stop and cross for Gerry Armstrong to score against Portugal would be remembered by Irish fans through the decades.

The squad gathered for preparations in Belfast. There was to be a testimonial for Jim Platt's brother John when Cliftonville took on Middlesbrough at Solitude, and Armstrong, O'Neill and Platt turned out for the match. On 24 May, a banquet was held in the team's honour at Belfast City Hall, followed by a government reception the next day as the dignitaries of Belfast and Northern Ireland gathered to wish the team well before the World Cup preparations began.

On match day in Wales on 27 May, Bingham informed the *Belfast Telegraph* that he would be shaking up his normal pairing at centre half. For some time, John O'Neill and Chris Nicholl had been a formidable combination at the back. However, their last two outings had been the back-to-back 4-0 thrashings earlier in the year. Against Scotland, with Nicholl injured, Bingham had played McClelland beside O'Neill and they had enjoyed a good evening. Now he wanted to try out the other permutation and dropped O'Neill. 'I want to see just how this formation would work. I know what O'Neill and Nicholl can do. Now I'll get another answer from this formation.'

Also back in the team was Jennings, who was in need of competitive action, and Bingham remarked, 'I'm more optimistic and encouraged by his reaction in training and this will be a proper test. It will be competitive, hard and there will be no hiding.' The captaincy was handed for the night to Sammy McIlroy when Martin O'Neill was ruled out with a toe injury but, despite the behind-the-scenes disagreements, it would have been a confident Northern Ireland who ran out at the Racecourse Ground, as Wales had failed to win any of their previous eight games.

For the second year in a row the FA Cup Final had gone to a replay as Spurs took on Second Division QPR, and the replay had been scheduled for the same day as the Northern Ireland/Wales match. It had been anticipated therefore that this dead rubber game in the Home International series would suffer an even lower attendance than normal. Nevertheless, the paltry turnout of just 2,315 set a new record low for a British Championship game and the empty stands added to the misery of what was to be another night to forget for Northern Ireland.

Wales started the game well and created a number of chances

before making an early breakthrough in the seventeenth minute. A cross from Leighton James was prodded on by Bryan Flynn to Alan Curtis who quickly dispatched the ball past Jennings on the angle from ten yards out. However, what none of the reports mentioned was that the ball had been helped on its way to Curtis by a ricochet off an Irish defender's boot.

Northern Ireland raised their game for the rest of the half and both teams created a number of chances. Billy Hamilton in particular was dangerous up front, with Armstrong and Healy also having shots. Nevertheless, it was fair to say that Wales were the better team and the young Ian Rush of Liverpool almost saw his shot go past Jennings, only for it to be cleared off the line by Mal Donaghy. A chance for an equaliser when Hamilton headed a corner cross came to nothing when Wales' debutant goalkeeper, Neville Southall, punched it away from under the bar.

In the second half, Bingham gave his reserve keeper, Platt, some match time, confident that Jennings was moving freely and looking good for the summer. Northern Ireland were still creating chances, with Healy involved in most of them, but he dropped back into midfield when Bobby Campbell came on to replace Cleary. The task for Northern Ireland soon became an uphill one, though, when John McClelland conceded a freekick and Flynn floated the ball into the box for Rush to head beyond Platt – his first international goal. It got worse with fifteen minutes to go when McIlroy, uncharacteristically, played a suicide ball, from inside the Irish box to the hemisphere just outside it, which found none of his own players. It was picked up by Peter Nicholas who struck the ball first time, picking up a deflection from the Irish defence to leave Platt stranded as it sailed into the net. It completed a disastrous evening as Northern Ireland lost 3–0 and finished bottom of the British Championship.

The only real positive to come out of the evening was the

return of Jennings. As he recounts today, he had come close to having his World Cup dream snatched away. 'After qualifying, when I ripped my groin, I absolutely panicked. I only played three or four games from then until May. Every six or seven weeks going out and breaking down. I thought I wasn't going to make the World Cup after trying to qualify since joining the international team in 1964. Billy played me for the first half against Wales and at half-time he said, "That'll do you, Pat. Now you've got a month to get yourself fully fit for Spain." That's how close I came to not making it.'

It was probably just as well that the squad was playing away from home as none of the players would have wanted to read what was waiting for them in the next day's press.

Under the *Belfast Telegraph's* headline, 'Irish hit an all-time low,' Malcolm Brodie unflinchingly attacked the team: 'Never has any side embarked on the World Cup Finals adventure so demoralised as Northern Ireland after this utter humiliation by Wales ... an Irish side which I can state categorically was the worst I've watched in post-war international football. All the other shambles down the years – and there have been many – paled into insignificance compared with this one.' There is at least some level of subjectivity involved in sports journalism but to suggest that this 3–0 defeat was the worst in forty years was clearly wide of the mark. However, the condemnation kept coming: 'There were no redeeming features about this Ireland team. When they should have been reaching the peak they plummeted to the depths. Few other sides have flopped so alarmingly in their build-up to the finals.' And the criticism seemed to get almost personal when Brodie concluded with, 'To see three lumbering figures such as Gerry Armstrong, Bobby Campbell and Hamilton in attack was beyond belief.'

The *Irish News* had a go at the players for daring to negotiate match fees while losing on the pitch: 'All their bluster about increased Spanish bonuses looked a little sick as the Welsh romped to their first win in nine games. Nothing in the Irish display strengthened their case for an increase in the IFA offer. After finishing with the wooden spoon in the Internationals, they will be lucky if the Irish officials don't make a further cut.'

A more measured tone held sway in the *Newsletter* where Jimmy Dubois highlighted the positives as well as boldly pointing out the areas where they had fallen short. Hamilton was praised as the team's best player, 'who literally ran himself into the ground in his efforts'. However, even Dubois couldn't disguise what had been a very deflating result and, while he gave credit for 'their usual hard-working performance', he was forced to add that they were 'suspect at the back' and 'never gained any measure of control in midfield'. He concluded that, 'Overall, the performance of Northern Ireland fell far short of that expected from a World Cup finals team and the magnitude of their task in Spain was fully illustrated by this result.'

Martin O'Neill reflects on how the players dealt with such savage reporting in the press, 'I always felt it was feast or famine. The famous one was the "Auf Wiedersehen, Pat" and Pat took umbrage at that and quite rightly. Then Pat goes on to play for the next seventy-five years! The criticism was sometimes so over the top that you had to leave it. To be fair, against Wales we were piddle poor so some of the criticism you do accept, but when it's constant you just shrug it off. It started to bother us less and less because we weren't based in Belfast, so you didn't hear it unless family let you know. No one likes that kind of criticism, but we sometimes took it with a pinch of salt. Malcolm was Scottish, although he'd spent a long, long time in Northern Ireland, and when we met up we used to quote to each other in the Scottish accent, "Another pitiful performance by Northern Ireland".'

As ever, Bingham was keen to highlight the few rays of sunshine in the evening's performance, 'There were some positive aspects, particularly Felix Healy. He is an Irish

League player but more than acquitted himself. He was very good, very steady. I thought Billy Hamilton had an excellent game.' However, he couldn't hide his disappointment and the normally upbeat manager was forced into the unusual position of criticising his players. 'It was one of the worst performances since I took over, but it must be remembered that the team has been changed about ... They know this was a bad result and will want to put it right before Spain.'

With the pre-World Cup programme ending in disaster there was only one thing left to do – address the ongoing dispute over match fees. One imagines that it was a deflated Irish squad who met with Harry Cavan immediately after the game. The fight appeared to have gone out of them in the face of a resolute International Committee and a president who vehemently denied ever making them an offer at all. Cavan reconfirmed that they wouldn't be getting a penny more than the SFA had offered the Scottish squad: £600 per match for any player starting the game, £400 for those coming on as a substitute and £300 for those not involved. It meant a maximum payment of £10,100 per match across the whole squad – less than half the £22,000 Cavan had promised the players in March.

'After the Wales game,' explains O'Neill, 'I think they thought they had us over a barrel – "If you're going into a World Cup and you can't even win your last game against Wales you should just be happy to play."' However, O'Neill's ex-team-mate and Scottish international, John Robertson, had managed to get him a copy of the Scottish contract, and O'Neill saw an opportunity to snatch a longer-term victory. 'Someone from the IFA had checked out Scotland's bonus system but there was a bit missing, an important piece. There was a misjudgement by the IFA of what Scotland could potentially get. Suddenly, it became worthwhile if we could qualify for the second stage. The IFA had missed out that part.'

'Martin came to us and he did a deal,' Gerry Armstrong

explains. 'The IFA thought, Yugoslavia, Spain, Honduras – no chance we'll qualify, [but] the deal was, if we qualified for the quarter-finals they had to pay us £110,000 [over the next two games] because they were guaranteed another £350,000 or something like that. Martin had negotiated about a third of whatever they were going to get. I remember Martin sitting with the lads and saying, "We can get a draw against Yugoslavia, we can beat Honduras, we only need a draw against Spain. We can qualify." That was the plan. Martin loved a gamble, and he took that gamble. The Irish FA never thought that it would happen.'

Cavan announced to the press the following day, 'There is no longer any disagreement. We have had a meeting with the players to explain the Association's position and clear up any misunderstanding.' On the face of it, the IFA appeared as if it had emerged on top, paying the players much less than the amount they had promised for the initial group phase. However, it speaks volumes, even as it succeeded in making the players accept the Scottish terms, that it hadn't taken any notice of what it would be liable to pay out if Northern Ireland qualified for the second phase – simply because it never expected that to happen. Just as in 1958, when many of the travelling IFA officials had to return home after the group phase as they had booked their flights in advance, it was only the manager and the players who believed they would progress.

There is a coda to the story, however. The players had always sought to share the pool of money for the match fees equally among all twenty-two members of the squad. Even with the pool now slashed in half they maintained this honourable principle. The IFA had a three-tier system for making the payments and it would have been easy for the big names in the squad to have shrugged their shoulders, mumbled that they'd done their best to get everyone the higher payment, and then pocketed the £600 per game they would be confident of receiving as regular first teamers. Instead, in an act of solidarity and fraternity, they turned down the three-tier system and split the money equally with the lower league and part-time Irish League players who made up the squad but would be unlikely to play. For some of the amateur players involved in the squad this extra money meant a lot.

'There was a camaraderie,' explains O'Neill, 'and we wanted to share everything along the way with those who, unless there was a host of injuries, would not be participating. If they were going to be in the squad, they should be sharing the same things as ourselves. Everyone, to a man, who was playing a decent level of football at that time agreed. Whatever we would get, we would share it – every single person. So myself, Sammy McIlroy, Pat Jennings, we would share exactly with whoever was sitting in the stand.'

The disagreement had never been about high-paid players coveting a big payout. It had simply been about getting what had been promised to them, and the players could hold their heads high, knowing that they had maintained their character and dignity throughout.

Nevertheless, it had been a bruising couple of months for the team. They had crashed down from the crest of a wave, been embroiled in disputes not of their making and been savaged by local journalists. Also, and they knew this themselves, they had severely underperformed. They would have to pick themselves up and start anew. The task ahead for Bingham was immense. To prove the doubters in the press wrong and navigate a way out of the group phase would put all his achievements so far in the shade. As he mulled over the selection of his final twenty-two-man squad he was in no doubt that ahead of them lay a mountain. One that, after the last five months, no one expected them to climb.

IT ALL GOES RIGHT

On 31 May 1982, Bingham announced the final twenty-two-man squad for the World Cup:

Goalkeepers
George Dunlop (Linfield, Irish League)
Pat Jennings (Arsenal, 1st Div.)
Jim Platt (Middlesbrough, 1st Div.)

Defenders
Mal Donaghy (Luton Town, 2nd Div.)
John McClelland (Rangers, Scottish Premier)
Sammy Nelson (Brighton & Hove Albion, 1st Div.)
Chris Nicholl (Southampton, 1st Div.)
Jimmy Nicholl (Toronto Blizzard, NASL)
John O'Neill (Leicester City, 2nd Div.)

Midfielders

Noel Brotherston (Blackburn Rovers, 2nd Div.)
Tommy Cassidy (Burnley, 3rd Div.)
Jim Cleary (Glentoran, Irish League)
Tommy Finney (Cambridge United, 2nd Div.)
Felix Healy (Coleraine, Irish League)
David McCreery (Tulsa Roughnecks, NASL)
Sammy McIlroy (Stoke City, 1st Div.)
Martin O'Neill (Norwich City, 2nd Div.)

Forwards

Gerry Armstrong (Watford Town, 2nd Div.)
Bobby Campbell (Bradford City, 4th Div.)
Billy Hamilton (Burnley, 3rd Div.)
Johnny Jameson (Glentoran, Irish League)
Norman Whiteside (Manchester United, 1st Div.)

Four selections had been made from the Irish League, a tremendous achievement for the part-time players involved. Even the best Irish League clubs of the time were playing to a standard no higher than the Third or Fourth Division in England, so the inclusion of so many players from local football was a career-defining moment for those involved. However, it also spoke of the problems Bingham faced when having to enlarge his squad to the full quota of twenty-two. Those making the trip to Spain were Jim Cleary and Johnny Jameson of Glentoran, Felix Healy of Coleraine and George Dunlop of Linfield. As Cleary told the press, 'My selection and that of the other locals is an honour for the Irish League. Six weeks ago, I never thought there was a chance of going to Spain.'

Two years previously, Bingham had inherited a squad that had generally been playing for better teams, including the European champions. Most of those players were still there, but they were no longer playing in the top division. Only six of the squad were now on the books of English First Division teams, and one of those – Middlesbrough – had finished bottom in the season just ended. It was true that several members of the squad had experienced good campaigns at club level in the Second and Third Divisions and gained promotion, but that would be for the season ahead and their most recent experiences had been at a level far removed from the challenges of taking on the host nation at a World Cup.

Another talking point of the list was the one that gained the greatest number of column inches: seventeen-year-old Norman Whiteside had booked his place for the summer tournament. It was an astonishing turnaround for a player who had only signed his professional contract a few weeks earlier and who had made just one starting appearance in first team football.

As Whiteside recalls today, he had been largely unaware of the gathering fates around him as he worked his way up through the system at Manchester United. 'Eric Harrison was our youth coach there and … he was very familiar with Billy Bingham because they'd worked together at Everton. Also, our physiotherapist at the time was Jim McGregor who Billy Bingham got on well with … Eric Harrison would say things like, "You know, son, keep going the way you're going, Northern Ireland's going to the World Cup during the summer." … Then I'd be in the medical room with Jim. "Nice couple of goals for the reserves last night. The international manager of Northern Ireland was watching." All these little tips, if you like, or clues, but I still didn't take it in.'

The inclusion of Bobby Campbell from Fourth Division runners-up, Bradford City, had certainly been on the cards following his recent selections in the British Championship, but it meant that one player who had long been a member of the Northern Ireland squad, even if rarely getting into the starting line-up in recent seasons, had to miss out. Derek Spence was a popular member of the Northern Ireland set-up and he had held high hopes that he would continue to be involved with the team, despite playing in the Third Division for Southend United. His commitment to Northern Ireland was unquestionable. In his autobiography, *From the Troubles to the Tower*, Spence described the aftermath of the game against France in which he had a header cleared off the line, 'At the airport on the way out of Paris, I shook hands with Billy Bingham and he said, "I'll see you in May." This I took to be confirmation that I would indeed be going to the World Cup.'

A few months later in April, Bingham was in the stands of a Third Division encounter featuring two of his prospective strikers as Billy Hamilton's high-flying Burnley took on Spence's Southend. Despite being reduced to ten men, Southend won the entertaining encounter 5–3 courtesy of two second-half goals by Spence. It was a good day to turn in a fine performance with the international manager watching, or so Spence thought. Unfortunately, Bingham had left at half-time.

'When it was time to announce the squad, Billy Bingham didn't contact me, so I learned my fate on Teletext,' Spence recalled. 'When I got to the bottom of the list, my worst fears were confirmed. My name was not there. I would not be going to the World Cup. I was so devastated by my omission that I couldn't bring myself to watch any of the games. Football is a bruising business, but nothing else I endured during my playing career ever hurt anything like as much. I felt lost, desolate even, and couldn't be consoled.'

The other members of the squad were also saddened when Spence missed the cut, his infectious humour usually a highlight of get-togethers. As John McClelland explains, 'I think they were looking for a goal-scorer, but Bobby [Campbell] ... should never have been there. We all felt for Derek Spence because he had been with the team for a long time and he was the one who missed out.'

Alongside Best, Spence was probably the one player connected to the squads of the period who felt that he should have made the trip to Spain but didn't. Nevertheless, managers have to make hard decisions as, ultimately, their own positions are on the line if they get it wrong and Bingham had made up his mind based on what he thought would give Northern Ireland the best chance in the tournament. His job now was to gel his twenty-two into a cohesive, well-drilled and fit unit ahead of the hot and humid conditions awaiting them in Spain.

He took them to Brighton.

The decision to take the Irish squad to the south coast of England for the pre-World Cup training camp certainly raised eyebrows at the time. Most nations were heading to sunnier climes in southern Europe or the US. However, Bingham had some ideas about how to train the team that made use of the facilities at Sussex University, and he felt that being in familiar surroundings, somewhere they could bring their families along, would be of benefit to the team. Then he enjoyed a stroke of good fortune as the south coast baked in a heatwave for the entire duration of their stay.

A happy Bingham was able to tell the *Newsletter*, 'We have got Spanish conditions without moving off our own doorstep. It is hotter here than in Barcelona and it is a perfect place to get acclimatised – though we could never have predicted that. If it stays like this until we leave, I shall be delighted.'

David McCreery remembers that the stick about going to Brighton was typical of the feelings towards the team in general, 'All you'd hear on the sports programmes was, "Northern Ireland are training at Brighton, ha, ha!" And Saint and Greavsie [Ian St John and Jimmy Greaves hosting their Saturday morning football show on ITV] were saying, "Northern Ireland only need to pack their toothbrush because they'll be coming back straight away." It made you even more determined to go out there and do your job.'

And doing the job was just what Northern Ireland did as they threw themselves into a rigorous training programme. 'We went and we trained very hard,' says McCreery. 'Billy knew what he was doing, how to get the players in physical condition. We went there and enjoyed it because the families were there as well. Everybody got on well together. Billy knew how to treat players … He knew when to take and when to give.'

Bingham had seen first-hand what makes a happy training camp for a World Cup when he was part of the team that went to Sweden in 1958. Peter Doherty had allowed the squad certain freedoms at night-time as he felt it was beneficial to morale and team bonding and now Bingham did the same, trusting the players not to abuse the privilege of being allowed out for a few hours at night. He told the *Newsletter*, 'I like to find a happy medium between laying down the law and letting the players relax.'

Billy Hamilton has particularly warm memories of the time in Sussex. 'When it came to training, Billy ran the socks off us, but he let us go out …[We] went out for a pint after training, had a few laughs … back for eleven, on the training pitch the next morning at nine and ready to go. We loved getting on to the training ground and bantering each other about the night before. I think we struck the ideal balance between having a few drinks and then training hard. And people respected Bingham for letting us do that, so we didn't break the curfew. The craic was mighty, the spirit was high, and everyone was starting to look forward to the competition.'

Of course, there was no getting away from the fact that the Irish build-up so far had been disastrous in terms of match results, but Bingham explained to the *Newsletter* that it was all about what happened from that point onwards. 'After last week's defeat in Wales I have made it plain that no one's place in the team is guaranteed. My side will be selected on what I see in the next ten days.' This chimes with Jimmy Nicholl's memory of the camp, 'When you were at Brighton and you had all the troops together, you were thinking, right, this is it, *this* is the preparation. It was that preparation in Brighton that was the most important.'

The training itself, conducted in the blistering and unusual heat, was exacting. Bingham made use of the training facilities at the university campus and got the team to train with expert cross-country runners, increasing the distances each day. Reporting after the first day, John McClelland told reporters, 'It may not have looked much, but it was really hot and trying out there. The boss has promised to make it harder day by day, and none us are looking forward to day ten.'

According to Billy Hamilton, 'Our training regime was, maybe, nine to half twelve, an hour's break and then one-thirty to three-thirty. It was quite a lot of time on the training pitch and we were going through quite a lot of tactical stuff ... We ended those sessions with maybe an eight-mile run round the training pitch.'

A camp of this intensity would certainly have been harder for some than for others. A lot of the players had just completed a long season at club level, or had been out of the game for a while due to injury, and Bingham's training was the equivalent of having them embark on another pre-season warm-up. Some, however, like Gerry Armstrong – always a hard trainer from his days in GAA and at Spurs – more than met the challenge. Martin O'Neill recalls, 'Gerry outran us all in the cross-country runs. With some of us, Gerry had finished, washed and showered and had tea by the time we got home. He loved it. He was incredibly fit, could go forever and a day.'

Armstrong credits his fitness to the strict fitness regime he already followed for club football and in preparation for Spain. 'I give credit to Graham Taylor at Watford. He had me going into those World Cup finals fitter than I'd ever been. Watford were going up that year and we were having a good year at club level and that goes on into the internationals. Then Billy told us to prepare for the World Cup, so I started training on my own. Two or three times a week, after training at Watford, I'd go and do a four or five-mile run. I timed myself and recorded it. Then a few days later I'd try and beat it. Over a few months I knocked nearly two minutes off my time. A lot of the players found it difficult in Brighton, but I loved it because I'd been doing it for two years at Watford.'

For the seventeen-year-old Whiteside, who would still have been at school if he hadn't chosen football as a career path, the biggest problem was not the intense training, but the unfamiliarity of it all: new faces, new surroundings, new routine. Even deciding what to pack for the camp had been a challenge. 'Because I'd never been involved with a competition like that it was a new experience, and I didn't know what to take with me. I didn't know how long I was going for, so I took everything I had … I was rooming with Jim Platt and Jim said, "Do you need all that, Norman? You're not going to carry *all* that to Spain with you? You've got about ten suitcases here!" So, I rustled through my gear, kept what I thought I would need, and I got the rest sent home.'

During the stay, Whiteside gravitated towards the half-familiar ex-United players, but even mealtimes brought the potential of making a faux pas. 'When the menu came round, I used to look at everybody else to see what they were ordering so that I wasn't out of place. I couldn't order a fish supper.' Yet on the training ground he was standing out for all the right reasons. 'I was just trying to be myself. Trying to impress, but just being myself. I remember scoring some goals against big Pat Jennings. I got the ball on the edge of the box, looked up, swerved the ball around the defender and big Pat couldn't get to it. Billy was on record since saying, "I knew when he swerved the ball past Pat Jennings from twenty-five yards, he had something about him."'

Billy Hamilton remembers the impact the young man made straight away: 'I had heard about Norman and read about Norman but when you actually saw him in the flesh you thought, my God, that's a man in boy's clothing. He had the physique and was a lovely lad. You knew when you got into the five-a-sides and the tackles went about, Norman could look after himself. Very, very quickly in Brighton it looked like Norman was going to play a part in the World Cup.'

Chris Nicholl, with a slight back injury, and Martin O'Neill, with the toe injury that had kept him out of the Wales game, had been the only minor worries as the team got together. However, as the days went by in the continuing heatwave and the players responded well to the training regime, everyone was declared fit and the only medical bulletin worthy of any mention in the Irish press was John McClelland's bad reaction to his suntan cream bringing him out in a rash.

The first real worry of any kind came when Chris Nicholl injured his ankle in a five-a-side game after training and he immediately had it packed in ice. As he told the *Newsletter* on 9 June, 'I have apparently tweaked a ligament and I can't run. The only answer is rest and treatment but, fortunately, I am a quick healer and, with luck, I'll be ready again in three days. The pitches are so hard this weather that there is always the risk of this happening. But we've nine days still before we meet Yugoslavia and, although it's annoying to pick up this injury, I am confident of being fit.'

In the meantime, the rest of the players were put through their paces with some warm-up games against a Sussex University team. As Bingham told the press, 'It gave us a chance to try out some of our free kicks and dead ball moves.' On the evening of 11 June, the players were then able to enjoy a special documentary about one of their number when the BBC broadcast *Number One*, a look back on the distinguished career of Pat Jennings on the eve of his thirty-seventh birthday.

The happy stay in Brighton came to an end on 12 June with another minor medical issue. Talking to the *Irish News* Bobby

Campbell reported, 'It's a dodgy ankle, which I've hurt before but it's normally all right after a couple of days if I go easy on it. But I shan't be going dancing tonight.' Bingham played down the injury in the *Newsletter*, saying, 'I brought him off as soon as it happened because I don't want to take any chances. But I think it is just a niggly injury caused by the hard grounds.'

It was now time for the team to decamp from Brighton and head to London for the evening before flying to Valencia the next day. Derided by many footballing pundits for basing their preparation in Sussex, the camp had nevertheless turned out to be an unqualified success. Fitness levels were soaring, the players were getting used to temperatures that were in excess even of those in Spain and Bingham was able to study the talented youngster, Whiteside, in training for the very first time. He was clearly impressed with what he saw and with the potential for creating a new dynamic in the team. Sammy McIlroy recalls that Bingham had even planned kit for the players to bring with them to protect them from the sun in Spain. 'I can remember down in Brighton that Billy, from his shop in Southport, supplied us with suntan cream, all the lotions and sunglasses to take to Spain … But we had to pay for it!'

Possibly the only element of the time spent on the south coast that hadn't worked out had been the inclusion of Bobby Campbell. The early desire to impress during the British Championship call-ups had given way to less disciplined behaviour now that he knew he was definitely going to Spain. Gerry Armstrong recalls the growing feeling that an error had been made. 'Bobby was out running around Brighton celebrating, he was out partying. He was wild. He was in and out of the hotel and he was coming in with a girl, picked her up in a nightclub or wherever. Late one night, we were all sitting there discussing tactics and football and Bobby comes in. "All right, Billy! What about ye, lads! She's a cracker, isn't she?" We just sat there and Billy was saying, "Oh my God." Billy knew then that he'd made a mistake, but he couldn't do anything about it.'

Several years later, Bingham enjoyed a heart-to-heart session with several of his senior players who were at the end of their international careers. Armstrong remembers asking him about the decision to select Campbell ahead of Spence for the squad and Bingham's honest answer. 'As a manager you make some good decisions and some bad decisions. He was scoring a lot of goals for Bradford at the time, he was a lot younger, I thought he could add something to the team. But that was one of my bad decisions.' By mid-June of 1982 it was too late to do anything about it and the players boarded the flight for Spain.

As far back as January, the *Belfast Telegraph* had been reporting on the work being done to make sure Northern Ireland's stay in the host country ran as smoothly as possible. The IFA secretary, Billy Drennan, had flown to Valencia, where their final game against Spain was to be played, in order to pip Yugoslavia to a hotel near the beach. He and Bingham had also checked hotels in Zaragoza, where two of Northern Ireland's other group games were to be played. However, a few days later, Drennan announced that Valencia would be their only base with twenty-minute flights taking them to Zaragoza instead of coach journeys of several hours. Bingham reported, 'The hotel is superb, with all the facilities and a training area nearby. It proved beneficial for us to make an early inspection and beat the others to it.'

So far, so good, and it mirrored Northern Ireland's previous World Cup appearance twenty-four years earlier when Drennan had similarly managed to nip in just ahead of Czechoslovakia and secure excellent accommodation for the team in a town where they were all taken to the hearts of the locals.

By May, Drennan was reporting continued pleasure with the arrangements. 'I'm delighted how things have worked out for us in Spain. Accommodation is excellent. We're setting up an

Irish FA administrative office here. We'll have our own banking facilities, a special training centre at Levante, and everything has been sorted out for the provision of a plane from Valencia to Zaragoza for the two matches there.' Upon arriving, there was the need for some diplomacy from the IFA when they discovered that the grass hadn't been cut and that Levante, who played in the Spanish Third Division, had no electricity as it had been cut off for the non-payment of bills. However, this was all quickly resolved and everyone was very pleased with both the accommodation and the facilities on offer.

The Irish squad arrived on 13 June, the day the tournament started with a match between Belgium and the defending champions, Argentina. Northern Ireland were the last of the twenty-four teams to check in to their bases in Spain, just four days before their first match, scheduled for 25 June. Again, what may have appeared as a mistake to outside observers proved to be a winning move for Bingham. As he had explained, 'Home environment is infinitely better, and families can be near at hand. Boredom doesn't set in.'

Since meeting up for the game against Wales in late May, the players had only had a few days off before heading to Brighton. For many of the players it would be a period of almost a month in each other's pockets, but Bingham had cleverly cut that down to just twelve days in Spain without their families. With the team better prepared in terms of fitness than at any point during his two-year reign, and with them now well used to training and playing in sweltering heat, Bingham began to align their body clocks to the evening kick offs.

Training at the Levante ground began with light sessions in the morning then a siesta to take the players out of the midday heat. A meal was taken at 5.30 p.m. and then the team would have a more arduous session at the Levante stadium at around 8 p.m. As Whiteside recalls, 'Billy was very meticulous in his training programmes, down to having the meal at the same time as you would have it before the game the next night, with the same food, the same energy you would need. This is all before sports nutritionists came aboard. We went and had lunch and then we'd play a game three hours later because that was what we were going to do against Honduras or whatever. Training was very common sense. Why would you train at midday when the game is at seven o'clock in the evening? The good thing about Billy was that he took most of it as well – he was very hands on. Martin Harvey was around, but Billy wanted the final say in everything, what time you got up, what time you went to bed.'

In between sessions and siesta, the players were allowed to relax around the pool, but even this was controlled in case someone accidentally suffered from sunburn. Jimmy Nicholl recollects, 'It was a good hotel, good facilities and training. Billy and his assistant Martin Harvey used to let us out, but Harv was on pool watch – "I think you've been out for more than an hour and half, you have to get in," which was right. At least you weren't locked up in your room all the time.'

As the opening match approached, team spirit was riding high, all defeats from earlier in the year now long forgotten. Camaraderie was strong among all the players, but especially those who had a long-established bond. As John McClelland remembers, 'We were like a family I thought. You could have six teams play for England, but Billy hadn't got that variety of choice, so we just met up for every international together. We met up and trained hard, but we enjoyed each other's company.'

Billy Bingham remembers that, 'It was a good camp and I've always found that when you've got a good camp it's a great start for you in the match. They were really geed up and I was geed up as well.'

Another card in Bingham's hand was the presence of Bertie Peacock. Not only could Bingham bounce ideas off his 1958 team-mate, who knew what it was like to manage the country, but he was there as a bridge to the players and an inspiration, as someone who had tasted the success of taking the small nation beyond the first stage of a World Cup. Bingham recalls, 'Bertie had a nice way with him. He was a guy who would talk to people. He was excellent. The job I created for him was to help me get through with a squad of players and talk to the ones who were out of the team maybe.' As Jennings confirms, 'Bertie was someone everyone respected, especially the older players who remembered him. He was a lovely bloke who knew the game inside out and everyone had respect for him.'

When Bingham and Peacock had played in the 1958 World Cup it was reckoned that perhaps only a couple of dozen fans had made the trip to Sweden to support them. The lack of easy and affordable transport had been the problem and several fans entered folklore by travelling through Europe on mopeds to reach Scandinavia. In the intervening twenty-four years, travel in Europe had been transformed by cheaper air flights and package tours and this time Northern Ireland would be cheered on by several thousand of their faithful fans.

Paul Vance, from Donaghadee in County Down, visited his local bank manager to ask for a loan of £300 to pay for the Spanish trip and recalls the arduous journey laid on by the tour operator: 'We were 150 fans, spread over three coaches despatched from Cambridge to collect us off the nine-hour Belfast–Liverpool ferry voyage on a sunny June Monday morning. Three hundred miles to Dover, another short ferry crossing to Calais and on again by coach to the Costa Dorada, some nine hundred miles south, interrupted only by a couple of hours break in Montpellier. We were tired, but young, and Northern Ireland were at the World Cup, so it mattered not! But even at that, for each of the actual games, there was a three-hour transfer from our base to the stadiums, Valencia or Zaragoza, the two cities that hosted our group games.'

Part of what made Northern Ireland such a formidable

proposition at Windsor Park was the impassioned support of the fans. For the first time in their history Northern Ireland would be playing games outside the United Kingdom where a sizeable portion of that support was travelling with them, and that could only be of benefit to the team.

As Northern Ireland fine-tuned their preparations and Bingham began to consider his best starting eleven for the game against Yugoslavia, the nation was enjoying a purple patch of success in the world of sport. Local boxers Hugh Russell and Barry McGuigan were gaining a lot of column inches as they worked their way up towards fighting for British titles. Jim Baker had finished runner-up in the World Indoor Bowls competition in the days when it was a major televised sport on the BBC. The Triple Crown and Five Nations Championship-winning Irish rugby team of 1982 contained players from the Ulster team. Alex Higgins had memorably conquered his demons long enough to win that year's Embassy World Snooker Championship. John Watson was the sole British driver in Formula 1 racing and, having won two Grands Prix so far that season, was sitting top of the Driver's Championship. They had all risen to the occasion and diverted attention away from the cycle of violence shared on the local news, giving the population something commendable and inspiring to look up to. Now the focus was on the football team as they stepped into the spotlight on a grand stage. Could they overcome the spiral of recent defeats and lift themselves, and Northern Ireland, to glory?

Sammy McIlroy had been interviewed several months earlier about the World Cup prospects and he had focused on the team's greatest strength. 'It's difficult to put your finger on any one reason for our success. But if I was forced to single something out, it would be the remarkable spirit in the dressing room. There's a tremendous never-say-die attitude and every player gives one hundred per cent. Getting through to Spain has been a tremendous boost to all of us, both players and public alike. But

I suppose the one I'm most pleased for is our goalkeeper, Pat Jennings. He thought he would never play in World Cup finals. Pat is a remarkable man. He is so calm and assured that he gives us all confidence. And the way that he is playing he could go on to the *next* World Cup finals.'

Much would be asked of Jennings and his team-mates in the coming weeks, but Bingham knew that everything would depend on fostering, harnessing and focusing the spirit that ran through the squad. They were about to be tested on the world stage.

YUGOSLAVIA

As Northern Ireland prepared to step out for their opening game of the tournament, management and players alike were aware that their competition could boil down to the result of this one match. The Irish and the Yugoslavs would have looked at the fixture list and both entertained hopes of beating Honduras. They would also both have been apprehensive about playing the host nation and, while hoping a draw or victory might be possible, accepted that they would be favourites to lose that game. Therefore, whoever came through victorious from this opening encounter would be superbly placed to qualify from the group.

Malcolm Brodie spelled out this position in the *Belfast Telegraph*: 'Everything will depend on that opening match. Take two points from Yugoslavia and the chance of going to Madrid for the quarter-finals would be high.' However, there was still an air of mystery surrounding the Yugoslav team, as Brodie pointed out, 'Just how good are Yugoslavia? Even the critics, it seems, cannot make up their minds for in one World Cup publication printed in Britain a colleague tells me they were written off on one page as ambitious amateurs while bracketed on another with Brazil and Spain as possible winners.'

Everyone who followed European club football knew that the club sides from Yugoslavia were respected opposition and that most of the players in Spain for the World Cup played for the big clubs in their homeland. Yugoslavia's World Cup pedigree was also incredibly sound. They had qualified for six of the ten previous World Cups and had only failed to get past the first phase on one occasion, reaching the semi-finals twice. The current team had impressed during qualifying, topping their group and finishing a point ahead of Italy while handing out five-goal thrashings to some of the weaker sides in the group on no less than three occasions.

However, at this point Yugoslavia had seemingly gone into hiding. While Northern Ireland's disappointing World Cup build-up had taken place in the glare of the international football community, Yugoslavia had hidden themselves away and their only warm-up games had been against local club sides. Reports had emerged that they had been unimpressive during this period but their manager, Miljan Miljanić, contested this and told the press, 'They have reached the peak at the right time and I dismiss those stories that we are playing like a group of strangers.'

What was known about them was that Zlatko Vujović was their main attacking threat. The Hajduk Split striker had netted seven times in the eight qualifying games and would pose a particular threat to the Irish defence. His defender brother, Zoran, had also scored in qualifying, while his team-mate at club level, Ivica Šurjak, was another key dangerman from midfield, able to contribute goals to the team.

Another threat was Red Star Belgrade's midfield star, Vladimir Petrović, who had recently struck a deal with Arsenal. At this stage he would have been largely unfamiliar to British players and fans, but he would earn a lingering reputation in a short spell and they would welcome him as a maverick and popular figure in December of that year. One player some of the Irish players would have known well was Manchester United's Nikola Jovanović, who had been the club's first ever overseas signing when their previous manager, Dave Sexton, had bought him in 1980 from Red Star Belgrade. Sammy McIlroy and Jimmy Nicholl had been contemporaries of his in the United first team, and Nicholl had played alongside him in defence. However, Jovanović's time in English football had not been a successful one, despite scoring four times in his first season, and he had quickly been offloaded by the new manager, Ron Atkinson, back to Yugoslavia, where he had spent the last six months on loan.

Injuries were the main concern for Northern Ireland in the days leading up to the game. Billy Hamilton had taken a knock on his calf from an accidental kick by Jimmy Nicholl in training, but Chris Nicholl and Bobby Campbell were back running and likely to be fit in time for the opening game. As speculation began to build on who would make the selection, rumours began to snowball about the inclusion of young Norman Whiteside. The word circulating was that he had continued to impress during training and there was now every chance of him being handed an international debut on the greatest stage, just as the young Derek Dougan had been given his own first game in the World Cup opener against Czechoslovakia twenty-four years earlier.

Whiteside's Manchester United manager, Ron Atkinson, was in Spain to conduct television commentary for ITV and was staying at the same hotel as the Irish squad. He was therefore better equipped than almost anyone to talk about the young lad's prospects, confidently telling the press that he could end up saving him a million pounds in the transfer market as he looked for a new striker, before going onto add, 'I have listened to the

Irish players talking about him. They are all very excited and impressed. If it was up [to] them, he'd be in.' Whiteside himself remained very grounded and was the dictionary definition of modesty when batting aside absurd comparisons to George Best, which he was quick to point out were being made simply because they were from the same city and had been discovered by the same Manchester United scout. 'I've no left foot,' he told the press, 'I'm not too good in the air and I am not that fast. I've loads of weaknesses.' Nevertheless, an unmistakable buzz was building and Bingham, alert to the potential danger of the spotlight shining too brightly on one so young, moved quickly to protect him and deflect the selection talk: 'It is all unfair on the boy. They are putting too much pressure on him and I have not even said he will be playing in the side. The other strikers have been in tremendous form in the workouts too.'

Bingham, ever someone who liked to study the opposition's tactics, had been thrown by the lack of visible evidence of what Yugoslavia had been up to that summer and was desperately awaiting the arrival of a videotape he had been promised by a friend in London. One piece of possible intelligence that arrived, however, aroused Bingham's suspicions. 'I have received a letter from a Yugoslav who is unknown to me, but it gave a complete breakdown of their team. However, I am a bit apprehensive about this information in case it's a ploy to put me on the wrong track about their strengths and weaknesses.'

One other report that had Bingham on his guard in the final days was the story of a monetary disagreement within the Yugoslav ranks. Apparently, their players had received no money at all in payments for the games, so had taken it upon themselves to accept a lucrative contract from a boot manufacturer to wear their products at the tournament. However, their football association had already signed a deal with a rival manufacturer for considerably less money and there was now a stand-off while revised terms could be demanded. Bingham smelled a ruse, however, and remarked, 'Let them have their worries but you will find they vanish when the team goes on the pitch.'

The opening match in the group, between Spain and Honduras, had already taken place the day before. The Spanish were expected to make short work of the modest threat posed by the unfancied Honduras team and this was reflected in how Martin O'Neill managed his expectations going into the game. 'It is important for us to get a result against the Yugoslavs, but it would also be nice if the Hondurans could limit the Spanish goal-scorers. This group could yet be decided on goal difference.'

Hungary had already played against El Salvador in a match that rekindled memories of the famous Magyars of the 1950s – Hungary had taken the unfortunate El Salvador apart and sent them into the World Cup history books with a crushing and humiliating 10–1 rout. Spanish fans now dreamt of a similar scoreline as Europe met Central America again. The Irish merely hoped that Honduras could keep the score down a bit against a Spanish onslaught, so it would have come as a massive surprise to see such a small footballing nation pull off a remarkable 1–1 draw.

In a night described by the Spanish press as 'ninety minutes of shame', Honduras had looked remarkably comfortable against their illustrious opponents, going 1–0 up through Héctor Zelaya's well-taken goal after just eight minutes and then holding on for much of the second half. Incredibly, the Spanish players had already made six penalty appeals, which had been turned down by the referee, but they were successful with a seventh in the sixty-fifth minute and the converted penalty allowed them back into the game. That was how it finished, though, and the local press were merciless in their appraisal. Bingham was clearly delighted at this most unexpected helping hand. 'This result has obviously got to give us a lot of heart, even before we meet Yugoslavia. It was an astonishing result. I thought Honduras put on a really outstanding show and were unlucky not to win.'

Pat Jennings remembered being slightly wary following this great upset. 'The Irish team watched that game with mixed feelings. We were all instinctively on the side of the underdogs, coming into that same category ourselves, but the quality of the Honduras performance underlined that we were going to have three difficult group games instead of two. It made it absolutely vital that we didn't lose our opening encounter with the Yugoslavs, even though our opponents would start as red-hot favourites.'

The group now took on a slightly different complexion – the winners of the Irish/Yugoslav face-off could potentially win the group now that the Spanish had dropped points. However, Bingham was careful to keep expectations grounded ahead of the clash, pointing out that a draw would be a good result. 'There is no profit in experimenting with romantic notions that we can somehow play like the Brazilians. I have not the players for pretty passes so why try it? I will not be preaching to my players to hurt anyone, but we will not change our style. We will give it everything we have and the Yugoslavs will know that they have been in a game. The foreign press have termed us a weak team and I just hope the other three teams in our group approach us in this fashion – they may be in for a shock.'

Miljanić was not falling into that sort of complacency though. He had managed Yugoslavia in two previous spells, one of them at the 1974 World Cup, and he had also managed Real Madrid, winning two Spanish League titles with them. He was too wily an operator to write off the opposition and he told the press, 'The Irish team is not as bad as those [recent] results. Let us not be led into wrong conclusions. We know how dangerous they are when pushed hard, when motivated, and they should be in that frame of mind for the World Cup. Northern Ireland cannot be under-estimated. To be honest, they lack a lot of skill, but make up for that with their spirit.'

Bertie Peacock was also happy to report to the press, 'I have never seen a team so sharp. They are perfectly honed. Everyone is mentally and physically alert. You know the adrenalin is pumping. They know they want to go out there and prove they are not a side of no-hopers or an embarrassment.'

Every member of the Northern Ireland team passed their final fitness tests and Bingham announced his starting line-up on the day of the game. Jennings would keep goal despite his low amount of first team football since January, while fit-again Chris Nicholl would play at centre half. The surprise was that Rangers' John McClelland would be alongside him in place of the reliable John O'Neill who had been an almost ever-present start since Bingham had taken over the team again in 1980. McClelland muses today that it was the intense recovery work following his horrific injury that led to him getting the nod over O'Neill. 'I didn't think I'd be getting to the World Cup at all but looking back in hindsight at what made Bingham pick me was that I was flying when running. I had just been running and doing weights and press-ups and one-arm pull-ups and all sorts. I was in the gym for six months. I'd done three pre-seasons and suddenly Billy is thinking, "Where is he going?" because of my speed.'

While McClelland's selection had been unexpected, the big shock was that Bingham gave Whiteside his debut, someone who hadn't even been born when Jennings had made his own debut for Northern Ireland. Pelé's famous record as the youngest World Cup player of all time would now be taken by the boy from Belfast. He would play alongside Armstrong and Hamilton in a very physical Irish forward line. Whiteside was an unassuming young man who had never thought such a selection was possible while in the reserves in Manchester. He reflects, 'It was great getting into the forty, then the twenty-two and travelling over to Spain. When Billy named the first eleven, then it becomes a bit of reality.'

Sammy McIlroy recalls, 'I remember we were getting on the

bus and Billy Bingham pulled me and he said, "I've picked the side and I've put big Norman in." He was asking me, "Is he nervous? Is he going to cope with the situation? Is everything going to be all right? How do you think he's going to do?" I said, "Billy you're more nervous than him. Don't worry about him.""

Whiteside had been told the night before the game as they gathered to watch Honduras play and the congratulations from the other players were instantaneous, but the modest teenager could only reply with, 'Thanks a million,' over and over like a catchphrase. Once the story broke in the press, however, Whiteside became an instant global sensation – even his parents back in Belfast were besieged by reporters.

For the other strikers in the team, Whiteside's inclusion was welcome news as Northern Ireland would now be playing with a front of three attacking players rather than two. Billy Hamilton remembers, 'It was a different dynamic we had [compared] to the qualifying rounds … Norman was a breath of fresh air. It didn't give teams much time to prepare against us. They'd probably been looking at tapes of us from qualifying. He added to the team in physicality and goal threat.'

Armstrong recalls how Bingham envisaged a new shape to the team with the inclusion of the teenager. 'Billy had a wee chat with me one night and said, "I've been thinking we could put Norman on the left and Billy in the middle. You're fitter than anyone. I need your energy. What about if I play you on the right side and you can support Jimmy Nicholl, playing in front of him. You'll get more space because people won't be picking you up." It gave me more opportunities to use my power, my pace, coming from deeper.' Armstrong had been used to playing on the wing and undertaking defensive duties during his time at Spurs and he immediately saw the benefit in being freed from the opposition marking, with a licence to surge forward when he could.

On the day of the match the squad boarded their chartered plane for the short half-hour trip to Zaragoza, and were surprised when, during the flight, the cabin crew played Irish pipe music as well as the Dana song, 'When Yer Man Gets the Ball', which the squad joined in singsong. Once they reached a local hotel, they could relax for the afternoon, but Bingham kept Whiteside indoors, shielded from the press until after the game. Whiteside recalls seeing the reporters and photographers gathered in the lobby and how Bingham called a security guard to help force him through the throng when it came time to board the coach for the stadium.

Now was the time Bingham needed to work his magic as he motivated his team for the most important game they had so far played together. 'It's hard to specify exactly how he did it,' recalls Whiteside. 'I don't think you could put his team talks together and sell them as general motivational guides ... They were tailored for the Northern Ireland football team and were about our country, its people, what they'd gone through over the past decade and what our being out there meant to them. People talk about the hairs on their neck standing up during Billy's speech and I had goosebumps. I felt so inspired to play that I could have kicked down the door for the honour of putting on a green shirt in the company of those ten fine men. The coaches, Martin Harvey and Bertie Peacock, went from player to player emphasising small details of the tactical plan and then Billy simply wished us well and the eleven players and five substitutes gave a full-throated, rousing "C'mon!" as we were summoned into the tunnel.'

Once on the pitch and surrounded by the noise of the fans, the players got their first real experience of the heat and humidity in which they would be playing this World Cup. Pat Jennings recalls, 'The heat was unbelievable. As soon as you put your shirt on, the sweat was dripping. And that was just for me. You can imagine what it would be like for the outfield players to run about in that. I remember whenever you brushed the grass there were mites coming up. It must have been the heat and the watering of the pitch. Every time you touched the grass these bugs came up. I don't know how the outfield players coped with it all the time.'

However, Martin O'Neill felt that the Yugoslavian style of play might aid them in this cauldron. 'It was so, so hot. Even kicking off at night it was so hot. I knew that the Yugoslavs would take their time with things. In terms of losing the ball, I felt that we could get back into a position again because the Yugoslavs would take their time. They wouldn't be thrusting at you every single minute, they would want to keep the ball, particularly in those conditions. Don't get me wrong, one or two of them could break you down in a moment but they were going to be a keep-the-ball team. I therefore felt we could get something in this game.'

The match kicked off at the Estadio La Romareda in Zaragoza at 9 p.m. on 21 June with the temperature inside the stadium at almost one hundred degrees Fahrenheit, and the opening exchanges saw a robust style of play from two teams not afraid to mix it up physically. Armstrong went in rather hard on the Yugoslav goalkeeper, Dragan Pantelić, in the first few minutes, and Miloš Hrstić required treatment following an accidental challenge by McCreery. These were important minutes, though, for Northern Ireland, setting out their stall as Bingham had demanded, playing the kind of physical game that the English leagues were all about, and letting their opponents know that they wouldn't be overawed in any way.

It was in the seventh minute that Northern Ireland were suddenly given a taste of the explosive pace and skill of Safet Sušić, who had just signed for Paris Saint-Germain. Plucking the ball out of the air in midfield, he quickly skipped past Martin O'Neill and then avoided a sliding tackle a second later from David McCreery. John McClelland also committed himself fully to a tackle and Sušić again danced past. As two further Irishmen closed in from opposite sides, he reached the edge of the box and unleashed his shot. Although it went narrowly wide, the warning had been fired.

Five minutes later, Jovanović stormed through the centre of the field to win the ball against Chris Nicholl. It was quite clear that he handled the ball in doing so but none of the officials seemed to share this opinion and he laid the ball off for Sušić who was waiting right on the edge of the box and who forced a good save from Jennings. There were flashes of Northern Irish inspiration in return when Armstrong brilliantly turned a man on the right wing only to overhit his cross to McIlroy, and when Whiteside embarked upon a surging run to the edge of the box before being hacked down for a free kick. However, it was in the twentieth minute when they first worried the Yugoslavs as Armstrong set off deep in his own half, beating one player and exchanging a pass with McIlroy who then threaded the ball through for him again upfield. Armstrong ghosted past two more Yugoslavian players before shooting and, despite the effort going wide, it no doubt had the same warning effect that Sušić's run had had upon Northern Ireland earlier.

Almost immediately afterwards, however, a long ball was pumped forward by Petrović to Zlatko Vujović and bounced deep into the Irish box, Jennings coming out well to make the save from the resulting header. Ron Atkinson on the commentary seemed to think the keeper had left coming out for the ball far too late, but the ball had not been there to win beforehand, and Jennings had clearly used all his experience to perfectly time his advance and snuff out the attack. Worse danger was to come, though, as the game neared the half-hour mark and Edhem Šljivo motored down the right wing and easily evaded Donaghy, who went to ground trying to tackle him. He was eventually forced to check back by McClelland, who had come over to the wing to meet him, but he then passed to the advancing Ivan Gudelj who worked a one-two with Sušić and knifed his way into the Irish box. Chris Nicholl came to meet him but completely misjudged his attempt to get a foot on the ball. Donaghy, who was also back in the mix deep inside his own penalty area, was forced now to raise his arms and stand off from the ball to avoid colliding with Jennings. However, all Jennings could do was force the player wide of the goal to the byline with Gudelj still in control of the ball and Jennings out of his net. He now laid it out wide and the ball was whipped back into the Irish six-yard box where Donaghy was forced to head it across the pitch for a throw-in. It had been the best chance of the game so far.

A Jennings save from a Gudelj header following a Yugoslav corner brought down the curtain on what had been a fiercely contested first half. Yugoslavia had created three good chances and although Northern Ireland were yet to carve out anything clear cut themselves, they had teased their opponents with a number of runs from Armstrong, and the two midfields had largely cancelled each other out. The nightmare for the Irish would have been conceding during the first half and watching their World Cup fade away from them before it had truly started. That had been avoided and they now had something to build upon for the second half.

Northern Ireland began the second period brightly with Armstrong doing a lot of good work on the right flank. From one such move in the fifty-fourth minute he was able to cross for Hamilton who attempted a dramatic overhead kick, but the chance to be remembered for the most spectacular Northern Ireland goal in living memory evaporated as the shot flashed wide. On the opposite wing, Norman Whiteside was beginning to get a real feel for the game, and he was regularly exchanging balls with McIlroy as he powered up and down, using his body strength to great effect. In one such move in the sixty-second minute, however, he lost out on the ball and in his enthusiasm at trying to win it back went in a little too hard on his opponent. Having let a number of Whiteside fouls go without too much fuss, the referee now felt he had to step in, and so Whiteside added to his list of records by becoming the youngest player ever to be booked at the World Cup.

As the game moved into its final quarter, the Yugoslavian players now visibly began to wilt in the heat. It was a very hot and humid night, but it was surprising that players used to a continental climate were the first to feel its effects. Petrović in particular seemed to be struggling to exert himself much in midfield and Northern Ireland took hold of the game. Armstrong was once more fouled as he sped down the right wing, and Chris Nicholl beat two defenders from the resulting free kick to send a looping header just over the bar.

Another move down the right wing, this time from Hamilton, saw the same answer from the Yugoslav defence who were quite happy to concede free kicks rather than let their opponents go past them. This time the set piece was played in towards Hamilton who passed it back to the edge of the box for McIlroy to shoot, but it was an easy one for the keeper to deal with, coming straight down the middle to where he was standing.

Yugoslavia contributed with their own attacks, but it was noticeable that they possessed less cleverness and pace than they had demonstrated in the first half, and the Irish defence was able to deal easily with anything that came into the box. Northern Ireland, on the other hand, even in the punishing heat, attacked down the wings with more energy and purpose, lacking only the final ball on each occasion. However, in the eighty-ninth minute they went very close indeed. Martin O'Neill worked his way along the right and then chipped the ball into the box. It was won by Armstrong and his header was on target, but Pantelić moved across to make the save for Yugoslavia, and when Hamilton challenged him, and the ball bounced free, it was adjudged to have been a foul.

Although the final chance of the game fell to Yugoslavia it was a header that went well over the bar and never troubled Jennings. Instead, it was the Irish who finished the game feeling that they had emerged on top and the sight of Whiteside beating two players on the left in the last seconds through sheer strength, despite his age, was proof of just how convincingly the Irish had passed this test against top-class opposition. When the referee blew his whistle for full-time, the Irish could take pride in a job well done, whereas their counterparts were left to wonder how they had faded so badly and failed to create the chances they had in the first half.

Bingham was quick to praise his players afterwards. 'We coped well and the longer the game went on we became stronger. It was a compliment to the British style and to British fitness. I was pleased with the application and overall determination of the players, and the back four were outstanding, as was Gerry Armstrong, who operated in a very demanding free-range role, which meant he had to cover a lot of ground.'

Bingham also had plenty to say about the boy making all the headlines. 'I don't normally single out players, but Norman is something special. It was no gamble to play him … He is aggressive and not overawed and his confidence and competence on the field of play made him a wonderful find.' These words were echoed by the elder statesman of the team, Jennings. 'I've seen some debuts in my time, but this boy is incredible. He takes on players with a skill and confidence expected from those much older and more experienced.'

The Yugoslavians weren't afraid to admit how they had struggled afterwards. Miljanić told reporters, 'It was too hot out there for my players and they were exhausted at the finish.' As to the Irish, he said, 'They did not make many chances, but I was impressed with their approach. They looked a good solid team.' His captain, Ivica Šurjak, went further and remarked, 'The Northern Ireland defence was too hard to crack. It was almost impossible to get past them.'

Jennings remembered, 'Our fitness was a plus in the steaming heat of Zaragoza and we lasted the pace far better than the Yugoslavs. Whilst delighted with the result, I was disappointed with the Yugoslavs. I'd expected a great deal more from them, but most of their players appeared to be ready to settle for a point well before the end.'

The press agreed that this had been a point earned against good opposition rather than a point dropped and, under a headline of 'On top of the world – no goals but spirit soars,' Malcolm Brodie lavished praise in the *Belfast Telegraph*, almost eating the words he had written after the defeats in the spring: 'Billy Bingham said the other day that friendly matches didn't really matter to him, it was when the crunch came that Northern Ireland would count – and that's just what happened last night in the furnace of La Romareda. A courageous, professional performance.'

Brodie then went on to extol the virtues of the young Whiteside, 'Few, certainly nobody in post-war Irish football, has ever made a debut of such elegance, class and impact. It was quite phenomenal, his running, challenging for position, his ability to accept and hand out punishment, lack of an inferiority complex and an amazing work ethic. There was no prima donna act either from him as the press descended at the end, no self-projection, no attempt at taking the credit. "I thought we all did brilliantly," he commented in a typical Belfast fashion. "I'm knackered," as he flopped in his chair.' Brodie also had praise for the rest of the team, singling McCreery out as being worthy of particular mention, noting that the job he had done in marking Petrović out of the game meant that 'This was McCreery's best game for Northern Ireland, even more so than when he did a shadowing job on Holland's Johan Cruyff some years ago.'

Looking back on that opening match, the players still feel that it had been a great start to the campaign. Sammy McIlroy offers, 'It's always good in the first game to get something on the board.

Yugoslavia were renowned to be a very good footballing side. It gave us a lot of confidence. Okay, we got a point, let's move on to the next game.'

It had been a successful evening's work for the Northern Ireland team. They hadn't acquired the win that would have taken the pressure off them in the group, but they were still in with a chance of qualifying. They had also proven themselves against a skilful team and demonstrated that they were the fitter side and better able to handle the conditions in Spain.

Whiteside remembers, 'I was absolutely spent after the game, almost in a trance. I passively watched the antics of our fans. The most I could manage in response to their shouts of encouragement was a weak smile and a frail thumbs-up. Martin Harvey took the seat next to me for the journey back to the airport and asked me how I felt. When I replied that I had never been so exhausted in my life, he patted me on the shoulder and said, "Right enough. That's how you're supposed to feel when you've given your all."'

HONDURAS

The days following the result against Yugoslavia were happy ones for the squad and the fans, as the press talked up their chances of progressing to the second phase. Whiteside found himself in a swirl of interviews with the world's press, under Bingham's watchful gaze, and the fitness of the team and their training schedule in Brighton and Spain were praised as a great success. Now, all focus was on the plucky Central Americans who had caused a seismic upset in their first game against the hosts.

In *Ireland's Saturday Night*, a few days before the game, Bingham expressed his respect for the group underdogs. 'I'm glad we did not meet them in our first match but had the opportunity of making an assessment against Spain. It was a red warning light for us, otherwise we could just perhaps have underrated them.' In the *Belfast Telegraph* he elaborated further. 'We have to be careful with this one. You cannot afford to slip up. Honduras played it tight against Spain, but I think they will open up against us. They are still in with a shout and they are a young side with quite a few quality players.'

Honduras had obviously been a team shrouded in mystery before the tournament began. Most of their warm-up matches had been against lower league Spanish sides and their players were generally unknown outside of their home country. The exception was Gilberto Yearwood, who played in the Spanish league with Real Valladolid; and their young striker, Armando Betancourt, who had recently been voted college player of the year while studying at university in the USA. Their potential, however, would only have been revealed to the Irish, and the rest of the world, in their brilliant display against Spain.

Jimmy Nicholl remembers the feeling going into the game: 'If we're going to do it this is our chance because you don't expect to beat Spain on the Friday night. So, this is your opportunity, you gotta do it. It's only when you're going up against them, you realise you're still going into that game a wee bit blind. You're thinking, I don't know what I'm up against. You've some preparation, but on the night ... these boys are better than Yugoslavia and we're expected to beat them.' McIlroy also recalls that the lack of knowledge about the opposition was a problem. 'No one knew anything about them. We knew what we were told about them – big, physical, strong side. One or two situations about set plays or whatever.'

Betancourt revealed to the press that the crushing defeat of their Central American neighbours, El Salvador, had actually given the team a fillip: 'That was shocking and made us wonder what fate had in store for us. It also made us more cautious and determined not to suffer the same humiliation. Matching Spain has lifted our expectations. We suspected that we could do something people did not expect, but it was vital to maximise our percentages. Our attack had little chance to shine. Spain were rolling all over us, but our defence proved it was not as weak as many people had said, and we do not think the Irish will find it easy either.'

Reading the contemporary press, it is clear that no one underestimated the Hondurans any more, and yet this game was still seen as the moment Northern Ireland could push for a place in the quarter-finals. Their chances were improved with the news that the Honduran defensive stalwart Fernando Bulnes would be missing through injury. Meanwhile, their own injury concerns following the first game had evaporated as McCreery overcame a calf muscle problem and Billy Hamilton had fully recovered from an ankle knock. Bingham was therefore able to announce a line-up unchanged from the team who had played in the first game, with Whiteside keeping his place among the eleven and John McClelland once again being preferred to John O'Neill at the back. With Noel Brotherston, Tommy Cassidy and Felix Healy all being placed on the bench, there was an indication that alternative attacking options would be more important than alternative defensive ones for this crucial game.

One distraction at this point, however, was the constant prodding by the *Belfast Telegraph* of players who had been left out of the team, looking for any sign of discontent and therefore an opportunity to fill a few column inches. Malcolm Brodie seemed to make it his business to interview anyone who perhaps had a claim on the first team. Thus, John O'Neill was put on the spot to provide a quote when he was left out for the second time running: 'I was disappointed I didn't get into the team for the Yugoslav match and now this has happened.' What this seasoned journalist, who had followed the team for decades, thought that would achieve other than disharmony is uncertain. Every team that has ever played, let alone in a World Cup, has more players left out of the starting line-up than those taking to the pitch. It is a fact of football that only eleven can play. Therefore, Brodie's constant search for dismayed players was hardly helpful to the team spirit.

In the build-up to the match, Tommy Cassidy had also been sounded out to reveal his disappointment and even, seemingly, to question the manager's tactics. Apparently he had been told that he would have played against Yugoslavia if Bingham had opted for a more attacking formation, and he said, 'David McCreery, who took over, played magnificently in such a system, but you cannot win World Cups by defence all the time. You must attack and where are the goals coming from in this set-up? Perhaps that will happen in the Honduras fixture. Whether he changes the side remains to be seen. However, we must attack – must go for goals – as it is essential to win this one.' It's perhaps as well that, in a world long before instant social media, the squad had no access to what was being written about them back in Belfast.

Setting aside the disappointment of those watching from the sidelines, and focusing on the issue of scoring, Billy Hamilton struck a more realistic tone when he told the press, 'Before we came to Spain people felt that if we got a result against [Yugoslavia] then we could pile up the goals against Honduras. That just won't happen, for they proved against Spain that they have discipline and some positively brilliant players. They are no mugs, and we will find it difficult to get the two points.'

Goals were the things people expected against Honduras and yet this was always unrealistic. A look at Northern Ireland's recent record would have shown why. In their last nine games they had scored just two goals, four goals in their last twelve, and they hadn't scored more than once in a game since October 1980, nearly two years previously. As Bingham told the *Irish News*, 'We have never had prolific scorers, but the men I rely on for strike power are producing fewer than I would hope for. Their ratio of goals per game is not high and we have to come to terms with that. I cannot make them into something they are not. But every player in the heat today must get into scoring positions.' However, he was also upbeat about the condition of his team, 'I told them in straight terms that they had been dreadful over the last few months and that selection would be based on the evidence produced during the training in Brighton and here. Obviously, it has worked, for they are all mentally and physically in top condition and now confidence is fully restored by that draw.'

The night before the Honduras match, Northern Ireland got some good news as Spain played Yugoslavia in a bad-tempered game with four bookings. Yugoslavia took the lead in the tenth minute from Gudelj; however, they did not hold on to it for long and the Danish referee gave a penalty many observers thought should have been a free kick. He had been standing very near to where the foul had taken place and with a clear and unheeded view of the incident. However, he had pointed to the spot, despite the fact that the foul had quite clearly taken place outside the box. When Spain's Roberto López Ufarte kicked the penalty wide, the referee then ordered it to be taken again and Spain equalised on the second attempt. Enrique Saura then won the game a few minutes after coming on as part of a double substitution in the sixty-fourth minute. Once more Spain's blushes had been spared, but Yugoslavia's chances of progressing now looked to have suffered a mortal wound.

As Bingham told the press the next day, 'I have to admit that I never thought the penalty was on. At first, I thought it was a good decision, but when I watched the video playback, I saw the trip was clearly outside the area and Alonso stumbled in. But I can't complain. Spain got the result that we Irish wanted. We have to beat Honduras and try to get as many goals as possible. If we do, then the pressure is on Yugoslavia for their last game. They are psychologically down and even more so if we triumph over the Hondurans.'

For those Irish fans who loved working out group permutations the result was a tonic. Victory over Honduras would mean that a draw against Spain would be enough to qualify regardless of what happened between Yugoslavia and Honduras. Even with a defeat in the last game, they might qualify if Yugoslavia didn't beat Honduras by too many goals or if Honduras narrowly won.

A final game defeat would also be sufficient if their two rivals drew. Suddenly, the prize was clearly on show for Northern Ireland – a place in the quarter-finals was possible if they could just beat Honduras. Of course, the Hondurans would have been entertaining similar thoughts, and they knew that a victory over Northern Ireland would put them in the driving seat for qualification if they could avoid defeat in the final game against Yugoslavia.

Flying back to Zaragoza on the day of the match for another evening kick off, Northern Ireland found the conditions almost as stifling as their first game, but this time the proceedings were played out in front of a mere fifteen thousand fans. Few Hondurans had made the trip to Europe and fewer Spaniards fancied the game between the group's two lesser nations.

Northern Ireland started the game brightly, and in the seventh minute they had a glorious opportunity to open the scoring. Whiteside floated in a lovely ball from the left wing and it was met by the incoming Martin O'Neill who was free and unmarked on the edge of the six-yard box. However, O'Neill headed over the bar when he really should have done better.

A few minutes later, Whiteside again provided the threat, this time on the left side of the penalty box. Pushing the ball beyond him, he was chopped down before he could pursue it, and the referee instantly blew for the free kick, with Whiteside furious that a penalty hadn't been given. However, it looked as though it was the right decision with the foul having taken place just on the line of the box. A first attempt to take the free kick, which midfielder Gilberto Yearwood headed into the Honduran keeper's hands, had to be retaken as the wall hadn't been the full ten yards back. On the second occasion, McIlroy tried something different and, after a stepover from Donaghy, he whipped in a powerful shot, which had the keeper beaten but clipped the crossbar and bounced down. In the scramble in the six-yard area, Chris Nicholl headed the ball back towards goal only for it to hit the bar again. This time the ball bounced upwards and then dropped down to the waiting Armstrong, practically standing on the line, who couldn't miss with his header.

Northern Ireland's goal-scoring account at the World Cup had finally been opened and at this moment it would have been easy to believe that they would now go on to score at least a few more against a Honduran team who looked much more rattled against the Irish than they had been against Spain. However, the goal stung the Central Americans into action and they almost recorded an instant reply in the thirteenth minute when Betancourt smashed an effort against the Northern Irish bar from a corner with Jennings well beaten. A few minutes later, José Roberto Figueroa burst through the Irish defence to loose a shot but it went straight along the grass and into Jennings' grasp. Shortly afterwards the same player would sting Jennings' hands with a well-taken free kick, but the goalkeeper didn't have to move too far from the centre of his goal to deal with it.

In the twenty-sixth minute, Prudencio Norales sped dangerously into the box and was forced wide of the goal by Jennings. The danger wasn't over, though, because the midfielder had maintained possession and Jennings was now caught out of his net. Norales laid the ball off to Figueroa who, from the edge of the right-hand side of the box audaciously chipped the ball over the retreating Jennings; it would have dipped accurately into the Irish goal if not for Jimmy Nicholl placing himself on the line to head clear. This had not been in the script most Irish fans had been typing in their heads following the Armstrong goal, and Honduras were causing all sorts of problems.

The next chance fell to Northern Ireland, though, when Chris Nicholl missed an opportunity to extend the lead – the ball had fizzed across the six-yard area just ahead of him when he had the goal at his mercy. In the thirty-third minute, the Honduran captain, Ramón Maradiaga, suffered a moment of temporary madness. Pinned down at his own corner flag by

O'Neill, he decided to back-heel the ball out of danger to a waiting defender. Unfortunately for him, the lack of accuracy of the back-heel took it straight into the path of McIlroy who wasted no time in sending in a cross to the far post where both Chris Nicholl and Whiteside went for the same ball. This probably spared the blushes of Maradiaga as the ball ended up going just over the crossbar when either one of them might have been more accurate if left to meet the ball alone.

There was perhaps a sense that Northern Ireland had reasserted themselves in the game, and in the forty-first minute Gerry Armstrong came close to scoring a truly great goal. Chesting down a cross twenty-five yards out from goal he held off the Honduran tackle from behind and began closing in on the edge of the box. He feinted to deceive Allan Costly and send him the wrong way, which opened up space to give him a clear sight of goal. His shot easily beat the keeper, Julio Arzú, but it hit the post and bounced back to Arzú, who took two attempts to smother the ball with Hamilton bearing down on him.

At half-time, Northern Ireland would have been pleased with what they had achieved so far. They had controlled the majority of possession and had further chances to score. However, even the contemporary reports of this match misrepresent what had happened in the first forty-five minutes. Watching it today you can see that, far from being some sort of potential goal cavalcade for Northern Ireland with Honduras on the ropes, it was actually the Central American team who had had the greater number of chances. While they had seemed content to allow the Irish to control midfield, their chances, when they broke, had been good enough and numerous enough that they could easily have been going in for the break comfortably in the lead. This was a game hanging in the balance, there for the taking by either side.

It was the Irish, however, who came out with a greater sense of purpose for the second half as McCreery, McIlroy and O'Neill found acres of space in midfield. Just on fifty-six minutes, the ball was crossed from the left for Armstrong at the far post who headed it down and back across the net. Whiteside was waiting, completely unmarked, and he carefully squared himself up and shot past Arzú with ease. However, it was ruled out immediately and the teenager was denied his first international goal. As the ball had been played backwards towards him it was impossible for Whiteside to have been offside so it can only have been given against Armstrong in the build-up. With the Spanish television images providing no replay, viewers at home were left none the wiser as to why the decision had been made.

After fifty-eight minutes, Honduras made a substitution and Eduardo Laing came on for Norales. Shortly afterwards, in a rare foray into the Irish half, they won a corner. It was well placed into the centre of the box and Betancourt showed his danger by skilfully carving out some space for himself and heading the ball powerfully towards the net. Jennings pulled off a great save and pushed the ball over the top for another corner. Unfortunately for Northern Ireland, the lesson of how good Honduras were from corners had not been learned. From the second corner, the substitute Laing stole to the near post and turned and powered the header past Jennings for the equaliser. McClelland remembers the frustration felt at the time. 'We thought "They've just done that corner! Why didn't we get hold of it and stop the exact same movement?"'

Bingham soon responded with a substitution of his own and introduced Noel Brotherston for Whiteside, who had taken a knock that had required treatment. Brotherston immediately showed some attacking intent down the right wing as Northern Ireland tried to retake the lead, and a good move by Hamilton and McIlroy on the edge of the box resulted in a decent shot from Hamilton, which flashed across goal and went just wide. A short time later, a magnificent turn by Armstrong just outside the front of the box saw him clear the way for a cracking shot that was well met by Arzú who pushed it wide into Hamilton's path. Arzú then did enough to pressure Hamilton to shoot from the angle, but it didn't clear the post and went behind for the goal kick.

Bingham gambled now by taking off his captain, O'Neill, and throwing on the inexperienced Irish League player, Felix Healy, who took up position on the left wing. O'Neill didn't appear overly happy about going off, but it later emerged that he had been playing with a slight calf strain. However, this was a massive chance to take – pitting a part-time player against an organised defence that had already absorbed whatever Spain had thrown at it. Northern Ireland, if anything, now appeared slightly less of a threat once the midfield calmness and vision of O'Neill was withdrawn.

With just five minutes to go, Betancourt won a free kick outside the box. The ball was pushed out to Figueroa, who rasped a shot just inches wide across the Northern Ireland goal. The replay suggested that Jennings may have got a slight touch to it. If so, Jennings had denied Honduras earning a winner completely against the run of play. Jennings remembered, 'I made my finest save of the World Cup, diving full length to turn a shot around the post with my fingertips. To my amazement, and to the annoyance of the Honduras players, the referee promptly awarded a goal kick. He had not realised that I'd reached the ball, even though it must have been apparent to the millions watching on TV. I was happy enough the referee got it wrong. I wasn't looking for personal glory at that moment and was relieved to avoid the risk of Honduras getting another goal from a corner kick.'

Betancourt then played a good through ball for Figueroa to run on to in the Irish box. Donaghy came back across and got an all-important foot on the ball in a perfectly timed tackle to send it out for a corner just as the situation began to look dangerous. Of course, the two previous Honduran corners had produced all sorts of problems for Northern Ireland and now their manager told them from the touchline exactly what he wanted from the set piece. It was taken short and then whipped into the box with Jennings forced to dive out and punch the ball away. Unfortunately, it dropped to a Honduran player on the far side of the six-yard box and was played straight back towards goal. This time it was met by a strong header from McClelland and this allowed Armstrong to run the ball away and relieve the pressure. It was the final chance of the game but left observers feeling that, for all their possessional dominance in the game, it had been the Irish who had been grateful to escape with a draw at the finish.

Needless to say, the local press were extremely pessimistic in their summations of Northern Ireland's World Cup chances following this result. The *Belfast Telegraph* led with a headline of 'Mission impossible', while the *Newsletter* declared in bold, 'Sub Laing has all but sunk glory hopes.'

The players were disappointed. Armstrong told the press, 'We should never have thrown it away – never at all. We had them on the rack and they were ready to disintegrate.' Chris Nicholl, meanwhile, referenced the goal as being, 'Like a knife in the ribs. For an hour we had the game won and we were creating chance after chance against an indifferent team. But that is all history now and we know we have to do it again against Spain.'

Malcolm Brodie was perhaps not as savage as expected in his appraisal, but he still pulled no punches when he wrote, 'If this is the end of the 1982 World Cup venture, and to all intents and purposes it is, we have only ourselves to blame. The age-old problem of lack of scoring forwards raised its ugly head yesterday.' However, he seemed much less reasonable when he singled Whiteside out for criticism: 'I'm afraid Whiteside had a somewhat disappointing second international performance. Whiteside may be the answer in the years to come but, at seventeen, is still much too immature for such a heavy burden to be placed on those broad shoulders.'

Coming so soon after the tribute the same journalist had delivered to the same player after the Yugoslavia game, the comments seemed mean and unmerited. The criticism still stung with Whiteside many years later as he remarked, 'You expect people to be fickle, but you'd think a consistent line could be maintained for a bit longer. I had heard the cliché about building you up to knock you down, but at times you want to say, "Make your mind up!" How could I go from a superstar to a child in such a short space of time?'

Brodie now sought to gain column inches by magnifying a disagreement between Bingham and O'Neill regarding the substitution. He wasn't alone in the press in doing this, but he went much further than any of the other local journalists when he tried to bait the two men with a series of unnecessary questions: 'Did any animosity exist?', 'Are you satisfied with his captaincy and his attitude in general?' The Spanish press must have loudly rejoiced to see an Irish journalist doing the job of undermining Northern Ireland for them.

However, as the footage of O'Neill leaving the field shows, he was a man bemused by, but ultimately accepting of, the decision. There was certainly no argument or tantrum involved and, although it would appear that O'Neill then queried the decision in the dressing room, Brodie seemed to be trying to create friction where none existed. Both O'Neill and Bingham were astonished by his questions but answered them with good grace – there was no hostility or bitterness at the substitution as it had ultimately been a case of crossed wires.

As O'Neill told the *Irish News*, 'In the general annoyance at the result and my substitution, in the heat of the moment, I let my feelings be known. Apparently, it was a misunderstanding because I had a tightening hamstring and the bench thought I was labouring. I am still disappointed but it's all over now. It's in the past.'

The players were frustrated and wary of what now lay before

them. As Pat Jennings reveals in his autobiography, 'We flew back to our hotel in Valencia feeling somewhat deflated by the result. Whatever the permutations if we drew our last match with Spain, the realistic view was that victory was the only way of guaranteeing our progress. And that seemed too big a task.'

Bingham, while frustrated at the time, is philosophical about the result: 'I played long enough in the game to know that there are wins and losses and there are times you deserve to win and you lose, and times you win and you deserve to lose. I thought it was just one of those games that we weren't lucky enough to get through.'

Norman Whiteside remembers, 'The common consensus was that we had missed our chance and we only had pride to play for in the last group game, one reporter going so far as to point out the positive to our fans, that while we lacked finesse at least "the side so far has not proved the embarrassment we expected".' Faint praise indeed.

Northern Ireland had been left disappointed by a draw in a game they could easily have won, but which they could also have lost if Honduras had been a little more fortunate with their own chances. The criticism from some quarters of the press rankled – the whole world had written them off. Now before them lay the greatest task that any Northern Ireland side had ever faced.

After watching the Spain game against Yugoslavia with its debatable penalty award, Bingham had remarked to journalists, 'Doesn't that crowd pressurise the referee? If anyone can win against Spain in Valencia it is a miracle. You won't get any favours there.' Bingham would find out the truth of his own words the hard way as Northern Ireland faced their moment of destiny.

THE NIGHT IN VALENCIA

At first, the draw against unfancied Honduras looked as though it had left Northern Ireland's World Cup dreams in tatters – they had squandered their lead in a game that had offered them the best chance to take maximum points. Yet Honduras had already shown against Spain that they were no pushovers, and Northern Ireland had done just as well against them as the Spanish had – and that was without the fanatical backing of home support behind them, and while playing in punishing and energy-sapping heat that, unlike their opponents, they were not used to.

Qualification for the second stage *was* still achievable, but as their final game was against Spain, the task ahead seemed to be nearly impossible. It was true that Spain had laboured in the first two games, perhaps under the pressure of being the hosts of the tournament. However, many felt that Northern Ireland had little more than a ghost of a chance. Three of the last four World Cups had been won by the host nation. Playing in front of home supporters and being familiar with your surroundings gave a team a boost that was impossible to overestimate. In fact, two of those three nations – England and Argentina – had never won a World Cup until they had staged a home tournament.

On television, veteran player Mick Channon was so dismissive of Northern Ireland's fate that he didn't even mention them when assessing the chances of the British teams going into the final group games. Norman Whiteside reveals that the negative opinions of the press acted to spur on the team, 'If it was to be our last match we must play without fear because we knew we had nothing to lose. As the game approached and we read more and more comments about being no-hopers our defiance grew. I looked around the practice field and could sense the boys were up for ramming the critics' words back down their throats.'

Following the exertions in high humidity during the first two games, the team were allowed to recover gradually ahead of the crunch match. On top of the exhaustion, there were also a few niggling injuries to essential personnel with Gerry Armstrong (right knee), Martin O'Neill (hamstring strain), Norman Whiteside (ankle) and David McCreery (bruised thigh) all nursing themselves back to 100 per cent fitness, but all expected to be in the line-up for the forthcoming game. Bingham knew that he had to conserve his players' stamina – the Spanish heat wouldn't pose the same problems for the host nation – so he ordered them to do only light training. There was also a sense that he was perhaps playing his cards close to his chest in terms of team tactics. If the Northern Ireland team weren't involved in full training sessions, then it would be impossible for the Spanish to learn anything to their advantage from their spies.

Taking this to the extreme, Bingham even refused the opportunity to use the match stadium as a training ground just before the game. All teams had been offered this so that they might familiarise themselves with their surroundings, and it probably raised a few eyebrows when Bingham turned it down. However, with the tactical battle likely to be as important as the physical one, it was an astute management decision. It was also a little bit of a mind game, especially concerning the opinions on Northern Ireland in the Spanish press.

It was no secret that the Spanish were slightly mystified by the Northern Ireland squad and had labelled them as lazy and too fond of their alcohol. The accusations were very unfair. Bingham felt it was important to not only train but to relax and build up camaraderie within the squad. As to the suggestion that they drank too much, this was a source of amusement to the team as it had been a prank played on Tommy Cassidy that had contributed to the rumour. As Billy Hamilton gleefully recalls, 'We were back in the hotel and … Bingy said to us, "Stay within the grounds of the hotel, but you can sit by the pool and have a few drinks, don't go overboard." So, we got the cassette player out, the sunglasses on, a few tins of beer, a great atmosphere and a bit of banter going on. As the afternoon went on, Tommy Cassidy got a sun lounger out and fell asleep on it. We got a frilly cowboy hat and stuck it on his head, and we put all our empty beer cans round his feet … The next thing, in walked the Spanish press. Of course, they made a beeline for Tommy and took a picture of him. The next morning in the newspapers, there's Tommy Cassidy on the front with the words, "This is how the Irish prepare for the big game." Billy went berserk.'

While the Spanish were incredulous, the Irish thought this was hilarious and Hamilton stresses that, while a few drinks each were taken by the squad, 'Nobody took advantage or went overboard. The team spirit that built up was brilliant … I don't think you would be able to do that now.' As the local press poured scorn on the Irishmen, team captain Martin O'Neill saw the funny side and couldn't help poking a bit of fun when asked for his reaction: 'We expected something like this. It gives us the added incentive we needed against Spain. We might have some champagne after the match tomorrow night, and we could send some into the Spanish dressing room as well.'

This was where Bingham's management of the squad as a collective entity was paying off. Keeping things light and easy, allowing the players a bit of slack, all helped to keep a happy and relaxed squad. As he said at the time, 'I'm keeping matters as low-key as possible as we build up slowly towards the final group match. I don't want the players to get anxious. We know what the pressure will be, and I feel Spain will be under more than us. They are expected to win and we are not. This might prove to our advantage.'

Unfortunately, a slight spanner was thrown into the works when, on the day of the match itself, it was reported that the second-choice goalkeeper, Jim Platt, had fallen out with Bingham. Quoted in the Irish press, Platt had apparently said, 'I don't want to be involved in any slanging match. But if you ask me will I play under Billy Bingham again, the answer is no.' Apparently, Platt had taken exception to his exclusion from the first team for the opening two fixtures, allegedly having been led to believe, after the final preparation game against Wales, that he would be the first choice ahead of Jennings. According to the press, the only reason he hadn't walked out on the squad and flown home was because his family were on holiday at a nearby hotel. However, a quote from Platt in the *Belfast Telegraph* was less confrontational: 'I felt I had a good chance of playing, but Billy Bingham is the man who picks the team and he only has eleven places to fill. It is a difficult situation for any manager.'

As Jennings was then in his late thirties, with injury problems limiting his build-up for the tournament, Platt could have been forgiven for believing that his moment had finally come to claim the first-team place – and on the biggest stage of all. If he had been led to believe that this would be the case, then it must have been a bitter pill to swallow. However, a fit Jennings really had to be given the call up, regardless of how able his back-up was. Jennings was still one of the greatest goalkeepers in the world, with experience to match his talent.

For his part, Jennings is convinced that Platt was misquoted as he had never been one to complain during his long time as understudy, and it had seemed so out of keeping with the general atmosphere within the camp. Jennings also claims that he knew nothing of the story until he got home after the World Cup so, while it was a headline in Belfast, it didn't disrupt the mood within the squad. They had no access to these stories, other than through expensive long distance phone calls to relatives. Nevertheless, it is true that Bingham and Platt exchanged words on the subject on the day of the match, and Platt's name was conspicuous by its absence from the list of substitutes, with third choice goalkeeper, George Dunlop, being picked for the bench instead.

One thing that did have an impact upon the Northern Ireland team on the day of the final group game was knowing the result of the Yugoslavia/Honduras game, the penultimate match of their group that had been played earlier. In those days, FIFA organised the two final games in a group to be played at different times in order to maximise TV revenue. With qualification often on a knife edge for the teams involved, it was obviously an advantage in 1982 to be in the second game of this last round of matches; to know how two of the other teams had finished. It allowed teams to adjust their tactics and hopefully manufacture exactly the result they needed.

Yugoslavia had defeated Honduras 1–0 with a last-gasp goal – a penalty in the eighty-eighth minute. It was desperately hard luck on the plucky South Americans who had surprised everyone by drawing their first two games but who were now out of the tournament. A win for Honduras would have made life exceedingly difficult for the Irish and it might even have meant that beating Spain wasn't enough to qualify if Honduras had won by a significant margin against the Yugoslavians. The 1–0 win for Yugoslavia still meant that Northern Ireland needed to win their final game to be sure of qualification, but it also opened the door to other methods of qualification and a high-scoring draw such as 2–2 or 3–3 would also see them qualify automatically in second place. Even a 1–1 draw would give them a chance as they would be placed into a pot with Yugoslavia, with lots drawn to see who would go through.

This had never happened in World Cup history, although the proviso had often been there, but it at least offered Northern Ireland a glimmer of a chance beyond beating Spain. Martin O'Neill, as always, was on top of the permutations and he told the press, 'It doesn't make it any easier in that we still have to score one goal in a drawn game. But now, even if Spain go in front, we will have something to fight for. If we score at least once and go into the hat we will have a 50/50 chance, and that is better than nothing.'

In the end, the 1982 World Cup was the last tournament in which FIFA's practice of playing the final games at separate times would occur. It was abolished following disgraceful scenes during the last match of Group 2, played earlier in the day before Northern Ireland faced Spain. The football world had been stunned when the highly-fancied West Germans lost their opening game to lowly Algeria. When the Algerians, who had become the darlings of the World Cup after their heroic David versus Goliath achievement, went on to win their final game against Chile, it meant that the double World Champions faced exiting the tournament in the opening round. Austria had won both of their opening games and it meant that they were almost certainly through, unless they were beaten 3–0 or more in their final game. For the Germans, however, nothing less than victory would do. The scenes that followed shamed football and brought disgrace to FIFA and the World Cup. When the Germans took an early tenth minute lead, both teams appeared to give up playing competitively for the entire remaining eighty minutes. The Austrians feared attacking in case they left themselves open to conceding the two further goals that would knock them out on goal difference behind the Algerians. The Germans feared attacking in case they conceded an equaliser which would bring about their exit. 1–0, however, was enough to put both teams through. And so, the two nations played out a farcical circus of a game in which they passed the ball around meaninglessly to ensure that they both progressed at the expense of the hard-working underdogs from Algeria.

The game was immediately christened 'the Disgrace of Gijón', and criticism from the press and fans around the world was immediate and severe, not to mention the reaction from the furious Algerians. German manager, Josef 'Jupp' Derwall, responded angrily to the accusations of a fixed or arranged outcome, 'This is a grave, serious insult.' And while Austrian manager Georg Schmidt did not admit to any wrongdoing, he did acknowledge that, 'It was a shameful showing … I told my side to try and win, but I have come out of this match rather disillusioned.'

The West German FIFA representative, Hermann Neuberger – who happened to be president of the West German FA, vice president of FIFA and also, no less, president of the organising committee for the World Cup – was not likely to show the Algerians much sympathy; however, his statement on the matter beggared belief: 'There are no FIFA rules which say teams cannot play as they please. FIFA cannot sanction a team if they did not fight properly.' He was, of course, correct, but the implicit admission that his national team had played out an arranged result was hardly likely to quell the voices raised in protest. Quite correctly, the rules were changed for the next World Cup and such a debacle would never happen again.

The relevance to the Spain/Northern Ireland game was that suddenly the world's press was alert to the possibility of teams arranging a mutually beneficial result. However, while there were various permutations of scores which would see both teams go through, there was no chance of these two nations coming to any kind of arrangement. First of all, Spain considered Northern Ireland to be a minnow of a team, who should be put to the sword by their very tough and talented side. Spain had also failed to impress in their opening two games and were now under intense pressure to deliver in a home tournament before the microscopic glare of a local media who expected nothing less than triumph.

The host nation had another reason for wanting to come out on top, one connected to the complex structure of the tournament at the time. The second phase of the 1982 tournament was the quarter-finals and, for this one tournament only, the quarter-finals would not be a set of straight knock-out matches but four round-robin groups of three teams each, with the four winners emerging into the semi-finals. Some runners-up from the first phase of groups would be lucky enough to find themselves in a quarter-final group with another runner-up and one group winner, but two of the groups would be more difficult and would see two group winners against one runner-up.

With other groups having already concluded their final matches, the jigsaw of the second round was almost complete as the names of countries were filled in on World Cup wallcharts around the globe. Northern Ireland and Spain both knew that the runner-up from their group would be facing two group winners in the quarter-final and therefore it was in the interests of both teams to try and top the group and get a slightly easier draw against two runners-up. Both England and West Germany had won their groups and would be awaiting the runners-up from Northern Ireland's group, strongly fancied by most people to be Yugoslavia. Winning the group, though, would mean a seemingly more favourable draw against Austria and France, and the French had already shown signs of struggling in the tournament.

Of course, it's probably true to say that Northern Ireland would have taken their chances against anyone at the quarter-final stage and would have been delighted just to be there, but, for Spain, the twin thrusts of pride in front of their home support and wishing to avoid a nightmare draw against England and West Germany meant that this was win at all costs for them. Nevertheless, they were facing a Northern Ireland team who had nothing to lose and everything to gain, as centre half Chris Nicholl summarised: 'It could be our last game. If we do not win, we will be on the plane home on Sunday. So, what have we to lose by giving it everything?'

Bingham needed to manage the mindset of the players as the game came ever closer and also plan his tactics for what was expected to be a physical and relentless game played in exhausting temperatures. Of course, the best tactics in the world are only of use if the team is disciplined enough to stick to them and put them into practice. What Bingham needed was a team that was both relaxed and focused, and it would require every shred of experience from his long career in football to get the result needed to progress. Speaking to the press before the match he explained, 'Spain are basically a counterattack team so to go forward with all flags flying would be a mistake. We'll look at them for a while and then start to go forward a bit more. We finished strongly against Yugoslavia in 100 degrees and in 95 degrees in our second game, which seemed to tire them [our opponents] even more. It's taken us two days to recover but I am happy to say we are ready again and looking forward to a good battle with Spain … Admittedly, it will take much effort, passion, commitment and skill, but we possess these qualities in abundance.'

Billy Hamilton remembers Bingham's strengths in confidence-building. 'He was very good at motivating players. He would make you feel ten feet tall when you went on to the pitch. He never made you feel second best. He had a very good tactical plan. He knew that if we could swamp the midfield, that would stop the Spaniards passing through us and getting into the box.'

The captain also worked hard with the players on their tactics and need for discipline. As Gerry Armstrong recalls, 'Martin O'Neill had spoken to us the night before and we more or less agreed that we would defend the best we could. We were very good at getting behind the ball and making it difficult. We knew we would create some chances and we had to take one.' He remembered O'Neill's words as being, 'Look, it's as simple as this. We are not good enough to beat them two or three nil, so forget about it. Look at the way they played the other night. They played like a team under a bit of pressure. What we've got to do is keep them under pressure for the first twenty-five minutes of the game, not allow them too many chances, let the crowd turn against them. You know what we're like, we'll create three or four chances on the counterattack, and we'll stick one of them in. That's how we'll beat them, 1–0 and through to the quarter-finals.'

All Irish hopes rested on neutralising Spain early in the game, weathering the expected storm, and then hoping that they could creep into the match by creating their own chances later in the game. In boxing terms, this is known as a 'puncher's chance' – trying to avoid being knocked out and hoping for the chance to land one solid punch when it mattered most.

The real fear for Northern Ireland was that Spain might get a helping hand thanks to the pressure exerted by their huge and vociferous support, 'We were worried more by the referee than the Spanish players,' recalls Jennings. 'The fear that he might award a penalty against us was uppermost in our minds. We had seen Spain get doubtful penalties in both their previous matches, and the last thing we wanted was to be the fall guys for a hat trick.' Martin O'Neill had shared the same concern, 'We do not fear the Spanish team but are a bit apprehensive about the influence of their fans on the referee here in Valencia … we have seen how referees buckle under pressure from the people on the terraces.'

The penalties awarded to Spain had already helped them salvage a draw and scrape a victory in their opening two fixtures, so Northern Ireland would have to adjust their tactics and anticipate the threat of someone who might throw themselves to the ground in the penalty area. As O'Neill put it at the time, 'We certainly have it all to do against Spain, but we thrive on these make-or-break situations.'

On match day all the minor knocks and strains for Irish players had cleared up and they were at full strength. The only possible change to the line-up was suggested by *The Times* who reported that morning that Norman Whiteside could be replaced by the more experienced Bobby Campbell. However, they were wrong, and Bingham kept the faith with his young forward who had now, incredibly, played more minutes for his country than he had for his club's first team. On the Spanish front, Enrique Saura, who had scored after coming on against Yugoslavia, was drafted into midfield for Jesús María Zamora, who had a knee injury.

For the first time in the tournament, the players were able to leave from their own hotel and cross Valencia by coach to their destination. However, they also had to move through streets filled with the fanatical support of a home nation – fans who did their utmost to intimidate the Irish players with their flags and chants. Billy Hamilton remembers how one moment of levity managed to release some of the pressure they were feeling. 'We're preparing for the biggest match of our careers and we're leaving on the coach for the ground. I remember the streets being thronged with supporters going to the game and the flags being waved, mostly Spanish. Out through the window there was a beautiful Spanish girl, waving a flag. She was in a short skirt and a bikini top. Bobby Campbell stuck his head out through the coach and says, "Whataboutye, darlin'?" Sammy Nelson was sitting behind him and said, "For fuck's sake, Bobby.

Pull your head in or they'll think this is a cattle truck." It broke the tension. Everyone was nervous, but that just got a real belly laugh from everybody.'

Campbell was involved in another memorable incident at the stadium, as Hamilton recalls: 'Bobby was a bit of a rogue. Bingy gave Bobby all the tickets for the non-playing substitutes. Bobby sold them. The non-playing substitutes couldn't get into the game. It was the [Northern Irish] press crew that got them into the press area, or they wouldn't have got to see the game at all.'

As the showdown approached, Martin O'Neill gave his final thoughts and he remained upbeat when he said, 'Let me put it this way, we would be very disappointed to come off the field at nil each. We would rather come off losing two or three and having attacked them. That seems like a paradox, but a goalless draw does us no good.' However, as BBC1 presented its build-up to their live coverage of the match, their experts in the studio sounded a lot less optimistic. Lawrie McMenemy suggested that, 'Northern Ireland are such a tiny soccer nation, they have won to get here really. Spain have done so badly and have had so much stick even from their own supporters that I think Ireland could just get the backlash tonight. I can see them possibly getting a draw. I would love them to win it, but I can't see it.'

In the dressing room, Bingham tried to inspire, to reassure, to drum in the tactics, to build up confidence in ability. It was the most important pre-match speech of his career, and he would have been casting back into the talks he had heard from Peter Doherty and Danny Blanchflower before taking to the pitch in 1958. Jimmy Nicholl recalls, 'He spoke about the pressure Spain were under. We were under no pressure, no one expected Northern Ireland to win it. "The pressure's on them. Get the crowd booing, try to keep possession, get the crowd against them." Billy's team talks were brilliant. I was pumped to the eyeballs. He was brilliant at that. Then he had to bring you down cos you're climbing the walls!'

The assistants also played a key role in motivating the players, as McIlroy remembers, 'Martin Harvey and Bertie Peacock were both experienced men and good footballers as well. They were always there going round individually, having a word with players or if you needed any help. Great gentlemen. It was good to have them around because they maybe spotted a little bit of nerves with the players and just had a word, one to one. They were there if you needed them.'

And the team would need all the encouragement and support they could get, as they prepared to face the Spanish team in the sweltering arena of the Estadio Luis Casanova in Valencia, packed solid with fifty thousand noisy and passionate Spanish fans.

On then into the cauldron and the white heat of battle – into the oven-like temperature of the stadium in Valencia, the noise a cacophony of Spanish voices, a moving tide of red and yellow flags everywhere you looked. Even today, experienced teams full of players of high standing at the top of the game can freeze when faced with such a degree of hostile and impassioned support. It is easy to be overwhelmed by surging attacks coupled with the clamour and tumult of noise thundering from the stands. In such situations it is simply time to stand up and be counted or to go under. What must have been going through the minds of the eleven Irishmen who walked out to the centre of the park that balmy June night, the hopes of a tiny nation resting on their shoulders, knowing that every conceivable set of odds was stacked against them? Were any of them suddenly paralysed with fear? No one in world football would have thought any less of these rank outsiders from Northern Ireland if they had buckled under the glare of an audience that was at least in the hundreds of millions and watching from every corner of the globe.

As John Motson began his match commentary for the

BBC, he stated the simple truth of the matter, 'Sitting here in the stadium tonight, you have to say the task facing Northern Ireland is monumental.' The Irish players, however, entered the arena as a determined unit. They had already defied the odds to qualify so were used to uphill tasks with their backs to the wall. They believed that they somehow had a chance. As they took to the pitch they were greeted with flags, cheers and the pounding drum of Spain's most famous fan, 'Manolo el del Bombo' (the Bass Drummer), a colourful character that the Spanish cameras picked out at every opportunity and whom Norman Whiteside remembers vividly, 'The guy was beating the drum, and there was like *bom-bom-bom* "España" *bom-bom-bom*. And it was just ringing in the background the whole game: "España".'

Billy Hamilton remembers how oppressive the noise was inside the steep-sided stadium. 'I remember getting stripped for the game and everyone was looking forward to it. What I wasn't prepared for was the atmosphere in that ground. It was really, really tight and the supporters came right down beside you at the pitch line and they were quite hostile. The goosebumps and the hairs on the back of the neck were really up during the national anthems for that game.'

In one corner of the ground, however, was something for the Irish players to focus on amid the sea of red and yellow. The travelling Northern Irish fans were somehow making themselves heard and were proudly waving their own flags and trying to make as much noise as possible. Norman Whiteside remembers the positive impact the fans had on the team, 'Though they were outnumbered ten to one it gave us a hell of a lift to be greeted by their barnstorming cheers and songs as we walked out of the tunnel.'

One fan, however, was missing from the ranks. Paul Vance recalls, 'One lad from Belfast had found romance, waving our three coaches off on their way to Valencia for the big game. None of us would've missed this for the world, but he'd sized up his options and given away his match ticket. We'd lose anyway, were going home in two days and he'd a chance to make sweet music with one of the local señoritas … I hope his evening lived up to expectations, because he missed out on the greatest night in Northern Ireland football's long international history.'

There was another edge to the vocal rivalry between the fans that night, something that has almost been forgotten today. Just eleven days had passed since the conflict over the Falkland Islands had ended with the surrender of the Argentinian forces, and even less time had elapsed since dictator General Leopoldo Galtieri's fall from power. Despite the fears before the tournament, none of the three home nations had faced Argentina on the field so this match, between Northern Ireland and Spain, was the closest it had got. The Spanish fans made no secret of their support for their Latin cousins and were perhaps also spurred on by Spain's own disagreement with the United Kingdom over Gibraltar's sovereignty. David Cathcart from Dundonald in east Belfast was just eleven years old when he made the trip to Spain with his family to follow Northern Ireland in the group phase. He remembers the hostility of the Spanish fans before the match, 'They were singing songs in support of Argentina and, of course, referring to the Falklands as "Las Malvinas" in their chants. But the Northern Ireland fans got their own back by chanting over to them, "Galtieri's on the dole."'

Something else that had the potential to work against the Irish was the Paraguayan referee, Héctor Ortiz. As John Motson reminded the viewers at home, 'Tonight's referee has never before taken charge of a match between European sides. He told me that the only English-speaking team he's taken charge of before was the New York Cosmos in the United States. There are still question marks then against the referees and FIFA's appointments.' Prior to that night's game, Ortiz hadn't refereed any game at all for the last two years, and to have a referee at this level of the game who had never before officiated between Europeans but who spoke Spanish naturally would invite accusations of favouritism towards Spain. It's something the authorities would be at pains to avoid today but which they clearly thought was acceptable in 1982. Northern Ireland's fears of crowd and player pressure on the referee were realistic and all eyes were now on the man in the middle to see if he gave way as he blew the whistle to start the game.

Northern Ireland made the first attack by directing a free kick into the Spanish box, but then the onslaught against them began with a Spanish counterattack – Miguel Ángel Alonso shot just wide of the Irish post. A marker had been laid down and Spain would now be relentlessly teasing and probing the Irish defence in a busy opening spell.

After just four minutes, Roberto López Ufarte broke through in what looked like a very good goal-scoring chance, but it was denied by Jennings, who was alert to the danger and quickly ran out to smother the ball at Ufarte's feet. What would have frightened Irish supporters, not to mention Bingham watching from the dugout, was the speed and fluidity of the Spanish move. The final burst into the Irish penalty area had cut through four defenders who were all left for dead. The chance may have ultimately come to nothing, but it was an ominous sign of Spanish intent and ability.

One minute later, Jesús Satrústegui headed just wide. There had been three clear chances in the opening five minutes – nightmare viewing for those at home and the three thousand loyal supporters who had followed them to Valencia. How much longer could Northern Ireland stand firm against this intense pressure? Often in football, when one team is caught staring into the headlights as the other rolls over them, it is only a matter of time before the goal is breached. It looked for all the world in these opening minutes that this would be the case, and the uphill task would surely become impossible if Northern Ireland were to concede the lead.

In addition to the goal-scoring threat the Spaniards posed, they also now began to turn the screw on their opponents by harassing them physically. Those who had feared the impartiality of the Latin referee were now given just cause for alarm as a succession of strong and crunching tackles were left unpunished by Ortiz. Alonso, along with José Ramón Alexanko and Miguel Tendillo, waged a war of attrition against the Irish forward line and midfield in an attempt to intimidate them. With the referee showing little sign that their robustness was going to be punished, they were encouraged to push the boundaries even further. As Motson told the television audience, 'There is not much football being played at the moment, certainly not by Spain. Like so many countries in the past, and particularly Argentina four years ago, they are pushing the referee as far as they dare.' Jimmy Hill, never one to pull back from speaking his mind, went much further when he said, 'The Spaniards are being ruthless and cynical and if we are not careful, from what we have seen already, I am afraid the game will go on to be a disgrace to football.'

In the twentieth minute, Juan Gómez González (Juanito) finally pushed even Ortiz too far when, for no apparent reason, he elbowed Sammy McIlroy in the head as he ran past, mere feet from where the referee was standing. It was such a blatant piece of off-the-ball foul play that Ortiz had little choice other than to book him, but the cynical fouling on Irish players continued. As Gerry Armstrong remembers, 'I saw Miguel Alonso kicking lumps out of Martin O'Neill near the corner flag, there were a lot of bad challenges between Alexanko and Tendillo and myself and Billy Hamilton. There was a lot of tension, they obviously wanted to win the game and show their superiority in front of their own fans. We were quite a physical side and I think they felt they also had to be physical.'

However, Norman Whiteside recalls that the tactics perhaps backfired a little when they saw that the Irish were equal to the assault being waged. 'By ignoring it we turned the tables on them. When we didn't shy away we sowed doubt in their minds, making them ask, "Who are these lunatics and what are they capable of?"'

In fact, just after Juanito was booked, Whiteside extracted a measure of revenge by going in very hard and late on him. Perhaps showing some signs of immaturity by losing his head, he sought to avenge his team-mate and was fortunate that the referee appeared to have just missed the tackle by following the path of the ball with his eyes. If Whiteside thought that this evened matters up, he was proved wrong as the Spanish simply upped the ante in the next few minutes by hurling themselves into one dangerous tackle after another. McIlroy was again targeted, then Tendillo took out Billy Hamilton from behind. Whiteside was attacked from behind by José Antonio Camacho. The referee let all of these offences go unpunished and the game now risked being derailed by the lack of control.

'The referee was atrocious,' remembers Hamilton. 'The number of fouls that weren't given to us in that game was amazing. It's almost as if the referee was cherry-picked.' McIlroy, too, is damning in his recollection: 'They were shocking. They just wanted to steamroller us. First whistle, they thought, whoosh, let's get into them and some of the tackles they were doing that night were absolutely unbelievable. I've never seen a Spanish team since try to play like that. They tried to unsettle us, but we stood up to them and that rocked them a little bit. We didn't lie down and let them steamroller us because we had too many characters in that team to let that happen.'

As well as the lunging tackles, viewed by those watching around the globe, there was also the unseen and subtle fouling and attempt to injure that had Whiteside most aggrieved: 'When they're nipping you and standing on your ankles, literally putting their studs on your toes … there's nothing worse. It's like breaking your toe. Alexanko and Tendillo were just thugs, absolute thugs, but they got away with it.'

However, Jimmy Nicholl explains today that the Irish players took heart from the Spanish players resorting to such tactics. 'That was a good sign that the pressure had got to them … If they can't beat us with the football, then they're going to try and just physically do something and then it suits us great.'

In the twenty-fifth minute, Satrústegui had another header flash wide, but shortly afterwards, Norman Whiteside found enough space to shoot. It was not a serious scoring chance but there were signs that Northern Ireland were beginning to feel their way into the game. Spain had tried to hit them hard with chance after chance early in the game – and they had certainly been hitting them hard physically – but the Irish had weathered the storm and now looked able to live with the Spanish threat, despite the heat.

However, the risk to both the Irish goal and the Irish bodies was ever present. David McCreery was blatantly fouled by Tente Sánchez; Alonso went in hard on O'Neill; and, after thirty-seven minutes, Alexanko headed just over the bar. In the face of such provocation, it was not long before the Irish began to retaliate, yet only they were punished by the referee. Hamilton was booked for a challenge on Tendillo, but Alexanko got away scot-free for kicking Hamilton in the back of the legs. Soon after, in retaliation for being badly fouled by Enrique Saura, McIlroy lashed out with his boot as his opponent lay on the ground, but it was only the Irishman who went into the referee's book. While McIlroy was clearly in the wrong and had to be booked for taking the law into his own hands, it was hard not to have some sympathy with him. The challenge by Saura had left one of McIlroy's socks round his ankle and he immediately showed the referee his calf, which was displaying a ten-inch mark where the Spanish player had raked his studs into him. However, the referee ignored this evidence and instead booked McIlroy with an ostentatious flourish of the yellow card as he arched his back and dramatically aimed the card into the sky, to the delight of the Spanish fans.

Worse was to come. Almost immediately after the McIlroy booking, David McCreery gathered the ball deep in his own half and embarked upon a speedy and skilful run far into Spanish territory all by himself. With the Spanish defence unable to keep pace with him, only one defender stood between him and a certain shot on goal as he neared the edge of the Spanish penalty area. It was at this moment that the defender, Alexanko, charged into McCreery's left shoulder, making absolutely no attempt to play the ball. McCreery fell to the ground in agony and was left rolling around in some distress. It was a certain free kick in a dangerous area in front of the Spanish goal, and it should have been a guaranteed yellow. Ortiz, however, decided that Alexanko's block didn't merit punishment and that it wasn't even a foul at all. When the ball ended up going out of play, he instead indicated that it should be a corner kick. It was a clear signal that almost any kind of foul on a Northern Irish player would be tolerated.

McCreery smiles today as he recollects the foul, 'I think it was coming up to half-time so I thought to myself I'll just try and run the clock down. For me, going all that distance, it was to take up time. When Alexanko came through on me I think it was really a relief because I don't think I could have gone any further. I was knackered.' Nevertheless, as the half-time whistle blew, Motson summed up the feelings of all Irish fans when he said, 'Some of the challenges really make you wonder what the Spanish players have to do to get sent off. If Spain go any further in this competition, FIFA have to be very careful with the choice of referee for their matches, because a Latin American referee was never going to be sensible.'

Northern Ireland had somehow made it to half-time with their goal intact and without serious injury. However, as well as they had done in keeping the Spanish at bay, they knew that, as things stood, they would still be heading home from the World Cup. Somehow in the second half, they were going to have to start attacking, but this, they knew, would leave them open to the deadly Spanish counterattacking style. For Bingham and the Irish, the dilemma was whether they should risk going forward early and possibly concede or leave it late in the game and always regret that they exited the tournament without giving it their all. With only forty-five minutes separating them from a World Cup departure they had to score, but this was much easier said than done against a talented Spanish team who also seemed able to operate outside the laws of the game without any sanction from the referee.

As the second half began, Northern Ireland seemed, if anything, to be playing even deeper in their own half than ever before. However, this ultimately proved to be an advantage. Gerry Armstrong had come right back to just in front of his own defence to help out and it was at this moment that the world changed for every Irishman on the pitch, in the stadium, or following on TV around the world. Enthusiastically involving himself in defensive duties, Armstrong stretched out his leg to its full limit to intercept a Spanish pass. When he had regained his balance, with the ball still at his feet, he looked up to see the immediate path ahead of him free all the way into midfield and he took off.

He realised that he could push deep into Spanish territory, with Alonso the only threat to his advance. He managed to race beyond Alonso, who tried to trip up the Irishman long after the ball had gone. Fortunately, this blatant attempt at a foul failed to make enough connection and Armstrong now had time and space. Meanwhile, Hamilton and Whiteside were both sprinting up the pitch on opposite wings. Bingham had drilled into his men that this match was about taking their chances, so they knew that Armstrong had to be provided with as much support on his run as possible. Every attack that played out might be their best chance to grab the victory they required.

Armstrong now faced three Spanish defenders and found himself being pushed slightly out to the right. There was nothing more he could do at this point other than release the ball to Hamilton on the right wing and try to make himself available again in the centre. Hamilton took up the running and Tendillo, another of the serial offenders throughout the match, made little effort to go for the ball and instead merely tried to block off Hamilton's run with his body. Hamilton reached out with his left arm and, as if swatting an annoying pest, firmly brushed Tendillo aside, leaving him stumbling, his obvious attempt at a tactical foul having failed. Hamilton was now in space himself and able to carry the ball down towards the byline before whipping the ball into the penalty box.

The cross from Hamilton was of good quality and into a space that tempted the Spanish goalkeeper, Luis Arconada, at that time considered to be the world's finest and also his country's captain that night. It was just close enough to his line to make him consider coming out to deal with any danger directly. Unfortunately for him, it was also just slightly too far out for him to cleanly claim the ball. It was a huge error on his part. To begin with, Armstrong hadn't followed far enough into the penalty box to meet the cross. Secondly, there were two Spanish defenders waiting beyond Arconada who could easily have trapped the ball and played it out, or kicked it back up the pitch. Arconada panicked, went for the ball, couldn't quite do enough to control it and, as he fell to the ground, palmed the ball slightly back towards the penalty spot. Armstrong was waiting.

Now there was clear and present danger for the Spanish. Arconada desperately tried to get back to his feet and spread his body in front of Armstrong as the two defenders frantically attempted to get behind him to help cover more of the goalmouth. Armstrong gave them little time to get into position, and hit the ball first time as it reached his feet, gratefully accepting the present from Arconada. The shot sailed between the legs of the despairing goalkeeper and the defender directly behind him was left standing on one leg as he vainly tried to anticipate the flight of the ball by lifting his other to block it. He had guessed wrong, and the ball would have gone between his legs as well if he had kept two feet on the ground. Instead, it sailed just millimetres past his standing leg and into the net as the impossible became reality.

Silence.

The unceasing wall of noise from the fanatical Spanish support was turned off as if by flicking a switch. At the other end of the ground a tiny pocket of supporters erupted in joy, but even their combined clamour appeared like a deadly hush compared with the cacophony of Spanish drumming and shouting just seconds earlier. The stillness of the night was both instant and disconcerting.

'When I hit the ball into the back of the net all I could hear was a sudden silence,' remembers Armstrong. 'I thought something had gone wrong and the referee had disallowed it. Then I heard Norman yelling, "Gerry, Gerry, it's a goal!" Then it sank in.' Whiteside, too, recalls the moment of jubilation, 'I was thrilled, but if you watch the match now, you'll get a sense of how exhausted we must have been because we were only forty-seven minutes into the match and none of us had the energy to sprint towards the hero. We were in shock as much as anyone in the ground.'

It was an incredible twist in the night's script. As things stood, Northern Ireland would now win the group. Spain would still go through in second place, but it would be into the difficult England/West Germany group and they also knew that defeat against the minnows of Northern Ireland, in a stadium they had deliberately made their base for the last year, would see them shredded by the Spanish press and fans alike. Northern Ireland may have taken the lead, but Spain would now throw everything against them to avoid the ignominy they were facing. There were forty-three minutes remaining in the match and, as Irishmen and supporters everywhere settled down after celebrating the goal, the reality of the nervous torment they now faced for the remainder of the game would have sunk in.

Unfortunately, Northern Ireland suffered an almost instant setback when they found they would have to see themselves through almost an entire half of the match without one of their most dependable and experienced performers. Sammy McIlroy, who had been badly hurt during the altercation that led to his booking just before half-time, was in trouble with his movement. As he recalls, 'Jimmy McGregor, who was the physio at the time, had said to me, "Oh dear," because I had two horrific stud marks from the top of my calf to the bottom. Jimmy said, "You're going to struggle here, because it is going to stiffen and swell," – which it did. Once we scored, I had to come off because I could hardly put my foot on the ground.'

Tommy Cassidy came on to take McIlroy's place and Jimmy Nicholl describes having to 'get the football head back on,' as the Irish prepared to execute the next stage of the game plan Bingham had drilled into them so well.

The next real chance for the Spanish came in the fifty-third minute, when Ufarte was again denied by Jennings. Sixteen yards from goal he saw his effort comfortably gathered by the goalkeeper. Northern Ireland were holding on for now, but all ten of the Spanish outfield players were operating inside the Irish half as Northern Ireland set themselves up for a backs-to-the-wall battle to hold on to their precious lead. Armstrong, who had already shown great willingness to pull back and do his fair share of defending in the first half now seemed to hurl himself into the fray. Perhaps buoyed by the confidence of the most important goal of his career, he slid around the midfield making one telling tackle after another. Jimmy Hill was already fulsome in his praise for how the team were holding the Spanish off when he said, 'They deserve everything they've got. They ignored the fouls against them, ignored the danger, ignored the pain and carried on with resolution. Perhaps they don't have the class, but they have all the will in the world to run for their country.'

Still, the flow of violent play continued against the Irish with the Spaniards perhaps now taking their frustration out on those who had had the audacity to score against them. There can be little other explanation for Alexanko who, as the ball evaded him in midfield, turned round and aimed a kick at Chris Nicholl's departing form. It was a straight red card offence, and the referee wasn't too far away. However, once more, nothing at all was given. Possibly, as with the Whiteside incident, the referee's eyes had been diverted by the path of the ball, which was moving away from Alexanko, but he had no problem penalising Armstrong with a free kick seconds later for a high boot, despite the fact that his foot had been raised to the exact same height as his Spanish opponent. Spain were rewarded with a free kick on the edge of the Irish box and then disaster struck.

Following the Spanish free kick, Mal Donaghy and Camacho had tussled on the touchline over on the far side of the pitch. Camacho had made contact with Donaghy who then overreacted by angrily shoving the Spaniard in the shoulder. It appeared to be a 'nothing' situation, and any sensible referee would simply have given the two players involved a ticking off, warn them that they risked going into the book if it happened again, or, at very worst, book one or both of them on the spot. And at first it looked as though nothing at all would happen other than a Spanish throw-in, and Donaghy simply retreated back towards his goalmouth to take up a defensive position. But Ortiz pulled out his red card and sent him off. No punishment at all, not even a talking to, was deemed necessary for Camacho. It was the kind of favourable decision for Spain the Irish had feared before the game, and anyone who had been baffled by Ortiz's decisions in the first half would have been left flabbergasted by this latest ruling.

Hill on the BBC was outraged. 'If I were Camacho, I wouldn't be able to sleep tonight, my conscience wouldn't allow it. We've only seen the incident once, but it looked to me like he created all the disturbance. Camacho got away with it and Ireland are up against it.' Bingham was distraught beside the Northern Ireland dugout – the enormity of having to face a Spanish onslaught with only ten men clearly sinking in. As the crestfallen Donaghy trooped off the pitch, Bingham seemed to be asking him to explain what had happened. What had he done? But the reality is that Donaghy had done very little. His push on Camacho had perhaps been ill-advised – it had been well drilled into the team that the Spanish would look for every possible opportunity to fashion decisions against them – but it should never have been a red card. He had simply given the Spanish the opportunity they craved.

The assault upon McCreery in the first half hadn't even been considered a foul let alone a card-worthy offence; Alexanko had escaped what should have been a red card just one minute earlier but Donaghy had been sent from the pitch for almost nothing at all. As Billy Bingham reflects today, 'I was so sorry for Mal because he was a decent player. He wasn't a dirty player, meaning that he didn't put the boot in as they say. He was a fair player and tackled hard but fair with people. Unfortunately, it turned against him.'

But how had it happened? What made Donaghy over-react and what convinced Ortiz that it was worthy of a red card? Televised football at the time provided little in the way of replays. Every free kick decision today is analysed by replaying the action in slow motion from many alternative angles in close-up. Watching a complete version of this match, however, shows that the Spanish TV producers had provided only one replay in the entire match so far – and that was for the Northern Ireland goal.

None of the contentious decisions were shown again. However, by slowing down the footage and watching it frame by frame we get to see the whole picture of what took place. Camacho throws himself in front of Donaghy to shield the ball and let it go out of play and the two almost collide with the advertising boards around the side of the pitch. As Camacho bounces back and finds his balance, he brings down his boot in an attempt to stamp his studs into Donaghy's foot, something that no one watching at home in 1982 would have noticed.

Incensed by this underhanded attempt to injure him, Donaghy lashes out, but shoving someone in the shoulder can still hardly be considered worthy of a red card. Again, watching frame by frame as Donaghy does the sensible thing and removes himself from the conflict, we then see Camacho holding out his hands in innocence and turning to the linesman as if to say, 'Did you see that?' He is seen mouthing repeatedly, making a complaint to the linesman who hadn't sought to take any action when the altercation took place but now, based entirely on Camacho's complaints, suddenly decides to raise his flag and bring the referee over. The linesman was another Spanish-speaking Latin American, Enrique Labo Revoredo from Peru. Ortiz consults with him briefly and then, to everyone's amazement, immediately brandishes the red card to Donaghy. What Camacho said to Revoredo is unknown, but it clearly had its intended impact.

Jimmy Nicholl describes the added pressure the players were now under. 'You've got to watch it because you're so frustrated now with the refereeing decision. It's hard enough without that going against you. You've got to watch now that every single decision that goes against you, you don't lose the head and get frustrated with the referee because you've got to concentrate on your job, and if you're not concentrating on your job and you're getting frustrated with the referee then it's all going to come apart.' However, for John McClelland, the sending off induced a strange sense of relief, 'I always knew something would happen.

When Mal was sent off, I relaxed then because I thought, that's the thing that was going to happen, the pressure to help the home team … If he'd given a penalty, it's a goal, whereas if he sends someone off and we're down to ten men we can live with that.' It was an opinion shared by O'Neill, who explains, 'The only consolation I drew then was that I knew it would have to be an absolute genuine penalty, somebody would have to be brought down by us, for the referee to award it against us. Not that I wanted Mal Donaghy sent off. Far from it. It was ridiculous that he was sent off. But I knew it would have to be a genuine penalty because of the injustice.'

Faced with a defensive hole, Bingham now instructed David McCreery to drop back into the left back position, and any attempt at scoring further goals would be limited to taking their chances on the break as Armstrong dropped even deeper to help. This restored the number of men available for defensive duties but also meant that there was little outlet up the pitch to take pressure off the defence. Northern Ireland now set themselves up as a barricade to Spanish attacks.

The permutations of the group also meant that if Northern Ireland did somehow manage to score a second goal then Spain would actually be knocked out on goal difference by Yugoslavia. This was not going to be an arranged result like the West Germany-Austria game from earlier in the day, though. Spain knew that the best way to avoid losing 2–0 was to draw back level at 1–1, or to go on and win the game.

Incredibly, it looked for a second as though Northern Ireland might just get that second goal. In a rare venture from their half, Hamilton was hacked down by Tendillo as he ran with the ball. From the resulting free kick Hamilton then headed over the bar. It was also at this stage that frustrated Spanish fans began to hurl oranges at Jennings' net as they became increasingly horrified at the indignity of losing. The tension ratcheted up ever further inside the stadium and as the Spanish substitute Enrique 'Quini'

González blazed a great chance over the bar from just ten yards out, Jimmy Hill made an appeal to those watching at home, 'If you find that your next-door neighbours have not got their set on, do them a favour and tell them to switch it on because this last twenty minutes is going to be exhilarating. Ten Northern Ireland players, all of them heroes, are holding out against the Spaniards to get through to the last stages. It's wonderful to look at, and let's hope they do it.'

Northern Ireland now made their second and final substitution as the experienced defensive veteran, Sammy Nelson, came on to win his fiftieth cap, a huge milestone at that time with a small and select membership. The player making way was Norman Whiteside. He had played heroically, his age almost hard to believe. In only his fourth start as a professional footballer, he had refused to be intimidated by a skilful and highly physical Spanish opposition and he had more than held his own, but a fresh pair of legs was needed for the all-important home straight of the match. With Nelson being a left back, it was natural to assume that he was being introduced as a replacement for the departed Donaghy, who played in that position. Certainly, that's how it was reported in the press at the time. However, watching the match footage shows that Nelson was actually a straight swap for Whiteside in midfield and that McCreery continued to occupy the fullback role. Quite simply, McCreery, who had been a constant harrier of the Spanish midfield throughout the match, was now playing one of the best games of his career in defence. His ceaseless running and tackling was so successful that Bingham saw no reason to replace him, even with someone who normally played in that position.

Despite the obvious tension with so much at stake, this was exactly the position Northern Ireland had always hoped to find themselves in. Two years of Bingham's philosophy and preaching of work ethic and players interchanging positions to always leave a solid line of defence were now being acted out. Spain were unfortunate enough to be faced with one of the most resolute defences in the competition. As McClelland explains. 'It's like in the playground, you kick the ball away and they just come at you again, attack versus defence. We just stood there and took it all. We're organised. You're going to have to do something special to get past us. And they were panicking as the Spanish crowd were putting more and more pressure on them. You could feel the frustration of the crowd getting to the Spanish players and that's why they kick you. That's why they get agitated – frustration. It was very calm for us. It was organised because they weren't penetrating us. Kick it out, pass it when we can, kick it down, just wait but don't lose that shape. That's what Billy was good at organising us to do.'

As Northern Ireland stood firm and maintained their defensive structure, the seconds ticked down, but agonisingly slowly for the players and their fans. 'That was one of the first grounds I'd played in with an electronic clock on it,' remembers Billy Hamilton. 'I looked up and thought, this must be near time and it said thirty-five minutes, another ten minutes to go. I thought I looked up five minutes later, but it was still thirty-five. The last ten minutes were painstakingly slow to go through.' As the game now moved inside these final ten minutes, Gordillo let loose with a shot but it was a comfortable save for Jennings as it was hit straight towards him. A minute later there was a real scare as Quini just failed to connect with a cross into the box. However, the ball travelled beyond him to Saura at the back post who somehow messed up the chance. No replays were shown at the time, but watching the footage slowly shows just how Saura managed to miss such a glorious opportunity – David McCreery was sticking to him like glue and getting in an important touch on the ball to deny him what would have been a great goal scoring chance.

Quini then headed badly wide from another cross. In the eighty-third minute there was another chance for Gordillo but again he failed to sufficiently test Jennings and the Irish goalkeeper made the save. The eighty-fifth minute saw Juanito dangerously weave his way into the Irish penalty area but Martin O'Neill was alert to the danger and managed to put the ball out for a corner. From that corner, Alexanko then headed wide.

As the clock ticked down to just four minutes to go, Motson gave a very honest summation, 'Nobody thought they would make it through, except perhaps the Irish themselves, and their belief has come through so strongly.' In the eighty-eighth minute Camacho attempted a long range shot but it was straight at Jennings again and there was now an air of desperation about the Spanish attempts. As Hamilton observes, 'The game went more or less to plan for us. Bingy said, "Don't let the Spaniards get within our eighteen-yard box. Try and restrict them to shooting from the eighteen-yard box and Big Pat will deal with everything that comes from out there."'

Now on the bench, Sammy McIlroy could no longer influence the proceedings, but he remembers, 'We had a solid back four. All experienced people. We were quite comfortable. Okay, there were a few scary moments, which you're going to have, but with big Pat in goal that gave us fantastic confidence. He was cool as a cucumber. He never used to get excited. We had plenty of faith in him.'

At this late stage, the possibility of defeat was beginning to fade for the Irish but to even concede one goal after having held on so bravely would be heartbreaking for the players and could possibly serve up the ultimate in hard-luck stories – going out of the tournament by drawing lots. There could be no lapse in concentration now. The full ninety minutes were now up but these were the days before officials held up boards informing the crowd and players how many extra minutes would be played for stoppages. How long would Ortiz grant the Spanish in their efforts to score and finish top of the group? With the Spanish now ready to try anything to salvage a result, Northern Ireland managed to get the ball up the pitch and were able to run down the clock yet further. Amazingly, with the ball down in the Spaniard's own corner, Martin O'Neill started playing 'keepy-up' with the ball to further frustrate the Spanish as they saw their last precious seconds dwindling away.

The captain, however, had a better plan than merely retaining possession up the field. As he explains today, 'I was hoping, because we were running out of time and Spain were getting so frustrated, genuinely, that the fellow would come over and sweep me into the stand so that we'd get a free kick there and we could take up some time. That was the reason for it. No one wants to be tackled that brutally, but I wanted to be taken out of the game so that we could take our time over the free kick. I thought the guy would think, "That's a bit arrogant," and come and hit me. You like to think that, with it being a World Cup, someone out there somewhere in the ether would think, that's a nice bit of skill. But that wasn't my intention. It was hopefully getting fouled up there and somebody coming in and cleaving me!'

Once Spain managed to win the ball back, and with the final whistle expected any second, in desperation Alonso pumped a hopeful ball into the Northern Ireland box. It bounced high and Pat Jennings, who had come forward off his line, was deceived by the height and began to backtrack quickly. The ball was heading into the top corner of the Irish goal. 'I don't need any replays to remember that,' says O'Neill. 'I absolutely remember that like it was half an hour ago. My heart was in my mouth as the ball was bouncing, I was saying "Pat, c'mon, c'mon, c'mon, come out and deal with it." It was frightening.' As millions of viewers throughout the British Isles covered their eyes and gasped in horror, Jennings somehow got himself back and managed to tip it up into the air as Juanito bore down on him in the goalmouth. As the ball fell, Jennings rebalanced himself and got in position to make the all-important catch, his finest moment in the match, just as Spain looked likely to equalise with almost the final kick.

The moment has become almost as famous as Armstrong's goal and Jennings recalls today, 'I was never getting up to the first bounce. I couldn't have made it from where I was. They would have got to it before I got to it, but I knew once it bounced and it got in the air that I was going to get there. I was frightened then that if I collided with their player that maybe the referee might give a penalty against me, so I literally knocked it over the top of him and picked it up on the other side. There was no panic on my part. I knew exactly what I had to do.'

Surprisingly, the referee awarded Jennings a free kick, calling a foul from Juanito – though few would be confident that he would have made the same decision if the ball had gone into the net. But this had been Spain's last attempt and the referee blew to signal the end of the game.

Northern Ireland had achieved the impossible dream, winning the group into the bargain, and one small corner of the stadium now erupted into wild delight. The Northern Ireland subs and management, unable to contain their own feelings of relief and joy, ran on to the pitch to embrace the heroes who had given their all. As Norman Whiteside recalls, none moved faster than the old speedy winger from the 1958 campaign, now manager, Billy Bingham. 'Even though I enjoyed a thirty-four-year age advantage over Billy Bingham, our manager still beat me to Gerry. The picture of the two of them hugging became the definitive image of the win, a victory which Northern Ireland fans cherish as our greatest achievement, our '66.'

The players basked in their glory, probably still only half-daring to believe that it was true. Jennings had been commanding throughout the game, a calming influence among his defence in a match that called for cool tempers and nerves of steel. He would later recollect, 'I've never been as proud to be a member of any side than I was at that moment. No words can really convey my feelings. It wasn't just national pride. It was a sense of belonging, of being part of something special. Nothing in soccer has given me greater satisfaction than victory in Valencia. I didn't want to leave the pitch when it was all over.'

With the Spanish fans whistling and booing the performance of their own team, the Irish now advanced upon their pocket of supporters to celebrate with them. Bingham even allegedly invited them back to the hotel to continue the revelries. As Paul Vance recalls, 'We climbed on the fence extending hands across to shake. Most of the Spanish left promptly on the final whistle, but plenty stayed to applaud the efforts of the Irish. Exhaustion and jubilation all around. Players, fans, coaching staff – completely drained. I was more intoxicated on the Valencia air that night than any amount of alcohol could ever do.'

Bingham was almost lost for words when interviewed after the match. 'What can I say? It is absolutely fantastic. The decisions by the referee were quite harsh against us, there was a lot of physical contact and the referee seemed to take it out on us, but we did marvellously well, particularly when we were down to ten men … They killed the Spanish bull in its own ring!'

The memory of the game is still fresh for Hamilton today. 'We had the belief that on our day we could beat anybody. If everybody did their job and the organisation was one hundred per cent, we could beat anybody. The only thing was we had to go that goal in front. If we went a goal behind, we weren't going to do it … It was an all-or-nothing game – if we didn't give our all we'd get nothing. And everyone did give their all. It was probably one of the proudest performances I ever had … Billy Bingham must have been really proud because I've been a manager as well and if you get a team giving that much for their country and their manager you can't ask for anything more.'

The team finally left the field after drinking up every last drop of atmosphere, and Jimmy Nicholl, a player who had been at the top of the game for a long time when he had played with Manchester United, summed up his feelings by saying, 'You can forget your FA Cup finals, your league titles. There was twice as much happiness and euphoria in our dressing room after that game than I have ever seen before.'

Gerry Armstrong and Tommy Cassidy, who had played most of the second half, had to wait for their post-match celebrations as they had been taken, immediately after the game, to provide urine samples for a drugs test. This was a routine formality for the players, but it was one test that Cassidy will never forget: 'We were both so dehydrated that it took us an hour and a half to give a sample. We were sat under armed guards, next to FIFA doctors and officials, and it was just so funny that it took us so long. We simply couldn't pee! We tried and tried, drinking water, lager and even wine to help us. Gerry drank so much alcohol that he was a little bit drunk. He was singing "Danny Boy" and all sorts. It was hilarious — even one of the guards began to sway to his singing. That will stick with me forever.'

It was in the early hours of the morning when the two players finally managed to provide a sample, and they found the rest of the team waiting for them, in a scene reminiscent of the night Northern Ireland had qualified for the 1958 World Cup quarter-finals. Back then, the team had waited into the small hours on their heroic goalkeeper, Norman Uprichard, coming back from hospital with his arm in plaster before making the journey back across Sweden to the team hotel. Now they had been similarly delayed with their celebrations, but they would make up for lost time.

As the team coach made its way through the streets of Valencia, which had seen furious Spanish fans burning a huge World Cup public art installation, the players were cheered by crowds gathering on corners as Irish fans danced and jumped into fountains. When they arrived back at the hotel and emerged from the coach, Jimmy Hill was waiting to greet them with champagne. Bingham insisted on opening up the venue to any of the waiting fans who wanted to join them – even going out and opening the gates to the complex himself. The players had worked hard and now it was time to party. They would not be partying alone. Hamilton warmly recalls the scene, 'By the time we got back, there must have been three hundred supporters around our hotel. The atmosphere was great. Some of them were able to get in, some of them didn't, but it was straight down to the bar and everybody having a laugh and a joke. It was a sort of surreal situation. It took a while, and God knows how many beers, but it was still only slowly sinking in what we'd done ... we'd qualified for the quarter-finals of the World Cup.'

Some of the players made phone calls back home and the sense of achievement became even greater when they heard of the reaction in Northern Ireland. Norman Whiteside was told that the nation had erupted in spontaneous celebration and people were dancing outside in the streets. Even Simon and Garfunkel, who were performing in Dublin that night on a reunion tour, got in on the act and dedicated a rendition of 'The Boxer' to 'yer men' when they heard the news of an Irish victory. Martin O'Neill jokes, 'There was a famous story of Malcolm Brodie reporting back to the fellow on the desk late at night at the *Belfast Telegraph*: "Take this report down." "All right, Malcolm, I'm ready to go." Malcolm says, "Magnifico! Magnifico! Magnifico!" and the man on the desk says, "Stop there, Malcolm, I heard you the first time."'

Back in Valencia the party got into full swing and Felix Healy grabbed a microphone to start the singing. Armstrong, understandably, was the centre of attention and was in ebullient form – so much so that all his wise-cracking inspired Sammy Nelson to give him the nickname 'Don Quick-Quote'.

But as the champagne flowed, one of the heroes, young Norman Whiteside, technically wasn't of legal drinking age. 'Yeah, the boys had a few beers that night,' he recalls. 'I believe so, because I was only seventeen, I didn't partake,' he says with a knowing and cheeky grin. 'I had to watch them get drunk. The

Spanish press gave us a kind of ugly press … they had a go at us about partying and drinking and everything else. But why not? Why wouldn't you celebrate? Billy was good. "Go and enjoy yourself, boys, and have a few days off."

Sammy McIlroy recounts how the local journalists continued to tarnish them, 'In the hotel, we're having a drink and the press were picking empty bottles up off other tables and putting them on our tables. And then next day in the paper, [there was a] massive photograph that Spain were beaten by this team who liked to drink. The photograph was of us surrounded by these bottles of beer. They could not believe that Northern Ireland beat Spain. I'll never forget that and that made the victory so much sweeter. They just could not believe that their team had been beaten by a so-called team of boozers.'

The party continued right through the night to dawn on Saturday and beyond, with many of the players moving straight on to breakfast, but if ever an Irish team had earned it, they had. Jimmy Nicholl laughs as he remembers suggesting, 'Aye, breakfast on Sunday, maybe!' Martin O'Neill would later describe it as, 'One of the most memorable nights in my life, where we shared great moments with the Northern Ireland supporters. In fact, there were about thirty-five in my bedroom at half past three in the morning.' For Gerry Armstrong, the morning after the night before provided one of his most abiding memories in football, 'I remember sitting on the balcony, listening to Malcolm Brodie typing. Pat Jennings said to me, "What a night. You don't get many nights like this in football. This is special." Then we ordered our tea and toast and sat watching the sun coming up.'

Norman Whiteside's brother Ken partied with the team into the wee hours. He had phoned his employers pretending to be sick in order to travel to Spain and support his brother but, thanks to the press coverage of the match and the morning after, had some awkward questions to answer upon his return to Belfast. 'I think it was Ulster TV who said, "Would you do a little piece?",' Whiteside recalls. 'Me and my brother walking up and down on the beach. He's supposed to be ill at home. The whole of Ulster TV have just seen him with his brown tan. I think that was a little bit of a giveaway!'

It's perhaps best to let Pat Jennings finish the tale of the epic victory in Valencia. The Spanish press had continued to give the Irish a hard time over insinuations that they were too fond of their alcohol and were not taking the World Cup seriously enough. Jennings recalls, 'When the Spanish reporters turned up at the hotel after our 1–0 win, one of our lads took them gently aside and said, "Just imagine what the score would have been if we'd stayed sober."'

AUSTRIA

Northern Ireland's success against Spain had shocked the football world, but none was as stunned as the IFA. The Irish administrators were clearly surprised, and as a result, were rather underprepared for the second phase of the tournament.

During the celebrations after their famous victory the players discovered the full extent of the IFA's lack of faith. Gerry Armstrong remembers, 'We were all partying and Billy Bingham was loving it and then, about one in the morning, I saw his face turning … He got us all together and he said, "You won't believe this. I've just spoken to Billy Drennan. He told me he's booked our flights for tomorrow to go back to London. He didn't think we would win … The even worse part is we haven't got a hotel in Madrid. He didn't book a hotel for us." That's the sort of stuff the Irish FA did in those days. So, we ended up having a shit hotel on the runway at Madrid airport because we didn't plan it properly. Billy Bingham was livid because he was very professional. He hated it.'

It seems that no lessons had been learned from the disastrous lack of preparation for the 1958 quarter-finals. Back then, the IFA had also neglected to plan for Northern Ireland's progression past the group stage and they, too, had lost their almost-perfect base. Instead, the team were undone by arduous coach journeys that did nothing at all to help them prepare for their final two matches, including the sad dénouement against France. The IFA secretary in 1958 was, as in 1982, Billy Drennan.

While the IFA may have complained that they were forced to take their accommodation for the second phase in 1982 from a list sanctioned by the official travel organisation for the tournament, it's hard to imagine that any of the top teams would have left anything to chance. Permutations of finishing spots in the group tables would have been analysed to forecast the likely venues for their quarter-final matches. Not so with Northern Ireland, and the players' efforts were once more undermined by the sloppiness of their officials. As Billy Bingham reminded the *Irish Times*, 'I helped to fix up the hotel we used in Valencia. But it was up to the IFA to sort out hotels for the second round.'

What is particularly unforgivable is that both potential scenarios that had Northern Ireland qualifying from the group phase had them playing their next two games in Madrid. If they won the group, as they did, their quarter-final group games would be played at the Estadio Vicente Calderón, the home ground of Atlético Madrid. If they had finished second (and had to face West Germany and England), they would have played their games at the Estadio Santiago Bernabéu, home of Real Madrid. Playing in Madrid was the only possible outcome for progressing to the quarter-finals – something which would have been known since the draw in January – so it's simply unthinkable that the IFA instead had left things to chance.

The hotel in question, the Alameda, was right beside an airport and was therefore noticeably light on the kind of amenities that athletes might require. While other teams had hotels with training facilities within the hotel complex, not to mention swimming pools, tennis courts and the like, the Irish were forced to train at local public parks and had nothing at the hotel to help them relax. As Bingham told the *Newsletter*. 'We were led to believe this hotel had a beautiful garden and pool, plus a games room. But there is no garden, no games room and the pool is a dark indoor dungeon.' Pat Jennings explained, 'The windows were treble glazed, to keep out the noise of passing aircraft, and everywhere was darkened to combat the stifling heat. It seemed like the middle of the night all the time.'

Malcolm Brodie was a little more upbeat about the hotel, but in a withering piece in the *Belfast Telegraph* he said, 'The hotel itself is all right, the food good, but the surroundings are dismal … Such a situation should not have been allowed to arise. Its root cause I think is that nobody, including officials, expected Northern Ireland to reach the quarter-finals.'

Jennings was in absolutely no doubt as to where the blame lay: 'Officials from the other countries had sent representatives to the Spanish capital a few months in advance to inspect the hotels allocated by ruling body FIFA and state their preference. Northern Ireland hadn't bothered – so we ended up with the last one on the list.' Bingham was quoted in the *Belfast Telegraph*, recounting how Ron Greenwood, the English manager, had told him that they had been given a choice of six hotels by FIFA and, after inspecting them, they thought this was the worst and had avoided it as a result.

Drennan tried to defend the situation in the press, yet only managed to confirm the allegations of negligence, 'They told us Alameda was the best hotel and we took it.' It's clear then that, while the other nations put feet on the ground to check that everything was as they required, the IFA took what it was given sight unseen. It's not hard to imagine FIFA being relieved when Drennan consented to take the hotel that all the other teams had turned down after spinning to him that it was 'the best'.

Bingham was very alert to how disastrous the choice of hotel could be to all his preparations for the upcoming matches, 'The surroundings are not conducive to keeping players here for a week. The morale would be very low.' The press reported that he toured Madrid in a car until one o'clock in the morning, trying to find alternative accommodation. 'It was a priority move and I think we have found a place. Now it's up to the officials to make the arrangements if at all possible. We want to get out of here.'

Among the Northern Ireland party was, of course, IFA President, Harry Cavan (also vice president of FIFA), and one would think that, in this matter, the team could count on his support. While he had launched an unconvincing defence of the IFA in the press, seemingly surprised by the reaction from Bingham and the players, he assured everyone that he was working behind the scenes, 'I doubt whether any other country could take this matter as high as I have done. If there are any concessions to be obtained, we can get them.'

Unfortunately, word soon came back that FIFA had refused the switch of hotels due to 'security concerns' and the IFA was told that no move could be authorised, not even for the team of its vice president. The idea that training in public areas was less of a security concern to the team than moving to private facilities seems slightly unconvincing and illogical, but it was now clear that the Irish would just have to sleep in the bed their administrators had made for them. As Bingham said, 'We'll just have to accept it and get on with the job.'

Ironically, Northern Ireland were not the only ones put out by FIFA's decision. The Yugoslavians had been so confident that they would progress to the next stage – that Northern Ireland wouldn't gain the required victory over Spain to knock them out – that they had gone ahead and booked into the Alameda hotel, only to find that they now had to vacate the premises. As Billy Hamilton recounts, 'We couldn't get into our room because the Yugoslavs were in there. We had to wait for them to move out before we could move in.' Whiteside adds, 'We literally passed them on the stairs.'

While the hotel situation was bad enough, there are also other elements of the preparations that show conclusively that the IFA administrators had not believed Northern Ireland would progress beyond the first stage and that they had made no preparations at all. Most damning, not to mention embarrassing, was the revelation that the IFA had to contact the kit manufacturer, Adidas, to get the famous green kit sent out to Spain for the second phase. The IFA had only brought the white away kit required for playing the first three games, with no consideration that the green kit might be required later in the tournament.

The format for the quarter-finals of the 1982 World Cup will strike modern fans as being slightly bizarre. Instead of the final eight teams battling it out in four head-to-head knock-out matches, the tournament pitched the final twelve teams into four groups of three, with each team playing two games – one against each of the other teams they had been grouped with.

In the 1974 and 1978 World Cups there had been two groups of four teams for the secondary phase, providing two group winners who contested the final. In 1982, however, the tournament had been enlarged from sixteen to twenty-four teams and, as the top two from each first-stage group would progress, this now meant twelve teams would go through rather than eight. To continue the practice of having four-team groups in the second phase would have meant there were three groups – this would have led to a complicated scenario of having three winners and the best second-placed team go forward to the semi-finals.

Instead, FIFA decided to opt for four groups of three, and the winner from each group would go through. It was to make for a strange set up, in which one team in each group would play their two games first, then sit back and watch the other two nations compete in the final game, with their fate potentially out of their hands.

Northern Ireland were to face France (in an echo of 1958) and Austria – teams that were not short on star players. The good news was that Austria and France would face off in the first game, meaning that the Irish would control their own fate for the final two games in the group. The downside to this was that the French team would have a longer period to recuperate before playing the final match against Northern Ireland.

Bingham was upbeat about the Irish prospects, telling the press, 'I honestly believe we can get to the semi-finals. If I had met France and Austria in the first phase I would be quite happy. They play European-type football and we can take them all right.' The opening game would also give Bingham the opportunity to check out the current form of the two group rivals.

Austria played France on 28 June – a match in which the Austrian team seemed unable to lift itself from the mood of their torpid defeat against West Germany in Gijón. It's possible that they suffered mentally from the tremendous outpouring of criticism from around the footballing world after that sham game, but they were a changed team from the one that had started the tournament brightly with two straight victories. They were lethargic against France, who were still missing their guiding light, Michel Platini, due to injury. Austria had thrown away all their forward momentum in the final group game, under highly suspicious circumstances, and were now unable to regain it when they needed it most. Speaking in the *Irish News*, John McClelland stated, 'Austria looked as if they could not be bothered, as if they wanted to go home already. If that is the case, we will be delighted to help them on to the plane.'

The game was unremarkable and ended in a 1–0 win for

France but the talking point – and danger – for Northern Ireland was not the lack of threat from Austria but the sensational thirty-ninth minute goal from Bernard Genghini. The twenty-five-yard free kick rocket into the top corner of the net suggested that Platini was not the only talent in the French team.

Preparation for the game against Austria brought a mixture of boredom and trouble for the Northern Ireland squad, both as a direct consequence of the choice of hotel. With no pool facilities, limited outdoor recreation, and a limit on how much sunbathing the players were permitted each day, the team would be at a loose end after training. Some of the players discovered a way up to the roof and, with nothing else to do, and a desire to extend the time they enjoyed in the sunshine, they would often go there to illicitly continue to lounge in the sun out of sight. Obviously, the West German team had been given similar sunbathing restrictions, as the Irish spotted them on the roof of their, much better, nearby hotel engaged in the same activity. The two teams would wave to each other from their respective roofs. Unfortunately, Bingham soon got word of what was going on and made a trip to the roof to evict his players.

The real trouble came from having to train in public areas. At first this was a good opportunity to mix with the locals and generate some goodwill, just as the squad had famously done in Sweden in 1958. It soon backfired. Some local children had been playing around with some of the balls kicked astray during training and one boy in particular seemed reluctant to give the ball back when John O'Neill asked for it. With a bit of cheek emanating from the youth, O'Neill moved as if to kick a ball at him – a nudge to suggest he'd better quickly give back what he had taken. However, this empty threat was reported back to the pitch-side adults, who then launched an angry invasion of the training area, squaring up for a fight. Although the storm was quickly calmed and tempers soothed, with Bingham deciding that perhaps it would be best to wind up training for the day, the events were unfortunately captured by a camera crew.

Jennings himself has written about the altercation. 'None of the players gave the affair another thought, so it was annoying to learn later it had been shown on television all over Europe. It was a classic case of making a mountain out of a molehill, but it was one of those things that could have been avoided if the Northern Ireland party had been in a more suitable hotel.' It ended up being something of a PR disaster. Spain in 1982 was a different arena to Sweden in 1958 and, thanks to the Falklands conflict, the public weren't well disposed towards the British teams. The lack of security around the pitchside that led to this incident is also strange, considering that security was FIFA's stated reason for not allowing Northern Ireland to switch to a new hotel with private facilities.

With preparations far from ideal, Northern Ireland at least knew that their squad was more or less intact for the match. Sammy McIlroy had injury concerns with the bruised and gashed calf he suffered against Spain, and David McCreery had a minor worry with his shoulder - in the event, both pulled through without any concern. The only predicted change was one enforced by suspension: Mal Donaghy had to sit the game out after his red card, though Sammy Nelson was an able and experienced replacement. Northern Ireland knew they would be at a disadvantage in having to play the final game against France with less recovery time, but the upside was that they had enjoyed a longer period than the Austrians before their first second phase game.

For Northern Ireland's opponents this was now the last chance saloon. The tame defeat against the French meant that Austria could now only qualify by beating Northern Ireland – preferably by a large number of goals – and then also hope that Northern Ireland beat France in the final game by a narrow margin. It seemed a forlorn hope, but their manager, Georg Schmidt, was determined to at least go down fighting for the cause, and he implemented some eyebrow-raising changes to the team in the hope of instilling a greater passion than that on show against France. Chief amongst these was the surprise omission of Hans Krankl, the superstar of Austrian football. He had played for footballing giants Barcelona until the previous year and so was also extremely familiar with the Spanish stadiums, climate and general footballing culture. His dismissal from the first team seemed a strange and desperate move, especially when he wasn't even placed on the bench as a substitute. The reaction from the Northern Ireland camp to this news can only have been great relief that such a talented player was no longer going to be an issue for them.

Rumours in the press suggested that Walter Schachner and Reinhold Hintermaier were also to be replaced in the team as the Austrians looked for a miracle. Schmidt had only been given the job earlier that year – the Austrian FA had been unhappy at the lack of attacking football from the team and were happy to sacrifice the manager who had guided them through qualification. Schmidt, therefore, must have felt the pressure, especially given the lethargic efforts of their last two games. Austria had a mountain to climb in order to qualify, and even then, their fate wasn't entirely in their own hands. Schmidt was sombre in his analysis of Bingham's team, 'I admit to being a little apprehensive about the Irish. They looked organised when we watched them on television against Yugoslavia, Honduras and Spain. Physical aggression is the Irish strength. They will be hard to score against, although they don't appear to have many players capable of getting goals.'

The Austrians were given a last-minute boost, however, when Northern Ireland's talismanic goalkeeper, Pat Jennings, was ruled out of the match with a recurrence of his longstanding groin problem. Bingham relayed the sad news to the press, 'We have nursed him through it at training, but last night we realised he was in pain every time he kicked a ball – and you cannot take a chance.' Northern Ireland were fortunate to have Jim Platt, the talented understudy who had already deputised on many previous occasions, but the loss of Jennings at such a crucial point was certainly a setback to the Irish plans. Nevertheless, Jennings was happy for his deputy, 'I was pleased that Jim got to play. He was brought on for so many games when I wasn't playing, and I was delighted for him that he got a game. There were never any problems between us.'

At quarter past five local time, on 1 July 1982, Northern Ireland stepped on to the pitch of Estadio Vicente Calderón in the 38 degree heat. The immediate task before them – to beat a weary-looking Austrian side – was certainly achievable.

As the game kicked off, under the gaze of East German referee Adolf Prokop, both teams set off at a leisurely pace in a bid to conserve energy in the sapping heat. Northern Ireland made the first telling attack as Gerry Armstrong, full of confidence after the heroics against Spain, dribbled through the Austrian defence in the fourth minute, and then shortly after again to the right-hand side of the box in a move that should have earned him a free kick.

Austria's first test of the Irish defence came in the ninth minute as Nelson cut out a cross and put it out for a throw-in deep in his own half. A corner was won immediately from the throw, but Platt gained some early confidence as he made the catch. More corners followed for Austria but without any great deal of threat and all were easily dealt with by the Irish defence. In fact, given the extreme jeopardy of Austria's position in the World Cup, their fans must surely have been anxious about the lack of cutting thrust in their play.

Instead, Northern Ireland began to feel their way into the game. Young Norman Whiteside won a ball and hit a great pass for McIlroy who was just offside with his run. Armstrong put Jimmy Nicholl through on the wing who managed to centre the ball for Billy Hamilton. The Burnley forward hit a decent header on target, but it was, unfortunately, straight at the Austrian keeper, Friedrich Koncilia, who dealt with it easily.

Just over halfway through the first half Northern Ireland started to gain some territory. Whiteside and McIlroy linked up again with a shot from McCreery, then Koncilia, gathering the ball and preparing to distribute it back into play, almost threw it behind him into his own net in what would have been one of the most unfortunate and replayed own goals of any World Cup tournament.

There was a sense, though, that Northern Ireland were asserting themselves and were more likely to produce a goal. In the twenty-eighth minute McIlroy hit a cross-field ball to Armstrong who set off on a sprint – he beat one man, leaving him for dead, then another near the byline with just enough time to get in his cross before running out of play. It was a decidedly well-hit ball, straight to the far post where Hamilton had taken up the perfect position. He leaped in the air to head home from an angle. For the third game in a row, Northern Ireland had taken the lead and Hamilton now set off on a memorable run of celebration, winding his right arm in a windmill motion of pure joy.

It was an unforgettable moment for the Third Division striker and he is grateful today to the man who set him up, 'Gerry got the ball on the halfway line and he left two Austrian defenders as if they were old-age pensioners. He knocked the ball past them and skinned them and then put the cross in for me ... it was coming perfectly for me, but I had to get the header timed correctly to get some pace on it. I remember the relief to get my goal in a World Cup.'

It's hard to know whether, in the elation of the moment, the Irishmen on the pitch were aware of what this goal had done to the group standings and future permutations, but BBC commentator Barry Davies spelt it out for those following at home – one more goal, without any reply from Austria, and

Northern Ireland would require only a draw with France to reach the semi-finals and it would be the French who would be required to win at all costs.

However, such talk was still wishful thinking and there remained a job to be done on the pitch with the Austrians showing glimpses that they still entertained hopes of progressing. In the thirty-fifth minute, a period of Northern Ireland pressure ended with Austria on the counterattack, forcing Platt to push the ball behind from Max Hagmayr. Six minutes later, Gernot Jurtin cut inside and shot from thirty yards – Platt was again forced into action, diving to palm the ball behind for a corner.

But the half belonged to Northern Ireland and the marauding Jimmy Nicholl made another run to the corner late in the period, getting a cross to the centre of the box for Hamilton to head downwards, although it was an easy save for the keeper. Then, on the stroke of half-time, Armstrong took the ball ten yards inside his own half, instantly avoiding a high-footed challenge to leave one Austrian behind. Brimming with self-confidence, he set off with pace, cut across the centre and drove forwards, drifting further left as he bore down on the box. He beat another Austrian and the final defender attempted to knock him off the ball, but Armstrong was stronger, and the Austrian tumbled to the ground instead. Armstrong let off a shot but, following such a great build-up, it was a tame effort and went straight along the ground to the keeper. Nevertheless, it was a fine way to end the half – they had sent a message to the Austrians and, while the game was certainly no classic in terms of excitement, it was going exactly the way Northern Ireland and Bingham had planned.

As the teams re-emerged for the second half it was clear that Schmidt was prepared to gamble everything. He must have been severely disappointed with what he had seen from his players in the first half and he decided to use both his substitutions in an all-or-nothing attempt to turn things around. Hintermaier came on for Hagmayr, and Kurt Welzl came on for Johann Pregesbauer, as Austria looked for goals and a miracle.

Whatever was said at half-time – either tactical suggestions or an impassioned plea to at least bow out of the tournament fighting – it was a much-changed Austrian side in the second half and they started to show some real attacking threat. In the fifty-first minute, McClelland just about managed to get his head to a high through ball, attempting to head it back up the pitch while running towards his own net. He only succeeded, however, in looping it up in the air and, disastrously, it fell invitingly for forward Walter Schachner. Standing just six yards out, level with the right post of the Northern Ireland net, he calmly poked it towards the unguarded left side of the goal and must surely have thought he'd just scored the equaliser, only to see it bounce back towards him off the post. Hesitating for just a second, it was enough time to allow Jimmy Nicholl in behind him to scamper the ball out for a corner and save the situation. It was a clear warning shot that the game was still in the balance but worse was to follow.

From the corner, the ball was played back outside the box to Ernst Baumeister who struck the ball goalwards, but only into a sea of bodies. However, Bruno Pezzey cleverly flicked the ball behind him and into the net. Barry Davies claimed in the television commentary that it was a deflection but, rather than being merely struck by the ball, Pezzey, like the talented player he was, had clearly diverted it with some degree of skill. Regardless of whether the goal was due to luck or panache, the end result was the same. Northern Ireland would now have to pick themselves up and start again.

This, though, was an Austrian side reborn. The goal had completely changed their mood and a Houdini-like escape from the group might just be possible if they could score another few goals. Just a few minutes later Platt was forced to stretch to tip a dipping corner away to put the ball out for another corner on the opposite side as the Austrian pressure increased.

In the fifty-eighth minute Hintermaier played a perfectly weighted ball through to Schachner, who struck it magnificently and placed it firmly past Platt. For a second, Northern Ireland faced the disaster of their lead being reversed, but it was only for a heartbeat as the linesman raised his flag and the goal was disallowed. Replays suggested that Schachner was only a fraction on the wrong side of the last Northern Ireland defender and it was another warning of the menace Austria now posed.

Shortly afterwards, Schachner managed to turn McClelland on the edge of the box and run inside, but Nicholl once more stormed back and calmly won the ball just at the moment of danger. He prodded it back to Platt, only for Schachner to hurl himself down, rolling over and over in the box. Fortunately, the referee wasn't in the least interested in the ridiculous penalty claim.

With Northern Ireland looking increasingly disjointed Bingham decided in the sixty-eighth minute to bring on the winger, Noel Brotherston, for Whiteside. His first job was to run back and join the line-up in the wall; McCreery had given away a free kick just outside the box. Just as Hintermaier prepared to take the kick, Pezzey ran up in front of the wall, perhaps causing the discipline to break, and two Irish players rushed forward. The kick was taken and unfortunately deflected off McCreery and past Platt, who was given no chance by the change of direction and could only watch as it crossed the line.

Northern Ireland were now in disarray – the game had completely turned and so too had the prospects in the group. Austria were provisionally sitting on two points alongside France and dreaming of qualifying, if only Northern Ireland could do them a favour in the final game. Northern Ireland's prospects suddenly looked dismal – if they conceded another goal against Austria, then not even beating France would be enough to qualify. Fortunately, the men in green girded their loins at this moment and hauled themselves back into the fray, redoubling their efforts to keep their dreams alive.

With Brotherston on the pitch and prepared to run at the Austrians, the Irishmen pushed forward more often but, as they chased the game, the danger was in being caught on the counterattack. Such an incident soon occurred, and Austria squandered a truly gilt-edged chance to put the match beyond the Irish when Erich Obermayer pulled the ball back to an unmarked Schachner deep inside the Irish box. However, Schachner's touch was poor, and he once more threw himself to the ground under no challenge, either to make a rather desperate penalty claim or perhaps simply to distract from the breakdown of the Austrian chance.

With the stakes high and the game turning towards a conclusion, the action and pace increased and in the seventy-fifth minute, another great chapter was written into the Northern Ireland history books. An Irish attack saw Armstrong take a speculative shot from twenty-five yards out. It seemed a very strange choice with three other Northern Ireland players level with him and available for passes, or an attempted through ball, as he closed in on the Austrian box. One of those players was Jimmy Nicholl, who had joined the attack by haring forward from defence. He perhaps arrived level with Armstrong just a fraction after he had already made his mind to shoot. The ball that should have been played is clearly a through ball to Nicholl, who was about to gallop right through the two Austrian defenders in front of him and into the penalty area. What was he even doing there? It seemed like caution had indeed been thrown to the wind for the right back to be suddenly appearing in a central attacking position. Regardless, Armstrong chose instead to shoot. Nicholl must surely have thought in that instant that his surging run had been for nothing, especially as Armstrong's shot wasn't one of his best and was blocked instantly by the Austrian captain, Obermayer.

Fortunately, however, the block by Obermayer looped up and fell into Nicholl's path anyway. In fact, it perhaps worked out even better for the Irish because, as the ball deflected up and towards the byline, Nicholl had to sprint to catch up with it before it ran out behind. Koncilia was instantly alert to the extreme danger of the situation, and of Nicholl making the connection with the ball, and he ran out of his goal, out of the six-yard box and over towards Nicholl on the line. He must have known at some point that it was a race he had lost, and his tactics changed to trying to block any cross Nicholl might make. He leapt up as Nicholl reached the ball, but it was in forlorn hope because the ex-Manchester United defender clipped it high above him and into the six-yard area where Hamilton was waiting completely unmarked. His falling header has become one of the most iconic of all Northern Ireland goals. His entire body straightened and, lashing downwards, his head met the ball with sledgehammer force and Pezzey, who had scrambled back to cover the goal line had no chance. It was a second goal for Hamilton, and he pumped one arm repeatedly straight into the air as he rushed to join his team-mates in celebration.

Hamilton remembers that goal vividly, even now. 'I'm standing in the middle of the goal, the ball's miles up in the air, the defender's making his way back on to the goal line and all of a sudden you've got all these options. Do you take it down? Do you volley it? Do you head it? I just took a chance and headed it back the way it came and luckily the defender had gone too far the other way. It was coming down at no speed and from a great height but I was able to get as much power as I could and head it into the bottom corner. They used to say it was like a tree falling. That was more a relief than anything because the first goal was all about getting up and trying to get your timing right and head it down. This one you had time to think about it.

Sometimes you can overthink it. I'm just glad I made the right choice and headed it.'

Just as Austria's first goal had reinvigorated them, the second Irish goal had almost the opposite effect and Austria now began to slump, unable to pick themselves up off the floor once more. Not surprisingly, Northern Ireland seemed brighter, keener, fitter and determined to go on and score the third goal to win the contest. On seventy-nine minutes, Armstrong made a great run into the box as the ball fell back to Nicholl who crossed for Hamilton, who unfortunately headed wide when a World Cup hat trick had surely beckoned.

With just four minutes to go, Armstrong won the ball inside his own half and made a dart through the Austrian defence. He was about to go clear with only the keeper to beat and, although it was still some distance from goal, Anton Pichler took no chances and cynically brought him down – he earned a yellow card, but he kept Austria's vanishing chances alive. From the resulting free kick Armstrong headed just wide. Shortly afterwards, though, he had an even better chance with a header but elected to head down into Hamilton's path – only for Pezzey to hook it away – rather than head for goal himself when he was standing clear.

As the clock ticked down, it was all attack from Northern Ireland. Austria sensed that the game was up for them, the tournament over, whereas a victory for the Irish could transform their chances against France. McIlroy ended the game by taking a punt from distance in the final minute, but the ball sailed safely over the bar.

In the end it was a battling 2–2 draw for Northern Ireland. 'In normal circumstances a draw would have been a wonderful result in a one-off game,' said Whiteside, 'and with penalties we might have scraped it, but we had France coming up on our tail.' McIlroy agrees: 'We were a little bit disappointed that day … because we thought we should have won the game.' Still, Northern Ireland had fought their way back from the brink of disaster and kept their hopes of a semi-final place alive. What's more, they had acquitted themselves bravely on the world stage. As Whiteside remembers, 'We finished as we started, knowing that if we could beat France we would go through.'

For the travelling Irish press the result held no disappointment at all and was greeted with celebratory headlines as Northern Ireland continued to punch above their weight. While the players may have felt a slight pang of regret that they couldn't deliver the victory in the final few minutes of the match, the hard-bitten press corps, with many years of experience of following the sport, were left in no doubt that the Irish should be congratulated. Thus, the *Irish News* led with, 'It was another magnificent, fighting performance by the Irish.' The *Belfast Telegraph* meanwhile enthused, 'Northern Ireland's stature rises with every match in this World Cup series. It was yet another superb, stunning performance and one of great tactical merit.'

While the task against the superstars of French football looked to be an onerous one, the mood among the fans and the people of Northern Ireland was one of optimism. The players may have been wary of the coming storm as they were all too familiar with the quality of the French players, but those following them believed. Having already beaten the host nation, anything was possible.

In fact, the only sour note to be struck back home was from a familiar quarter – one that had been similarly sour back in 1958 when Northern Ireland had encountered strong criticism for playing matches on a Sunday. With the forthcoming game also being played on a Sunday, the Reverend Ian Paisley wasn't happy. He was quoted as saying, 'While all Northern Ireland rightly rejoices in the success of the team, it is to be regretted that their next match is to be on the Lord's Day. This is completely out of tune with Ulster tradition and, more so, is a desecration of the Lord's Day.' The more things change, the more they stay the same.

One thing the Irish squad hoped would definitely be changing, though, was the outcome of the quarter-final. In 1958 they had lost by four goals to France. Bingham had been part of that team and he now hoped to avenge the loss and plot a course for the semi-finals.

FRANCE

Gerry Armstrong recalls a conversation he had with his captain, Martin O'Neill, on the journey to the game against France, 'We're on the way to the stadium, we're like ten minutes from it, and Martin is bubbly and positive as always. He was never negative ... He says, "Just think, we're ninety minutes away from the semi-final of the World Cup." I say, "What?" He says, "Well, if we beat France today, we'll be in the semis." I hadn't thought of that. You wouldn't think that was possible, but in the aftermath of the Spain match I was not worrying about what lay ahead for us. We all lived for today, and that included Martin, but he also had his eye on tomorrow.'

O'Neill was certainly confident in all his interviews with the press, but contemporary reporting was tinged with realism. Journalists, players, pundits and even Billy Bingham pulled no punches when emphasising just how difficult the road to the semi-finals would be. France were a remarkable side. Sammy McIlroy explains, 'The difference between France and Spain was that France had players who could win you games. Over the next four or five years they were right up there in every competition.'

Spain had represented a particular problem – they were a solidly good team with fanatical home support to back them. On the other hand, France were a team full of superstars who possessed sublime skills and creative guile far beyond that of the hosts. They may have started the tournament in truly disastrous fashion – falling behind to arch-rivals England after just twenty-seven seconds as Bryan Robson scored what was then the tournament's fastest ever goal, and finishing the game as 3–1 losers – but they had won handsomely against Kuwait in one of the most bizarre games in the history of the tournament. Genghini, Platini and Six had put France 3–0 up and when Kuwait pulled one back with fifteen minutes remaining it seemed scant consolation, especially when Giresse appeared to have opened the gap to three goals again mere minutes later. However, this was the cue for a sensational series of events.

The Kuwaiti defence stopped playing during the fourth goal, claiming that they had heard a whistle and had assumed that play was being stopped. When told that this hadn't been the case, they refused to continue with the game.

Kuwait's Prince Fahad, also head of the Kuwaiti FA, came on to the pitch to remonstrate with the officials and to seemingly urge his players to abandon the game. Under such pressure, with Spanish security guards surrounding the players and officials, the Ukrainian referee succumbed and overruled the goal. France went on to score a fourth goal for a second time through Bossis, but it was a huge embarrassment for FIFA, albeit not on the scale they would encounter when Austria played West Germany four days later.

The French had then made routine work of securing the draw they needed to progress to the quarter-finals in their final group game against Czechoslovakia and the Czechs only equalised in the final minutes after Didier Six had put the French ahead halfway through the second half. Then came their quarter-final defeat of Austria, though most observers felt that the 1–0 scoreline didn't fully reflect the French superiority. In a reversal of fortunes, England were now struggling in the quarter-finals, while the team they had put to the sword so ruthlessly in that first game were beginning to ooze class as the tournament progressed.

Today Michel Platini stands as the disgraced former head of UEFA, banned from footballing activities for the same financial irregularities that provided the final smoking gun evidence against Sepp Blatter, his counterpart at FIFA. However, in 1982 he was one of the stars of international football, rightly lauded as a mercurial prince of the game, able to devastate oppositions from his midfield playground as well as posting scoring statistics that were simply astonishing for a midfield player. At the time of the 1982 World Cup he had just left Saint Etienne in France to join the Italian giants Juventus – there he would go on to win European Player of the Year three years in a row. He was a player in a different league to anything Northern Ireland had encountered so far.

But Platini was not alone. Alongside him in midfield was Alain Giresse, who had just been awarded the title of French Footballer of the Year. One intelligent playmaker was bad enough, but Northern Ireland would be facing two of them. And it didn't stop there. Making up the other two positions in midfield were Jean Tigana and Bernard Genghini. Already deadly enough, this quartet of stars was merely the midfield engine feeding through to the two French forwards, which included the impressive Dominique Rocheteau and Didier Six among the squad members vying for selection in attack. As Bingham told the *Belfast Telegraph*, 'France will be tough. There is no use denying that. They have a magnificently balanced side, improve with every game in this tournament and possess, in my opinion, the best midfield quartet in the world.'

There was, however, still optimism surrounding the exploits of the Irish. 'The odds were stacked against us because we needed to win,' recalls Jennings. 'But we certainly didn't believe it was an impossible task.' And as Sammy McIlroy told the press, 'We have done it once and we could do it again. We will certainly put up a better showing than we did last March when we lost 4–0 in Paris. But even if we do not make it, we feel that we can go home with our heads held high after four unbeaten games in Spain. Our biggest fear would be to have a drubbing on Sunday.'

Bingham's worries, though, were not just about the quality of their opponents – in a problem a little closer to home, he was struggling to sort out his goalkeeping problems. There seemed to be little hope that Jennings would make the game against France, and now there was also a worry over his deputy, Jim Platt, who had sustained a twisted back against Austria. Northern Ireland's third choice keeper was George Dunlop of Irish League side, Linfield. A redundant shipyard worker from Belfast, Dunlop was ready to step up and serve and was quoted in the *Irish News* as saying, 'I'll have no worries if I'm called up. I know I'm good enough not to let the lads down.' He was certainly a very well-respected keeper within local football and there is little doubt that he was prepared to give his best effort for his country. His story even had an element of the fairytale about it as the reason he was out of work was because his shipyard bosses had refused his request for leave for the World Cup and had paid him off instead. For Dunlop to bounce back from this personal disaster and step out in a World Cup quarter-final would have had an element of *Roy of the Rovers* about it. However, the gulf between part-time football and the quality that would be charging forth from the French midfield should not be expressed too lightly. Northern Ireland would need every second of international goalkeeping experience they could muster if they were to have any chance of surviving against the might of France. It was no place to throw an untested keeper from several levels down the footballing ladder.

Fortunately, it seemed as though Platt was going to pass his fitness test. Then, even better news emerged as Jennings refused to give up his own struggle. 'Two nights before the game Bingham took me aside and said, "It doesn't look like you will be able to make it." I didn't share his pessimism and requested that no decision be made until after a brief training spell on the eve of the match. I got through it with no worries, kicked about twenty balls to prove to myself there was no reaction from the groin, and I knew I was ready to play.'

Jennings recalls how he was backed in his fitness battle by the Northern Ireland physio, Jim McGregor, who said: '"Pat will get through the ninety minutes, there's no question about that. If he doesn't, you can blame me – I'll take the responsibility."' That support made a huge difference to Jennings. 'It was a smashing gesture by Jim McGregor to go right out on a limb on my behalf, and I really appreciated it. With a vital game only a few hours away it was the kind of vote of confidence which makes any player feel good.'

Whiteside provided some more good news for Bingham when he overcame a calf muscle injury and, with Donaghy now available again following his one-game suspension, Northern Ireland had managed to pull together their first-choice line-up for the momentous game. It was bad news for the experienced Sammy Nelson who had deputised so ably for Donaghy against Austria and Donaghy said as much to *Ireland's Saturday Night*: 'Sammy Nelson took my place against Austria and did nothing wrong. He is now in possession and, if I were him, I would be very disappointed if I were dropped for the game against France. Honestly, I sat in the stands [against Austria] hoping the team would win 3–0. Then they would be buzzing and Billy Bingham would not have to worry about changing the line-up.' These generous words from a fair-minded professional did nothing to change Bingham's mind and he reverted to the team that had enjoyed such glory against Spain.

One late selection problem for the Northern Ireland bench

came up when Noel Brotherston, who had twice come on as a substitute during the competition was unavailable through injury. Glentoran's Johnny Jameson was offered the opportunity to take his place in the dugout and perhaps become the second Irish League star to step on to the pitch that summer. However, Jameson was a born-again Christian and, as the match was to be played on a Sunday, he refused based on religious grounds. It was unquestionably a brave choice by Jameson. For a part-time footballer – for any footballer, really – taking part in a World Cup quarter-final was a once-in-a-lifetime opportunity, and he might well have been mocked for taking a stand on the issue. However, Jameson did take up a place in the squad knowing that Sunday games were a possibility and he was using up a position that could instead have been allocated to someone willing to pull on the green shirt, regardless of the day of the week. George Best, for instance, was watching the tournament at home, and Bingham had taken a risk on an Irish League player who now said he didn't wish to be made available for selection.

On the French side, manager Michel Hidalgo had the kind of selection problems the Irish would have killed for. With Platini now back to fitness, the only problem was trying to accommodate the embarrassment of riches within his squad, with Rocheteau and Gérard Soler making up the forward line ahead of Didier Six. Hidalgo's comments to the press were respectful of Northern Ireland but made with the confidence of a man who knew exactly the level of talent he had at his disposal. 'The Irish are powerful, solid and willing and we will have to go flat out for ninety minutes. The game against Austria neither reassured me nor frightened me. Hamilton was very impressive, and I feel the collective teamwork of the Irish will be our main threat. But our destiny is in our own hands.'

The semi-final now beckoned for both nations.

★

Kick off for the final quarter-final group game came at 17:15 local time in the same stadium used to host the two previous matches. As with most games at this World Cup, plenty of empty spaces could be spotted among the crowd, officially recorded at thirty-seven thousand. Martin O'Neill and Michel Platini, the two captains, went through the usual formalities of exchanging pennants and, watching at the time, you might have allowed yourself a glimmer of hope. For all the talk of the genius of Platini, he was someone without any major honours outside of France. O'Neill, on the other hand, had twice been part of a Nottingham Forest side that had won the European Cup. While the skill of the French was abundantly obvious, the steely determination and teamwork of the Irish was perhaps its equal, with players who were current or ex-Manchester United and Arsenal first teamers, and with one of the world's greatest goalkeepers marshalling their defence. Was it time to believe more in their own strengths than worry about those of the opposition?

As Polish referee Alojzy Jarguz got the game underway, the early minutes saw the same sort of cagey shadow-boxing that had characterised Northern Ireland's game against Austria. On a sunny day in the scorching Spanish heat, no one seemed too determined to burn through their energy reserves early in the game when there was a place in the last four at stake. However, as Northern Ireland worked on keeping the French attack at arm's length, it was immediately obvious that the engine of the French team, their famous midfield line-up, had many gears they could effortlessly move through.

Both Platini and Tigana showed signs of acceleration in these opening periods, which would have worried Bingham from his position on the bench. Northern Irish players were always on hand to outnumber any runner, but the sheer pace and movement of the midfield was evidence that their reputation had been fairly gained.

It was in the eighth minute when France finally began to flex their muscles as Platini and Genghini exchanged passes and moved quickly forward. Platini then cut through the Irish defence as he attacked the right-hand side of the penalty area, but the attack was wasted when he tried to chip Jennings from a tight angle when other options had been open to him. Nevertheless, this was the first mark of intent from the French. Important games are often opened by a phony war where the two teams try to gain a measure of each other. This was France saying that they had now found that measure and that further raids of this nature could be expected.

Nevertheless, the onslaught that some had expected did not begin immediately. Whiteside was even able to break through the French lines in the tenth minute, but his rolled ball across the goal found no one following in. A few minutes later, though, a nervous Donaghy played the ball back to Jennings when Rocheteau threatened the Irish goal. It wasn't firmly played and Jennings had to quickly throw himself down to smother it. It was perhaps a worrying sign that the Irish defence was growing more nervous.

Despite this scare, it was the twenty-fourth minute before the Irish were seriously troubled again. The danger occurred when McCreery conceded a free kick in a central position thirty yards out. The ball was floated to an unmarked Rocheteau six yards from the left post and he volleyed it straight at Nicholl. The ball then ping-ponged around the box before finding its way over to the opposite side where Platini executed an imperious piece of skill by turning and volleying the ball as it dropped over his shoulder. This time, his flash of skill was exactly the right choice and very much on target, but Jennings was alert to the situation, and pulled off a fine save as he raced out from the goal. The cleverness of the free kick, not to mention the speed of thought and wonderful skill of Platini, was another alarm call for an Irish side who had been gradually edging their way into the game, step by cautious step. With a quarter of the match gone it also marked the end of the two teams circling each other in the ring. The game now opened up.

What is the greatest goal ever scored by Northern Ireland on the world stage? For most people, the answer comes as easily and automatically as breathing – Gerry Armstrong against Spain. But in terms of technical execution, while also factoring in a higher level of opposition, Martin O'Neill's goal against France to put his nation on the brink of the semi-final of the 1982 World Cup wins hands down. Those who weren't watching in Madrid that day or following the events on television might ask, 'What is this Martin O'Neill goal?' The history books certainly record no such event. The fact that they don't is a matter of pain to Northern Ireland fans to this day.

A Jimmy Nicholl free kick down the right wing to Whiteside was the beginning of a bold move by Northern Ireland. Over halfway through the first half, France had shown dangerous attacking ability but had largely been successfully kept at bay. Every pundit had declared that Northern Ireland's best hope would be to keep things safe in the early stages and then try to grab a goal on the break by taking any opportunity that came their way. Against such opposition, chances might be few and far between, so the importance of finishing was paramount.

From the wing, Whiteside took out two French players facing him with a piece of audacious skill that seemed almost impossible for a seventeen-year-old boy who had played only a handful of internationals. Or perhaps it was *because* he was a seventeen-year-old boy with no experience that he felt unshackled by the normal 'dos and don'ts' of this level of the game. Either way, his choice of ball was inspired. Seeing Martin O'Neill running forward with space opening up, he back-heeled the ball adeptly into his path. O'Neill then passed the ball into a central position outside the box where Armstrong was waiting and continued his run. Armstrong was alert to the opportunity for a quick one-two and immediately touched the ball perfectly back into his path in a move that expertly split the French defence. O'Neill took one touch to control the ball before calmly placing it beyond keeper Jean-Luc Ettori into the net. It was a goal of beauty, executed with exquisite precision by Whiteside, Armstrong and O'Neill.

We're now in a world upside down. The impossible has happened again. It's 1–0 to Northern Ireland. For all the grandeur of the French team, what had they actually done in the game? Northern Ireland have them exactly where they want them, keeping them at arm's length and hitting them with a sucker punch. It is now the Irish who just need to see out the rest of the game to move on to Seville for a match that could take them to the World Cup final.

The travelling fans punched the air, and in pubs and homes across Northern Ireland screaming erupted as men, women and children clasped one another and danced and hugged and shouted in glee. The joy of football. The miracle of football.

Embrace those precious seconds. Wallow in the brilliance of a moment of artistry, of the accomplishment of hard work and team spirit shining through. Drift back into that slowed-down landscape of celebration and elation. Clutch it and hold it close. Stay there awhile and savour the scene. Remember forever how good it felt. Mere seconds is all it lasted.

French players were already raising their hands for offside as O'Neill broke through their ranks. Sometimes defenders who have been caught out by the opposition will try to trick the referee into giving offside as a way of saving face or just out of sheer desperation to keep their team in the game. Sometimes defenders claim for offside as they genuinely can't comprehend that the attacking player can have been anything else, having apparently come from nowhere and timed his run to perfection. Whatever was the case here, the referee and linesman instantly agreed and Northern Ireland's superbly executed goal was wiped from history within short seconds of it happening, not even granting the Irish players enough time to join O'Neill in triumph.

Offside decisions can often be marginal. Before the introduction of VAR (video assistant referees) it was possible to have sympathy with the decision-makers confronted with a fast-moving passage of play where the attacker is either fractionally onside or offside. With only a split second to make a decision on something some distance away, and with no ability to view it again, mistakes could easily be made. However, some mistakes are less easy to sympathise with, especially when the officials at World Cup games are meant to be the absolute best the world has to offer. When the ball was played, O'Neill was exactly on top of the white line of the French penalty area, which makes it even easier to see that not just one, but *both* French centre backs are clearly standing a yard in front of him.

It looked like a great run to beat offside when viewed in real time, but the replay proves conclusively that O'Neill was comfortably onside when he broke through to score. It was a heartbreaking decision for Northern Ireland and remains so to this day. As O'Neill laments, 'Television replays proved I was a yard onside. It still rankles with me greatly; not being in the record books as scoring in the World Cup is soul destroying.'

Northern Ireland had taken a chance with the kind of deadly attacking thrust that would have had footballing pundits salivating over replays if it had been scored by a linkup between Platini, Tigana and Giresse. It might have been the only chance they would get, and they had been robbed. O'Neill was still visibly grumbling as he walked past the referee a minute later, probably worried that the footballing Fates were against them. He was right to be concerned.

In the thirty-fourth minute Platini took the ball and surged towards the Irish box. McCreery kept pace with him and forced him wide and down towards the line where Donaghy was also waiting. McCreery seemed to ease off to leave the business of stopping Platini to the better-placed Donaghy, who made a sliding tackle. But Platini had long gone and the Juventus-bound midfielder crossed the ball to Giresse who placed it past Jennings. Martin O'Neill's goal had seemingly woken the French up. But for the generosity of the referee, they would have been staring at an exit from the tournament. The time for direct action had come and they cleanly and surgically dissected the Irish defence, who had gone from being seemingly 1–0 ahead to being 1–0 behind in a matter of minutes – a cruel blow indeed.

It would have been a depressing scene in the Irish dressing room at half-time. The French goal had showed their attacking abilities, but the Irish goal had been an even more cleverly and skilfully played move. And yet only one had counted.

Northern Ireland now had a monumental task ahead of them in the second half. If scoring one goal to beat France had seemed like a difficult mission before the game, they now had just forty-five minutes to score at least two goals to turn the game around. Not only that, but they knew that increasing the frequency of their own attacks and changing their shape on the pitch would leave them open to the pace of the French on the counterattack.

What would any manager do in these dire straits? Order his team to once more edge slowly into the game, keep the French at bay and look for a chance – two chances now – as the clock ticked down? Or take the game directly to the French and pray that they could deflect the almost certain counterpunches that would be delivered? It soon became academic because, within just two minutes of the restart, Marius Trésor played a ball up the wing to Rocheteau who controlled the ball and turned at the same time in a breathtaking exhibition of skill and acceleration to set off into the Irish half, leaving a bewildered McCreery in his wake. Running on into the box he found Chris Nicholl waiting for him and, almost unbelievably, McCreery, who had managed to catch up and draw level. Jennings was aware of the problem and seemed to have his near post well covered. But

Rocheteau, despite pressure from two players and a keeper of supreme experience, placed it into the net via the near post. It was an absolutely stunning individual goal, combining touch, pace and accuracy. This was what France were capable of and why they were much more formidable opponents than the Spanish.

Northern Ireland now needed three goals. Any debate about tactics was now put aside. There was only one way back into the game and that was all-out attack, but it was surely a forlorn hope. Five minutes later it almost got worse when a cross for Genghini saw the Frenchman use a wonderful piece of skill to control the ball, turn and shoot. It's likely he would have beaten Jennings if he had had a better angle to shoot from.

Despite the hopelessness of the situation, Northern Ireland started taking the game to France – Armstrong was at the forefront with some darting runs from deep. The gallant heroes of this small nation were going to go down fighting. However, always there remained the threat of the French midfield who now found more space opening up before them. With the game looking as if it were already in the bag, Hidalgo began to experiment with one eye on the next match and Didier Six replaced Soler upfront. Within minutes Six had provided a wonderful cross for Rocheteau who glanced it across the net when almost any header on target would probably have been a goal.

The threat from the French now seemed relentless and three minutes later, a free kick was awarded just outside the right-hand side of Northern Ireland's penalty area. It was played short and across to the edge of the box for Rocheteau. McCreery and McClelland both immediately converged upon the dangerman but McCreery rashly committed himself to the tackle. Rocheteau nimbly stepped aside and, with a devastating burst of speed, ghosted past McClelland. Jimmy Nicholl, so often the Irish saviour in defence for moments of extreme peril, came charging back from the wall to slide in but Rocheteau had already shot and once more beaten Jennings at the near post. It was another moment of individual brilliance from Rocheteau. Some goals you can't help applauding, no matter how painful the consequences for those you wish to win.

The contest was now over because no matter what sort of spirit the Irish were capable of conjuring, four goals in the final twenty minutes against such a team was impossible. In the seventy-fourth minute the French managed to keep possession for a spell with some simple passes, and chants of 'Olé!' were heard in the stadium. As the crowd grew louder, the French players seemed to respond, and their passes became more elaborate to further incite the crowd. It's easy to imagine that many of the 'neutral' fans in the stadium were local Spaniards who were greatly enjoying the retribution being handed out to their conquerors.

And yet it seems that nothing could quite dim the fire in the Irish hearts. Just a minute later, perhaps even roused into greater effort by the 'Olé!' chants, Northern Ireland stepped forward again. Attacking on the left wing, Whiteside took on two French players and strode towards the box, unleashing a cross into a dangerous area that just managed to miss Hamilton's outstretched foot. However, the ball travelled on and fell instead to Armstrong. The Watford striker shot hard from the angle and the ball appeared to clip Hamilton's ankle on the way, before it was once more in the French net. This time there would be no harsh reversal from the referee.

The goal was everything the players deserved. For the second time that day they had scored against these daunting opponents. They had been victims of an appalling error by the referee, yet had kept going, and the goal gave the scoreline a greater degree of dignity.

Nobody really expected any kind of dramatic late comeback. It's possible that the players would have given the world to get just one more goal, let alone the three they needed, to make the game look closer for the history books. However, the French hadn't quite finished, and when Northern Ireland committed five men to the French box on an attack, perhaps buoyed by their goal into overstretching themselves, a quick break put Rocheteau through once more. This time Jennings got the better of him and his save put the ball out for a corner. From the resulting kick the ball was moved around the outside of the area and eventually played out to the French right wing. From here, it was crossed for Giresse. The Frenchman wandered unmarked to about eight yards out and, unchallenged, was able to plant a firm header goalwards. Jennings managed to get a hand to it, but it was not enough, and the ball ricocheted in off the underside of the bar in dramatic fashion.

Even a blind optimist would have seen no hope at this point, but Whiteside's courage was still very much in evidence. Having had, by his own admission, a rather subdued performance against the Austrians, on this day he was in sparkling form against much better opposition, displaying all the raw talent his young frame possessed. In the eighty-fifth minute he turned two French defenders as he cut in from the left and, with two more bearing down on him, he let loose a shot from a narrow angle, which the French keeper pushed behind for a corner. The World Cup was drifting towards a conclusion for Northern Ireland, but their future was there for all to see in these last minutes.

The final whistle saw the players exchanging shirts and thoughts in what had been a clean but competitive game. The French had eased their way to a World Cup semi-final for the first time since 1958, but not without that first-half scare. The Irishmen knew that they had witnessed performances from true artists of the game, and they could hold their heads up high for what they had achieved that day, and for what they had accomplished throughout the rest of their stay in Spain. The scoreline may have been heavy, but they could be justly proud of their endeavours.

Bingham's immediate reaction was forthright. 'We were outplayed I thought ... We started a little bit slowly and I think we got slower. We just didn't get a grip of that game at all.' Meanwhile, in the dressing room Armstrong and Hamilton were debating about just who was responsible for Northern Ireland's goal, 'Gerry and I laugh about the consolation goal we got,' Hamilton reveals. 'It came off my ankle and into the net. I didn't celebrate much because we were 3–0 down. We got into the dressing room after the match and Billy Bingham came over and said, "Who got the goal?" and I said, "I did." I remember Malcolm Brodie being there and he said, "Naw, it's Gerry's goal, I've already written my report." So, Gerry has been awarded a goal extra and I've been awarded a goal less because of Malcolm Brodie's report. I would have got the Golden Boot for the British players. When you get beaten it's not the sort of thing you argue about, but I know it myself!'

The players had no qualms about losing to such opposition. As David McCreery remembers, 'That was us running out of petrol. We'd gone four games, physically drained, but [we were] very, very happy, because we'd got so far ... It was hard. I think our legs had gone. I think we'd gone the distance. We were beaten by a better team. But it might have been different if that goal had stood and maybe had our backs against the wall, like we did against Spain. It might have given us a wee bit more fight. I think once they scored, we made a few attempts, feeble attempts to box them, but for me that was the ending of the journey.'

Jennings is also realistic in his appraisal: 'The truth of the matter is that France had too many stars. We couldn't tie them down and they had that extra yard of pace which made all the difference. We held out until Giresse gave them a lead – after that we were chasing shadows. You can't expect the gods to smile on you all the time.'

The defeat is still hardest to take for O'Neill, for obvious reasons. 'If VAR had been there then it would have immediately given me the goal – I'm halfway round Madrid celebrating before they tell me they've disallowed the goal. Two minutes later they score at the other end, and in that heat and us trying to chase the game in the second half, France were just picking us off. For me, Brazil were far and away the best team in the tournament but, player for player, talent for talent, France were the second best. I've spoken to a couple of the French boys since that. Although they fancied their chances of beating us because they had the talent, because it was so hot, [they knew] it would be a really difficult second half. If [we'd been] 1–0 at half-time … it would have been a difficult second half for them in the blazing sun. We could defend leads, as we proved against Spain even with ten men. We were adept at doing that and it would have been an interesting second half.'

Norman Whiteside especially warmed to the theme of what could have been. 'Anything might have happened had it stood and I'm not being facetious when I say we could have just kicked the ball out of play every time we got it during the remaining sixty-odd minutes to cling to victory. I know it never works out that way, but it would have been nice to have had a lead to defend.'

However, he too is realistic about the talent of the French that day. 'Their midfield was so fluid and skilful and it was almost a privilege to watch how graceful yet devastating Platini's movement, passing and shooting could be. He was the greatest player I ever faced, absolutely supreme. Although we were soundly beaten, I'm proud that we gave it a go against such a formidable team. I'm full of respect for our achievement in getting to a spot where we were two victories away from the World Cup final.'

Unfortunately for Northern Ireland, they just couldn't replicate the same performance they had given against Spain. While Whiteside and Armstrong both played strong games, it's fair to say that the rest of the players didn't quite scale the same heights as earlier in the tournament. Whether this was a result of France just not allowing them to play, or the effects of a fifth physically draining game in the Spanish heat, there is no blame to be attached to anyone. The squad had given everything for their shirts, for the fans, for the people back home, and embarked upon a truly wondrous journey that had given so much joy to so many. They had done all they could to keep that journey going, but it was ultimately beyond them. They could leave Spain with admiration from the footballing world ringing in their ears, and deservedly so.

Reaction in the press back home was exactly as it should have been – acknowledgement that Northern Ireland had been outplayed on the day but glowing in pride for what they had achieved. The *Irish News* perhaps had the most accurate description of the game as it lamented, 'Beaten but not bowed, Northern Ireland came to the end of the road in Spain when quite simply, they could not live with a French side that is flowering at just the right time in these finals. Once again, they ran themselves into the ground, only this time more was needed, more than the Irish possessed.'

Malcolm Brodie, meanwhile, observed in the *Belfast Telegraph*, 'At this stage of soccer's greatest showpiece the cream floats to the surface and Northern Ireland's heroic and fighting side of limited talent just does not live in the company of the elite. To have come, however, within two matches of the World Cup final is a momentous achievement and one which makes them part of football legend.'

It was now time to turn thoughts towards returning home and life after the World Cup. After more than a month of living in each other's space it was important to plan time with families and relax, as Norman Whiteside remembers all too well: 'It would have been nice to stay but … after the game against France it was time to go home as well. We were drained physically, mentally, because we'd never experienced all this hype and press and this situation before … Some of the senior pros had had a really long season and then a really long World Cup and I do remember on some faces people were happy, looking forward to going home, seeing their families and then having a holiday. So, it was great to be part of it, but it was nice when it came to that end.'

As the team left for home, they continued to generate headlines. For Armstrong there was the flattering attention of Spanish team Espanyol de Barcelona who were reportedly keen on securing his services. In an age when so very few British players signed for continental clubs this was high praise indeed. There was also welcome news for the IFA's finances, with talk of a World Cup windfall of £500,000. This was to be invested in the building of a new stand at Windsor Park, with a promise of government funds to make up the rest of the projected £2.5 million costs.

Other headlines were stranger and less welcome for the administrators, as local artist Rowel Friers had started legal action against the IFA for its use of his 'Yer Man' mascot creation, claiming that he should be due royalties from all of its uses. The legal action was adjourned on the grounds that the IFA president, Harry Cavan, and secretary, Billy Drennan, were to remain in Spain until 20 July, over a week after the final, on FIFA business. The top two IFA administrators who had not secured accommodation for the actual players were staying on for a whole month beyond the first phase.

It may also come as no surprise that the IFA failed to organise a suitable welcome home in the streets of Belfast for the returning heroes. While it was true that the players yearned to return to their families, the majority of whom were in England, one might have imagined that, between them, the IFA and Belfast City Council could have quickly put some plan into action before the squad split up. But with the administrators remaining in the sunshine of Spain, nothing took place, and the players slipped home with none of the public outpouring of recognition that people expected.

In the end, the eventual open-topped bus parade took place on a wet midweek afternoon in November when the squad was next gathered together in Belfast for a European Championship qualifying game. For John McClelland, not sharing in the experience back in Belfast is his one regret. 'Everyone said the place was a big party. The reaction from Northern Ireland, the country, that's what I probably missed, I think. We were so isolated from the reality of what we did to get that reaction back home. It's always disappointing to think I never saw that. You're thinking, why didn't they have a civic reception? We had to wait until later in the year.'

Despite the enthusiasm of the sparse crowds who braved the November weather, many having to take time off work, it was not the reception the team deserved. A summer reception would have seen many tens of thousands of fans thronging the centre of Belfast, chanting, waving flags and wallowing in the immediacy of the events, but it seemed that there would always be a discrepancy between the efforts of the players on the pitch and those of the administrators off the field.

However, as Martin O'Neill remarked after the game against France, nothing could dim the achievement. 'They can never take away from us what we have done here. That victory over Spain in Valencia will live with me forever – the greatest night in my life and that goes for every player who took part.'

EPILOGUE

The 1982 World Cup remains one of the most memorable to this day, not just for the Irish and not always for the right reasons. With the exquisite Brazilians crushing the Maradona-led Argentinians 3–1 in the first of their quarter-final matches, connoisseurs of the beautiful game would have eagerly anticipated a final between the two most artistic teams of the era, Brazil and France.

This was arguably the most talented Brazilian team to ever appear at a World Cup and their confidence would have been sky-high after so ruthlessly dispatching their South American rivals. However, in one of the best games of the tournament, the class of Zico, Sócrates et al was swept side by the more pragmatic Italians, who hadn't managed to record a single victory while scraping their way through the first phase. The end result was 3–2, and all three Italian goals had come courtesy of Juventus striker, Paolo Rossi, who had only been able to take part in the tournament when a three-year ban for match-fixing was cut short by the Italian FA in April of that year.

With West Germany emerging from the quarter-final group that had contained England and Spain, the French now pitted themselves in one of the classic 'irresistible force versus unstoppable object' encounters. Controversy had dogged the games of both teams: the French had been both victims and beneficiaries of bizarre decisions against Kuwait and Northern Ireland, and the Germans had found it hard to shake off the stigma of the infamous Austrian game. However, that was all about to be eclipsed as what happened in front of seventy thousand fans in Seville on 8 July is still talked of as one of the worst decisions in World Cup history.

With the score at 1–1 in the fifty-seventh minute, a beautiful ball flighted from midfield by Platini saw the French substitute, Patrick Battiston, bear down on the German goal, having cut through from the last defender. The West German goalkeeper, Harald Schumacher, came storming out to face Battiston who attempted to chip him. As it turned out, the effort on goal went wide of the net, but Schumacher continued his run, even though he must have known that he would reach Battiston long after the ball had gone. The act of violence which followed has lost none of its sickening ferocity in the intervening years.

Schumacher launched himself into the air for what can only be described as an assault upon the Frenchman, smashing his hip forcefully into his chest and head. Battiston collapsed to the ground unconscious where he remained for some time. His injuries included two missing teeth, three cracked ribs and a damaged vertebrae. The referee, who had a clear and uninterrupted view of the incident, declared that no foul had been committed. No penalty was awarded, even though the foul had taken place inside the penalty area, and Schumacher, who clearly deserved a straight red card for one of the most audacious and savage fouls ever committed in the latter stages of a World Cup, was simply instructed to take a goal kick.

Although Platini later revealed that he originally thought

Battiston was dead, Schumacher showed no concern for the player he had just attacked, instead displaying signs of impatience as he waited to take the goal kick while Red Cross attendants worked on the stricken French player.

The referee's calculation that it hadn't even been a foul stunned the football world. While the French managed to regroup and lead 3–1 as the game went into extra time, there is no doubt that the incident cast a shadow over the remainder of the match. West Germany went on to win the game 5–4 on penalties and contest a final with Italy.

The 1982 World Cup ended in dismay for the purists who did not get the Brazil/France game most neutrals had been hoping for. Instead of Zico taking to the field opposite Platini, the tournament served up the previously banned Rossi against the disgraced figure of Schumacher, with the Italians triumphing. The German coach, Jupp Derwall, had famously said after the controversial game against Austria, 'We wanted to progress, not play football.' He succeeded in doing that.

However, the Brazilian and French squads will be immortalised long after those who knocked them out have been forgotten, and, while the tournament that year will always be identified with scandal and bad decisions, it is distinguished by the supreme skill of those two teams, and for the monumental spirit of the Northern Irish squad. Writing your skill large in the history books or giving all of your heart for a tiny nation to produce huge upsets are more worthy aspirations than merely progressing at all costs via an arranged match and an act of thuggery. Sometimes it really isn't about the winning but about creating impressions and memories that last forever. Being remembered is the ultimate victory.

At a time of great division and tension, Northern Ireland's heroic exploits in Spain acted as a force for unity of spirit.

For two and a half weeks, old descriptors such as 'British' or 'Irish' faded, replaced by a shared vision of being Northern Irish – an identity that could be proudly embraced. The nation's ambassadors on the field of play replaced the bleak headlines for which Northern Ireland was infamous with ones that instead espoused togetherness.

While the religious background of the players wouldn't be an issue anywhere else it is unavoidable that it was, and remains, worthy of comment in Northern Ireland. Despite the problems the international team encountered in the 1970s, and again in the 1980s, with cancelled matches and a deteriorating political scene, the team were always proudly united. As Billy Bingham told the *Sunday Telegraph*, 'The team could not have done what it had if I had eleven Protestants or eleven Catholics. You had Gerry Armstrong, from the Falls Road, and Norman Whiteside, from the Shankill. It didn't matter to us. I knew that if I was going to have a team, it had to come from all communities. I said when I took over, it will have to be from both persuasions. It was an absolutely mixed team and I never had an ounce of trouble.'

This is a subject that Martin O'Neill is keen to pursue. 'The religious divide between us, it never sprung up. Those lads like McIlroy, McCreery, big Norman, Jimmy Nicholl, John McClelland, I consider them to still be friends of mine and I hope that they consider me the same. We had a terrific spirit and wanted to play for each other. And that was against the backdrop of really difficult times.' As Norman Whiteside remembers, the post-match parties during this period saw a cross-community harmony often at odds with what was going on across the country. 'Martin and Gerry would be singing. There'd be Proddy songs, Catholic songs, Irish songs. It was just one big happy family.'

This, therefore, was a team that represented everything good about Northern Ireland. They showed the world what the small nation was capable of and brought people together. They could never hope to heal such a fractured nation by themselves, but, for several weeks in the summer of 1982, they gave a glimpse of what could be. As Van Morrison asked a few years later, 'Wouldn't it be great if it was like this all the time?'

Billy Bingham reflects today on the special group of players who wore the shirt with pride. 'We were very tough. Pat played so well for us, he saved us in many games, and Jim Platt always did a good job when he came in. The back four of Donaghy, McClelland, Chris Nicholl and Jimmy Nicholl was the best I ever had. They weren't a slow back four, they were very quick. Any speedy players who played against them, they could handle it. And they had that good goalkeeper behind them. That's why we were hard to beat.

'Martin was a good captain for me. He wanted to win. It was always on his mind: "How are we going to win this match, Bill?" David McCreery was a busy bee. He buzzed about the midfield. He didn't waste many balls and he was always on the go. A good team player. Billy Hamilton was always a handful. He was very strong in the air and he could hold the ball up, look around him for a pass. And he could finish. Gerry was an all-round player; he was underrated in many ways. When you have a player like that, you can move him around a little bit. And he could handle himself very well. He was robust enough to handle anyone who was going to be rough with him. It was a very good group. They all had a laugh at times, but they were serious about their football. To play well for your country, to say you gave it everything you could, we had that.'

Of course, Bingham himself was one of the most vital ingredients in the recipe of the team's success. He had seen what was required to take a small group of players to the world stage when manager after manager before him had failed, even when assets like George Best were available. Gerry Armstrong is in no doubt about the credit due to him: 'Billy was a very clever man. He knew how to get the best out of those players, with what he had in the squad.' Armstrong also credits O'Neill's appointment as another of Bingham's masterstrokes. 'He had the captain qualities and he always made sense. We had belief in him, the fact that he had won the European Cup twice. There was a lot of credibility about Martin for me. The players hung off every word he said. Martin dug deeper than anybody in terms of the ins and outs of the games, he covered all the angles.'

With a captain who led by example and who skilfully conveyed the manager's vision to the team, Northern Ireland quickly flourished, despite having a very small squad with only a handful of good players beyond the eleven on the pitch. The team would always be limited in what it could achieve, but Bingham's great strength was that he saw how the players' talents could be harnessed in certain directions and how they could be forged into a cohesive unit.

The team began to believe in their own potential and in the pressure-cooker atmosphere of the Estadio Luis Casanova in Valencia as the world watched on, they had the strength to imagine that their organisation and work ethic was equal to the task in front of them. Ability, tactics, courage were the three pillars of Northern Ireland's success.

The players today are in no doubt that the bond the team shared was instrumental in what they achieved. There are very few days in Gerry Armstrong's life when he isn't asked about the goal he scored against Spain. He is the only man on earth who had a first-person view as the ball disappeared through the legs of Spanish players and rippled the netting. His name has passed into legend and he has rightly taken his place as a folk hero to generations of Northern Ireland supporters. But ask him for his abiding memory and he recalls instantly, 'Pride of being part of a team that had that spirit and attitude. A small country that achieved greatness. Good hard-working professionals who complemented each other. It was teamwork which got us where we were.'

This is backed up by Jimmy Nicholl, 'When you're with a team like Manchester United, or another top team, and you have eight or nine players playing well, even if two or three aren't, you still might win the game of football. But with Northern Ireland that wasn't the case. We all had to be at the top of our game at all times. We were always underdogs and that's where I get my satisfaction from. The consistency of some players can sometimes be as good as the brilliance of others.'

It's remarkable that today even the most experienced members of the Northern Ireland squad, who had long and successful careers at club level, winning honours with giants of the English game, single out this period with Northern Ireland as their career highlight. Pat Jennings says, 'I was never as proud to be part of a team as I was being part of that team. I'd been trying to qualify for a World Cup since 1964 so eventually getting there and doing as well as we did, it's a time you'll never forget.'

Sammy McIlroy had played alongside George Best at Manchester United and scored a mesmerising goal in an FA Cup final, but he feels the same. 'A lot of my memories are with Northern Ireland. The fans, the camaraderie we had, the success we had. I had some great times with Manchester United, but when you're talking about playing for your country, the fun and games and laughter. I'm sure every guy from that squad could write a couple of books. The only thing is, they couldn't tell the truth! We had that much fun!'

The times are perhaps best encapsulated by Billy Hamilton: 'It's a testament to the achievement that people are still talking about it. It's hard to explain. It's a lot to do with the bonding. Meeting at the hotels, catching up with each other, playing practical jokes on each other, having a good laugh, going out for a pint together. Not only were they good team-mates but they were good friends and it's stayed like that to this day. I don't think that achievement would have been possible if that bonding wasn't in place before the Spanish game. We were like brothers, more than friends, it was that intense. I think that's what got us our glory on that night.'

Martin O'Neill has experienced more success than any other member of the squad, with a glittering array of medals at club level. Yet he is left with a greater fondness for his time with Northern Ireland: 'The European Cup was the pinnacle of anyone's club career. Those medals were for the likes of Puskas, George Best, Bobby Charlton, Di Stefano and Eusebio, and for me to be involved and win the European Cup was sensational. However, to qualify for the World Cup, to beat Spain, to qualify for a quarter-final with the team that we had, the spirit that we had, the camaraderie that we had, it was like a club team we got to know each other so well. I played for Nottingham Forest for ten years with a great team spirit enhanced by a great manager, but I had the same sort of bonding with the Northern Ireland group who would fight tooth and nail for each other. To be captain of that team was fantastic. I can give up the moment of the goal I scored in that match against France – and I have to rue that for the rest of my life – for all the great moments I *did* have.'

The exploits in Spain will burn forever in the memories of the players and the fans who shared such an incredible journey. However, the road ahead looked challenging. The average age of the first choice Northern Ireland eleven in Spain was twenty-seven. This is an almost perfect age in footballing terms, representing a player's peak when youthfulness is combined in equal measure with experience. The same eleven, though, would share an average age of thirty-one by the time the next World Cup was played. Question marks hung over how long seasoned campaigners such as Pat Jennings and Chris Nicholl could continue, and there were only limited signs of younger players coming through to swell the ranks. More immediately, Northern Ireland had been drawn in a daunting European Championship qualifying group alongside their recent rivals, Austria, and the reigning European champions and World Cup runners-up, West Germany. Only one team could qualify.

With such a summit of achievement behind them, any observer of football could have forgiven the players if they had decided to rest on their laurels and trade on these glories for the rest of their careers rather than adding to them. But Northern Ireland were far from finished and new chapters in their story were just around the corner. They'd followed their dream to Spain. Now Mexico was faintly calling.

APPENDIX 1

Northern Ireland Internationals under Billy Bingham, March 1980 to July 1982

26/03/80
Israel

1. Jennings
2. Nicholl, J.
3. Nelson
4. Nicholl, C.
5. O'Neill, J.
6. O'Neill, M.
7. McIlroy
8. Cassidy
9. Armstrong
10. Finney (Spence)
11. Cochrane

Ramat Gan Stadium,
Tel Aviv
0–0

16/05/80
Scotland

1. Platt
2. Nicholl, J.
3. Donaghy
4. Nicholl, C.
5. O'Neill, J.
6. Cassidy (McCreery)
7. McIlroy
8. Hamilton, W.
(McClelland)
9. Armstrong
10. Finney
11. Brotherston

Windsor Park
1–0
Hamilton, W.

20/05/80
England

1. Platt
2. Nicholl, J.
3. Donaghy
4. Nicholl, C.
5. O'Neill, J.
6. Cassidy (McCreery)
7. McIlroy
8. Hamilton, W.
(Cochrane)
9. Armstrong
10. Finney
11. Brotherston

Wembley
1–1
Cochrane

23/05/80
Wales

1. Platt
2. Nicholl, J.
3. Donaghy
4. Nicholl, C.
5. O'Neill, J.
6. Cassidy (McCreery)
7. McIlroy
8. Hamilton, W.
(Cochrane)
9. Armstrong
10. Finney
11. Brotherston

Ninian Park
1–0
Brotherston

11/06/80
Australia

1. Platt
2. Nicholl, J.
3. O'Neill, J.
4. Nicholl, C.
5. McClelland
6. Cassidy (McCreery)
7. Brotherston
(Cochrane)
8. Hamilton, W.
9. Armstrong (Spence)
10. Finney (Hamilton, B.)
11. O'Neill, M.

Sydney Cricket
Ground
2–1
Nicholl, C.; O'Neill, M.

15/06/80
Australia

1. Platt
2. Nicholl, J.
3. O'Neill, J.
4. Nicholl, C.
5. McClelland
6. Cassidy
7. Brotherston
8. McCreery (Cochrane)
9. Armstrong
10. Finney
11. O'Neill, M.

Olympic Park,
Melbourne
1–1
O'Neill, M.

18/06/80
Australia

1. Platt
2. Nicholl, J.
3. O'Neill, J.
4. Nicholl, C.
5. McClelland
6. Cassidy (Hamilton, B.)
7. Cochrane
8. Hamilton, W.
(McCurdy)
9. Armstrong
10. O'Neill, M.
11. Brotherston

Hindmarsh Stadium,
Adelaide
2–1
Brotherston; McCurdy

22/06/80
Western Australia

1. Platt (Dunlop)
2. Nicholl, J.
3. Nicholl, C. (McCreery)
4. O'Neill, J.
5. McClelland
6. O'Neill, M.
7. Cassidy (Sloan)
8. Cochrane
9. Armstrong (Finney)
10. McCurdy
(Hamilton, B.)
11. Brotherston

WACA Ground, Perth
4–0
Armstrong; Cochrane 2;
O'Neill, J.

15/10/80
Sweden

1. Platt
2. Nicholl, J.
3. Donaghy
4. Nicholl, C.
5. McClelland
6. Cassidy (McCreery)
7. Brotherston
8. O'Neill, M.
9. Hamilton (Cochrane)
10. Armstrong
11. McIlroy

Windsor Park
3–0
Brotherston; McIlroy;
Nicholl, J.

19/11/80
Portugal

1. Platt
2. Nicholl, J.
3. Donaghy
4. Nicholl, C.
5. O'Neill, J.
6. Cassidy (McCreery)
7. Brotherston
8. O'Neill, M.
9. Hamilton (Cochrane)
10. Armstrong
11. McIlroy

Estádio da Luz, Lisbon
0–1

25/03/81
Scotland

1. Jennings
2. Nicholl, J.
3. Nelson
4. Nicholl, C.
5. McClelland
6. O'Neill, J.
7. Cochrane
8. McCreery
9. Hamilton (Spence)
10. Armstrong
11. McIlroy

Hampden Park
1–1
Hamilton

29/04/81
Portugal

1. Jennings
2. Nicholl, J.
3. Nelson
4. Nicholl, C.
5. O'Neill, J.
6. McCreery
7. Cochrane
8. O'Neill, M.
9. Hamilton
10. Armstrong
11. McIlroy

Windsor Park
1–0
Armstrong

19/05/81
Scotland

1. Jennings
2. Nicholl, J.
3. Nelson (Donaghy)
4. Nicholl, C.
5. McClelland
6. O'Neill, J.
7. Cochrane
8. O'Neill, M.
9. Hamilton
10. Armstrong
11. McIlroy

Hampden Park
0–2

03/06/81
Sweden

1. Jennings
2. Nicholl, J. (McClelland)
3. Nelson
4. Nicholl, C.
5. O'Neill, J.
6. McCreery
7. Cochrane
8. O'Neill, M.
9. Hamilton (Spence)
10. Armstrong
11. McIlroy

Råsunda Stadium,
Stockholm
0–1

14/10/81
Scotland

1. Jennings
2. Nicholl, J.
3. Donaghy
4. Nicholl, C.
5. O'Neill, J.
6. McCreery
7. Brotherston
8. O'Neill, M.
9. Hamilton
10. Armstrong
11. McIlroy

Windsor Park
0–0

18/11/81
Israel

1. Jennings
2. Nicholl, J.
3. Donaghy
4. Nicholl, C.
5. O'Neill, J.
6. McCreery
7. Brotherston
8. Cassidy
9. Hamilton
10. Armstrong
11. McIlroy

Windsor Park
1–0
Armstrong

23/02/82
England

1. Jennings
2. Nicholl, J.
3. Nelson
4. Nicholl, C.
5. O'Neill, J.
6. Donaghy
7. Brotherston
   (Cochrane)
8. O'Neill, M.
   (McCreery)
9. Hamilton
10. Armstrong
11. McIlroy

Wembley
0–4

24/03/82
France

1. Platt
2. Nicholl, J.
3. Donaghy
4. Nicholl, C.
5. O'Neill, J.
6. McCreery (Caskey)
7. Brotherston
8. O'Neill, M.
9. Armstrong
10. McIlroy (Spence)
11. Cochrane (Stewart)

Parc des Princes, Paris
0–4

28/04/82
Scotland

1. Platt
2. Donaghy
3. Nelson
4. O'Neill, J.
5. McClelland
6. Cleary
7. Brotherston
8. O'Neill, M.
9. Campbell
10. McIlroy
11. Healy

Windsor Park
1–1
McIlroy

27/05/82
Wales

1. Jennings (Platt)
2. Nicholl, J.
3. Donaghy
4. Nicholl, C.
5. McClelland
6. Cleary (Campbell)
7. Brotherston
8. Healy
9. Hamilton
10. Armstrong
11. McIlroy

Racecourse Ground,
Wrexham
0–3

17/06/82
Yugoslavia

1. Jennings
2. Nicholl, J.
3. Donaghy
4. Nicholl, C.
5. McClelland
6. McCreery
7. Whiteside
8. O'Neill, M.
9. Hamilton
10. Armstrong
11. McIlroy

Estadio La Romareda,
Zaragoza
0–0

21/06/82
Honduras

1. Jennings
2. Nicholl, J.
3. Donaghy
4. Nicholl, C.
5. McClelland
6. McCreery
7. Whiteside
(Brotherston)
8. O'Neill, M. (Healy)
9. Hamilton
10. Armstrong
11. McIlroy

Estadio La Romareda,
Zaragoza
1–1
Armstrong

25/06/82
Spain

1. Jennings
2. Nicholl, J.
3. Donaghy
4. Nicholl, C.
5. McClelland
6. McCreery
7. Whiteside (Nelson)
8. O'Neill, M.
9. Hamilton
10. Armstrong
11. McIlroy (Cassidy)

Estadio Luis Casanova,
Valencia
1–0
Armstrong

01/07/82
Austria

1. Platt
2. Nicholl, J.
3. Nelson
4. Nicholl, C.
5. McClelland
6. McCreery
7. Whiteside
(Brotherston)
8. O'Neill, M.
9. Hamilton
10. Armstrong
11. McIlroy

Estadio Vicente
Calderón, Madrid
2–2
Hamilton 2

04/07/82
France

1. Jennings
2. Nicholl, J.
3. Donaghy
4. Nicholl, C.
5. McClelland
6. McCreery (O'Neill, J.)
7. Whiteside
8. O'Neill, M.
9. Hamilton
10. Armstrong
11. McIlroy

Estadio Vicente
Calderón, Madrid
1–4
Armstrong

APPENDIX 2

Player Appearances

A list of all the players picked to play for Northern Ireland in the twenty-four international matches Billy Bingham managed between March 1980 and July 1982. The players are listed in descending order of number of appearances.

Player	Appearances 1980–82	Total Appearances	Goals 1980–82	Total Goals	Dates of International Career
Armstrong, Gerry	23	63	5	12	1976–86
Nicholl, Chris	23	51	1	3	1974–83
Nicholl, Jimmy	23	73	1	1	1976–86
McIlroy, Sammy	21	88	2	5	1972–86
Hamilton, Billy	20	41	4	5	1978–86
McCreery, David	19	67	–	–	1976–90
O'Neill, John	18	39	–	2	1980–86
O'Neill, Martin	18	64	2	7	1971–84
Brotherston, Noel	16	27	3	3	1980–85
Donaghy, Mal	16	91	–	–	1980–94
Cochrane, Terry	14	26	1	1	1975–84
McClelland, John	14	53	–	1	1980–90
Jennings, Pat	13	119	–	–	1964–86
Platt, Jim	12	23	–	–	1976–86
Cassidy, Tommy	11	24	–	1	1971–82
Nelson, Sammy	9	51	–	1	1970–82
Finney, Tommy	6	14	–	2	1974–80
Spence, Derek	5	29	–	3	1975–82
Whiteside, Norman	5	38	–	9	1982–89
Healy, Felix	4	4	–	–	1982

Player	Appearances 1980–82	Total Appearances	Goals 1980–82	Total Goals	Dates of International Career
Campbell, Bobby	2	2	–	–	1982
Cleary, Jim	2	5	–	–	1982–84
Hamilton, Bryan	2	50	–	4	1968–80
Caskey, Billy	1	7	–	1	1978–82
McCurdy, Colin	1	1	1	1	1980
Stewart, Ian	1	31	–	2	1982–87

ACKNOWLEDGEMENTS

As with my previous book, *Spirit of '58*, I would like to extend a huge thank you to all at Blackstaff Press who have helped guide this title into existence through coaxing, editing and proofreading – Jenny McCullough, Michelle Griffin and Patsy Horton. Your patience and skills have been much appreciated.

Special thanks to my good friend in football and music, Jim Meredith, who was tasked with coming up with a title for the book at short notice when my mind was a blank. Something non-specific to the subject matter, encapsulating the joy of football and, if possible, a reference to something poetic or lyrical from Northern Ireland, preferably contemporary to the events: that was the challenging brief I gave him. Within ten minutes he was back with the perfect *Fields of Wonder*. And the lyrical connection to Northern Ireland is that the line comes from a Van Morrison song, 'Across the Bridge Where Angels Dwell' on the *Beautiful Vision* album, released in 1982.

Quotes in this book from players and managers have largely been taken from interviews conducted by myself between 2017 and 2021 for my forthcoming feature documentary, *Fields of Wonder*. I would like to thank the following interviewees for their time: Gerry Armstrong, Billy Bingham, Billy Hamilton, Pat Jennings, John McClelland, David McCreery, Sammy McIlroy, Jimmy Nicholl, Martin O'Neill and Norman Whiteside. They are all remarkable men. It is encouraging that they have remained connected to the world of football in one way or another over the years – Pat Jennings, for instance, is a regular visitor to Northern Ireland in his capacity as an official ambassador for the excellent McDonalds Grassroots Football initiative – and that they continue to inspire future generations of footballers.

Thanks are due again to Ben Price, the very able cameraman who recorded the interviews.

Thank you also to two gentlemen who travelled to Spain as fans – Paul Vance and Brian Monroe. Always a pleasure to listen to your memories and thanks to Paul for allowing me to quote one of his fine articles and to Brian for opening up his precious photo album.

I have drawn on a wide variety of sources in the writing of this book, in particular newspaper articles from the time. The following player biographies and autobiographies were also invaluable and provided important context and information that I was able to use to supplement what players had told me in interviews:

Allen, Robert, *Billy: A Biography of Billy Bingham* (1986)

Best, George, *Where Do I Go from Here?* (1981)

Best, George, *Blessed* (2001)

Bowler, Dave, *Danny Blanchflower, A Biography of a Visionary* (1997)

Cochrane, Terry, *See You at the Far Post* (2014)

Dougan, Derek, *The Sash He Never Wore… Twenty-Five Years On* (1997)

Firth, Paul, *Bobby Campbell: They Don't Make Them Like Him Anymore* (2012)

Harrison, David and Gordos, *Steve – The Doog* (2008)

Jennings, Pat, *An Autobiography* (1983)

Lovejoy, Joe, *Bestie: A Portrait of a Legend* (1998)

McIlroy, Sammy, *Manchester United: My Team* (1980)

Montgomery, Alex, *Martin O'Neill: The Biography* (2003)

Moss, Simon, *Martin O'Neill: The Biography* (2010)

Munro, John Neil, *When George Came to Edinburgh, George Best at Hibs* (2010)

Neill, Terry, *Revelations of a Football Manager* (1985)

Spence, Derek, *From the Troubles to the Tower* (2019)

Tossell, David, *In Sunshine or in Shadow, A Journey Through the Life of Derek Dougan* (2012)

Whiteside, Norman, *Determined* (2007)

Arriving too late to be included in the writing of this book, the following titles will be of huge interest to any fan of this period of Northern Ireland international football and are recommended as further reading:

Armstrong, Gerry, *My Story, My Journey* (2021)

McIlroy, Sammy, *The Last Busby Babe* (2022)

Also, the following books provide overviews on some of the subjects covered in this book and are well worth checking out:

Hanna, Ronnie, *Six Glorious Years: Following Northern Ireland 1980–86* (1994)

Jamieson, Teddy, *Whose Side Are You On? Sport, the Troubles and Me* (2011)

Roberts, Benjamin, *Gunshots & Goalposts: The Story of Northern Irish Football* (2017)

Walker, Michael, *Green Shoots: Irish Football Histories* (2017)

Many thanks to the ever-helpful staff at the Belfast Newspaper Library for enabling access to the back issues of the *Belfast Telegraph*, *Irish News*, *News Letter* and *Ireland's Saturday Night* and the priceless contemporary information they contain.

Two online pools of knowledge have been invaluable, as always. Huge thanks to all who have helped in making them the wonderful resources they are. No fan of Northern Irish international football should be without a bookmarked link to these two sites:

Northern Ireland's Footballing History (which incorporates Today in Our Footballing History)
https://northernirelandsfootballinghistory.wordpress.com

Northern Ireland's Footballing Greats
http://nifootball.blogspot.co.uk

Thanks are also in order to those who have contributed to financing the filming of *Fields of Wonder*, too many to list here. However, special mention must be made of The Amalgamation of Northern Ireland Supporters' Clubs and the Our Wee Country Facebook page for always being on hand to help. Also, some wonderful service was provided by the Northern Ireland Fans – Everywhere We Go Facebook page who answered my call for some information (and then some) within minutes.

Finally, thanks to Northern Ireland fan, football enthusiast and former Newspaper Library staff member, Brian Girvin. Your interest and kind words for both book projects have helped make the work worthwhile.